Peaceful Parent, Happ

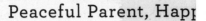

"This book delivers hope and help. Laura Markham brilliantly applies her respectful, attuned, limit-setting approach to sibling dynamics. Full of realistic scenarios and scripts for how parents can turn conflict into opportunities to build skills, and turn parental dread into meaningful intervention, *Peaceful Parent, Happy Siblings* masterfully coaches parents on how to honor each child's experience, set limits, reduce conflict, and build skills for life."

—Tina Payne Bryson, PhD, coauthor of
The Whole-Brain Child and *No-Drama Discipline*

"Parents need all the help they can get to be the kind of parents they want to be, and to use parenting skills that influence their children to be good citizens of the world. Dr. Laura's book is filled with this kind of help—practical, inspiring, and encouraging through real-life examples. It would have helped me a lot when I was raising my children."

—Dr. Jane Nelsen, author and coauthor of the *Positive Discipline* series

"Finally, a book that answers your questions around sibling rivalry! In this insightful book, Dr. Markham draws on scientific research to craft smart strategies that any parent can use to help their children resolve their conflicts with empathy, mindfulness, and peace. A must-read for every parent."

—Dr. Shefali Tsabary, author of *The Conscious Parent* and *Out of Control*

"Adding a child to the family creates a cascade of challenges. Dr. Laura Markham shows parents how to avoid common sibling difficulties, and how to convey their love, even in stressful situations, so children truly feel supported. Open this book, and you'll find clarity, wisdom, workable ideas, and generous helpings of respect for parents and children."

—Patty Wipfler, founder of Hand in Hand Parenting

MAY   2015

continued . . .

"Refreshingly positive and respectful in its tone, *Peaceful Parents, Happy Siblings* lovingly guides parents by using scripts and practical examples, essential tools for any parent with more than one child. Dr. Laura's compassionate approach is empowering for parents, and liberating for children."

—Lysa Parker and Barbara Nicholson, founders of Attachment Parenting International and authors of *Attached at the Heart*

"Brothers and sisters, rejoice! Here's a family roadmap to transform bickering kids into a connected sibling team. One third of kids have a warm caring relationship with their siblings. Read this book and your family can join the ranks."

—Heather Shumaker, author of *It's Okay Not to Share*

"A phenomenal book for parents with multiple children! Dr. Markham addresses all of the common sibling issues with sensible solutions to bring peace and foster healthy relationships between siblings. This book will be my constant companion for years to come."

—Rebecca Eanes, author of *Lasting Bonds: Building Connected Families Through Positive Parenting*

"Whether you are just beginning to contemplate having a second child or you are already frustrated by nonstop sibling fighting, this book is for you. I marveled at the amount of wisdom, compassion, and practical ideas packed into its pages. The wisdom begins with her gentle reminder that we have to start with ourselves if we want to make meaningful changes in our children's relationships with each other. The compassion is in Dr. Laura's empathy for everyone in the mix—including angry and worried parents. And the ideas aren't just practical and usable—many of them are downright fun. You'll laugh out loud just reading them, and everyone will laugh when you try them out. Wouldn't that be a nice change from bickering and clobbering?"

—Lawrence J. Cohen, PhD, author of *Playful Parenting*

"As a parenting coach, I know that sibling struggles can be heart-wrenching for parents. Dr. Laura's strategies are right on the money to help today's parents create more peaceful homes—and stronger sibling relationships. Great work!"

—Amy McCready, founder of Positive Parenting Solutions and author of *If I Have to Tell You One More Time* and *The "Me, Me, Me" Epidemic*

"This book walks parents through sibling scenarios—even ones for very intense children—and breaks down the specifics of how to approach common struggles, without making parents feel guilty or overwhelmed. It is a wonderful resource that gives parents the tools to not only help our children while in the midst of conflict, but also helps us teach our children how to be the loving, kind, and respectful brothers and sisters we know they can be."

—Gina Osher, *The Twin Coach*

"If you are the parent of more than one child, this is the book for you. Laura Markham begins at the beginning—the how and when to tell your child that they are about to become a big brother or sister—and then offers concrete suggestions to help you lay down the foundation for a healthy sibling relationship throughout your children's lives. I know that I will highly recommend this book to all my clients."

—Rev. Susan Nason, parent educator

"Dr. Laura's examples and coaching-based methodology make parenting siblings far less daunting. . . . Her book reassures us that doing our best with the right tools, including self-regulation, connection, and coaching, can build a much happier and more peaceful family."

—Nancy Peplinsky, founder and executive director of Holistic Moms Network

Peaceful Parent,
HAPPY SIBLINGS

*How to Stop the Fighting
and Raise Friends for Life*

DR. LAURA MARKHAM

A Perigee Book

A PERIGEE BOOK
Published by the Penguin Group
Penguin Group (USA) LLC
375 Hudson Street, New York, New York 10014

USA • Canada • UK • Ireland • Australia • New Zealand • India • South Africa • China

penguin.com

A Penguin Random House Company

PEACEFUL PARENT, HAPPY SIBLINGS

ISBN: 978-0-399-16845-1

This book has been registered with the Library of Congress.

First edition: May 2015

PRINTED IN THE UNITED STATES OF AMERICA

10 9 8 7 6 5 4 3 2 1

Text design by Laura K. Corless
Illustrations by Bryndon D.M. Everett

When you have one child, you're a parent. When you have two, you're a referee.

—DAVID FROST

Before you can teach your kids to listen, identify the problem, express their feelings, generate solutions, and find common ground, you have to learn those problem-solving skills yourself.

—LAURA DAVIS AND JANIS KEYSER,
BECOMING THE PARENT YOU WANT TO BE

You mean the baby could be a boy? But I'm your boy. I guess it's okay . . . We can always send him back, right?

—THE AUTHOR'S SON, AGE THREE

CONTENTS

PART THREE: BEFORE THE NEW BABY AND THROUGH THE FIRST YEAR

I wasn't prepared for my son's reaction when his little sister was born. At four, he'd had only a few tantrums in his entire life. But when the baby appeared, he seemed to panic. He was clingy, he was angry, he was scared. I was trained as a psychologist, but I was out of my league.

Like me, most parents look forward to the awe on our older child's face as he or she gazes for the first time at our newborn. We imagine the baby laughing as her big brother entertains her with funny faces. When one child gets hurt, the other will replay the care he's received from us, offering his sibling a hug and a blankie. Over time, romping through the sprinkler will give way to bike rides and camping out, which will give way to arguing over who gets the car on Saturday night and consoling each other over lost games and broken hearts. They may head their separate ways after high school, but that bond will continue through all the ups and downs of adulthood. We want to believe that we're giving our children a priceless gift: a friend for life.

But sometime in the first year—maybe even before the baby arrives—most parents begin to realize things may not be quite so simple, as I hear from the families I coach:

- *"She loves her brother . . . In fact, she hugs him so hard that it scares us . . . Her hands always seem to end up around his neck."*
- *"I can't even drive the car safely because they can't keep their hands off each other."*
- *"He really pushed me to my limit when I came out of the shower and realized he had peed on his nine-month-old brother!"*

There's no way around it. Sibling rivalry is universal. After all, every human is genetically programmed to protect resources that will help him survive, and your children *depend on* and *compete for* what are, in fact, precious resources—your time and attention. Even when there's plenty of love to go around, young humans haven't developed much impulse control, so they're bound to get into conflicts. Finally, temperament colors every relationship. Children who tend to be challenging will be even more challenging when you introduce a brother or a sister, and some siblings simply clash.

Unfortunately, many parents don't know how to help kids with these strong emotions, so hurt feelings can lead to aggressive acts, which can spiral into negative patterns of interacting with each other. Those hard feelings can set the tone in a sibling relationship right through the teen years, and even have a way of popping up at family stress points across a lifespan.

But there's good news, too. The sibling relationship is where the rough edges of our early self-centeredness are smoothed off, and where we learn to manage our most difficult emotions. Siblings often become good friends, and because they know each other so well, they can provide each other a deep sense of comfort. Even siblings who fight a lot usually do gain respect for each other and eventually get along. When they're grown, many siblings feel a deep connection to the only other people who understand what it was like to grow up in their home.

And here's the best news of all. Parents can make a tremendous difference in shaping the sibling relationship. Sibling jealousy is unavoidable, but it's almost always possible to help children develop a strong, positive bond that trumps the natural jealousy. It's not always easy to raise siblings who appreciate each other, who become friends for life—but a committed parent can make all the difference. I wrote this book to show you how.

When I was struggling after the birth of my second child, the only book on siblings that I could find was *Siblings Without Rivalry* by Adele Faber and Elaine Mazlish, and it stayed on my bedside table for years. This is still the book I recommend first to parents of school-age children whose kids are having a hard time with each other. But as a mother with a baby and a young child, I faced daily challenges such as how to keep my son busy while I nursed his sister, how to help him learn to be gentle when he gave her those overzealous hugs, how to handle it when she started crawling and went after his toys. There were constant challenges in those early days as a growing family; I wanted specific strategies to transform those challenges into closeness between my children. I had read enough research to know that the foundation of my children's relationship was being laid in that first year or two, but I couldn't find a roadmap.

As the years went by, I finished my PhD in clinical psychology at Columbia University and founded the website AhaParenting.com. My practice as a parenting coach gave me a window into tens of thousands of families, so I saw firsthand what worked, and what didn't, when families found themselves struggling. I built on the empathic model promoted by Faber and Mazlish and their mentor,

Haim Ginott, one of the grandfathers of today's positive parenting movement, to integrate new findings from research on emotion, attachment, and brain development (please see the acknowledgments). Observing the dynamics in the families I worked with, combined with my own mindfulness practice, taught me how parents can take control to shift the patterns in their families, not by controlling their children, but by changing their own thoughts, feelings, words, and actions. I've found that parenting gets a lot easier when we as parents can do three very hard things:

1. Regulate our own emotions.
2. Stay connected with our child, even when we're setting limits or the child is upset.
3. Coach instead of controlling, by fostering emotional intelligence, guiding with empathic limits instead of punishment, and supporting mastery.

These three ideas will transform your relationship with your children so they're happier, emotionally healthier, and more cooperative—and you're calmer and more fulfilled in your parenting. They're fully explained in my first book, *Peaceful Parent, Happy Kids: How to Stop Yelling and Start Connecting*. To me, these ideas are the key to finding the joy in parenting. And because they're the foundation of raising happy children, they're also essential to a happy sibling relationship, as described by one of my readers:

After applying your three big ideas (self-regulation, connection, coaching), my six-, five-, and three-year-old all get along more often now. As each of them felt stronger in their connection to me, they seemed to feel less anxiety inside and thus less of a need to act out by fighting with their siblings.
    –Anna

As transformative as these ideas can be for a family, parents still ask me the kinds of questions I struggled with when my children were young. How can they:

- Help young children develop the skills to express their needs and stand up for themselves—and also listen to their siblings?
- Help two small children, or even three, work through strong emotions at the same time?
- Create a family culture of cooperation and support that gives sibling love a chance to win out over sibling rivalry?

Luckily, there are solutions that really help. Every family has unique challenges, but there are proven, research-based ways to get your kids' relationship with each other started off on the right foot, and to keep them on track to a satisfying relationship. Even when kids are temperamentally mismatched or fiercely competitive, there are strategies that work to minimize sibling rivalry and maximize positive connection. Not all siblings can be best friends, but they can all learn to respect each other and honor their differences. This book details those strategies, giving you practical step-by-step blueprints to transform your children's relationship with each other.

As you've no doubt already figured out, just ordering children to "get along" doesn't help them learn to manage their emotions, communicate their needs, or resolve their differences. Peace doesn't come from pushing conflicts under the surface; they inevitably erupt again, all too often while you're driving, pushing the supermarket cart, or eating dinner at Grandma's. But if you give kids the skills to navigate the complex terrain of human emotion and relationships, you'll raise children who can work things out with each other. They'll be able to advocate for their own needs while respecting the needs of others. And they'll learn to look for win/win solutions rather than settling into bully and victim roles. In short, you'll raise kids who love deeply, regulate their emotions, and have healthy relationships. Not only will your children forge a close and lifelong sibling bond, but they'll thrive with peers, coworkers, and their eventual partner. They'll be the kind of person we need more of in the world.

Families are the crucibles that transform infants into mature human beings. No matter how hard things are in your family right now, it *is* possible to create a home where differences are resolved amicably, and to raise children who are friends for life.

If You're Welcoming a New Baby

If you're able to read this book before your baby arrives, or during your first year with a new baby in the family, then Part 3 is especially for you. If your family is at a different stage, I suggest you skip Part 3, and focus instead on the ideas in Parts 1 and 2.

If Your Children Are Constantly Fighting

What works for us is my being there to intervene, coach, model, prevent the breakdowns and fights on the days that are rough. For me this has made a huge *difference. I don't see many of my mom friends doing that . . . even the really, really awesome ones. Not because they don't care but because we are all so busy! It's like someone needs to give us permission to just let everything else go and focus on the relationships.*

—Beth

If your children are fighting a lot, you're probably feeling discouraged. It may help to remember that no matter how you parent, all children will fight sometimes—just as all couples will fight sometimes, no matter how solid a relationship they have. Fighting doesn't mean anyone is a bad person—not you, and not your children.

Maybe you find yourself wondering why your child is always the one hitting the baby while everyone else's children seem to love their new siblings. Remember, though, that you can't see inside anyone else's family. All children get jealous sometimes, no matter how loving they may act in public.

Maybe you're ready to scream because your toddler keeps hitting, no matter how many times you patiently teach him that hitting hurts. Don't give up. Research shows that young children often hit, no matter what parents do, presumably because they're still developing the prefrontal cortex that will give them more self-control. But as parents keep modeling and teaching a more peaceful approach, their children show more kindness to their siblings and more ability to regulate their emotions than children who have been raised with conventional discipline.[1] Your patience *is* making a difference, even if you can't see it yet.

Or maybe your children can't get through a day without some unpleasantness toward each other, so you wonder if you've done something wrong. The answer is No. You've done as well as you could with the resources you had. After all, your children were born with certain temperaments, and you were just trying to get dinner on the table without falling apart yourself. You're not perfect, but neither is anyone else. Most likely you simply have more challenging children. Parents who have easier children may not understand this, but I talk to thousands of parents, and it's quite clear that some children are more challenging than others.

The truth is, parenting as well as we can is always hard—really, truly, the hardest thing any of us has ever done. It's physically and emotionally exhausting. Too often we're pushed to put our own needs second, or third, or—unsustainably—even off the list. Raising children challenges us to rise above our natural human feelings of need and want, to give, give, give to another human who is too young to show any gratitude.

So life with children is always challenging, even under the best of circumstances—and most of us don't live in the best of circumstances. Most of us have multiple stressors in our lives and are so busy trying to keep up that sometimes it seems as if we end up raising our kids in our spare time. Like all humans, we get stressed and emotionally "dysregulated." That makes us lose our easy, enjoyable connection with our kids. Since our children depend on that connection to stay regulated themselves, they get emotionally off-kilter, too, so they act out, toward us and toward each other.

One of the solutions to this is to remember that our children are, in fact, our most important job; we're raising humans. We're shaping not only their relationships with each other, but their very brains. *Coaching your children so they develop emotional intelligence is what transforms their relationship with each other.* Who cares if you serve your children cheese and crackers and carrot sticks for dinner again? What matters most for who your children become and the relationship they develop with each other is their daily life as children. Sure, genetics has a lot to do with it. But the interaction of those genes with environment is what shapes your children.

This book has the tools you need to transform your family life. I hope you'll find some Aha! Moments. I know you'll also find that it takes real time and commitment to put these powerful tools to work. So I'm giving you explicit permission to prioritize your children, and their relationship with each other. There will be some days when you simply can't get to the dishes, the laundry, the emails. The only way to keep your children from bashing each other will be to sit on the floor with them to prevent the fights, to coach them to express their needs without attacking, and to find ways to transform tension into closeness with laughter or with tears. This is heroic work, especially because it's so private—no one is there to see what it costs you. But it's not as invisible as it seems. Just as a tree's rings record environmental conditions year by year, your children's experience now is creating the people they're growing into. Every day, you are literally shaping who your children will be for the rest of their lives. And don't worry, there's also a very immediate payoff, which you'll see in increasingly positive interactions between your children.

I say this well aware that you'll still have days when your kids will be on each other every five minutes. That doesn't mean you're not doing a good job. It means this is very hard work. If you keep prioritizing relationships in your family over whatever else you think you "should" be doing, if you keep digging deep for your own emotional generosity, you'll see your kids begin to soften toward each other. It might be hard to imagine your children becoming best friends, but the foundation stone of emotional intelligence that you're building will at the very least support a respectful relationship—and maybe something much closer.

Is it easy? No. Self-regulation is the hardest work any of us ever do, but that's the essential first ingredient for peaceful parenting. Don't worry. You don't have to be perfect at it. It's always a work in progress. There is no perfect parent, because there are no perfect humans. What matters is that we notice when we're off track, get ourselves back in balance, and reconnect with our kids.

Luckily, our children learn a lot from the times we miss the mark, because they'll miss the mark, too. Role modeling how to gracefully navigate the shoals of human imperfection is one of the most valuable gifts we can give each child—and their sibling relationship—because it teaches them how to forgive themselves and each other.

So please summon up all your compassion and forgive yourself, right now, for being human. Decide right now that instead of criticism, you'll give yourself extra nurturing when you're not at your best—which happens, on a regular basis, to every parent. Really. No matter what. I don't care what you've done while you were exhausted or furious. You're human, which means you make mistakes, and you can grow. You don't have to have parented perfectly, and you don't have to be perfect in the future. Whatever is happening in your family right now, that's where you start.

Figure out what support you need. Self-care? Information? Counseling? A written agreement with your partner about how to handle certain problems? Or maybe simply strategies to handle the situations that stump you? (This book will give you lots of those.) Once you give yourself that support, you can start turning things around with your children.

Whether your children are toddlers, preschoolers, or much older, you can teach them the skills to get along with each other. You can create a family culture of support and respect. Even more important, you can help each child with the emotions that cause hostility toward their sibling. And you can deepen your closeness with each child, so he feels safe enough to work through those emotions, and so he never, ever fears that you might love his sibling more than you love him. All of this begins with your ability to manage your own emotions and find ways to connect with each child.

Worried that the damage is done? It is never too late. What matters is that you admit that you're not happy with the way things are, and that you commit to intervening to make things better. Castigating your child to become a better sibling won't work. Neither will shame, blame, or punishment—of your child, or of yourself. But changing your own actions, to meet your child's needs and help him with his emotions, will always work. Is it a lot of work? A tremendous amount. Is it worth it? See what this mom has to say.

When Grant was born we went through an extremely difficult period with Dean—it was to the point that I literally couldn't turn

my back without him hitting the little one. At the time we were
doing time-outs, etc.—often carrying him kicking and screaming
to another room—and today I feel so much guilt about that! I used
to get very upset and yell at him when he would hit his brother and
have explosive tantrums. I do worry that a full year of getting so
upset at him has done some damage.

The same mom, two years later:

I've worked very, very hard to cultivate a sense that we treat each
other respectfully and fairly—the way we'd like to be treated. I
praise them regularly for being kind to each other and encourage
them to do little favors for each other. For example, three-year-old
Grant decides he wants to take his pickup truck when we're ready
to head out the door, and five-year-old Dean runs upstairs to get
it. I sing Dean's praises—literally—doing a "best big brother"
dance. We encourage them to hug and kiss and to be thoughtful of
each other. In general we just focus a lot on how great it is to have
a brother and playmate . . . and how we're all in this together.

Grant and Dean are lucky to have a mother who didn't give up,
or give in to her frustration and hopelessness. Instead, she got down
to work, every single day. She regulated herself. She helped her boys
with their big emotions. She met their individual needs. She created
a family culture of appreciation and support. And she's raising sons
who will be friends for life.

You can, too.

My first book, *Peaceful Parent, Happy Kids: How to Stop Yelling and
Start Connecting*, describes how to notice the big emotions that
highjack us, restore yourself to a state of calm, connect with your

child, and emotion-coach your child so he develops self-discipline and *wants* to cooperate without any need for punishment. In this book, you'll find out how to apply those lessons to raising siblings. There isn't space to fully restate the foundation for parenting outlined in *Peaceful Parent, Happy Kids*; I hope you will, or already have, read that book. While this book is a comprehensive source of tools to help you facilitate a happy relationship between your children, you'll find that it becomes much more powerful when you combine it with the tools for self-regulation, connection, and coaching that are outlined in depth in *Peaceful Parent, Happy Kids*.

PART ONE

PEACEFUL PARENTING 101

All siblings will do some fighting, no matter what their parents do. Conflict is a part of every human relationship, and you can't stop your children from having needs and desires that sometimes clash. What you *can* do is give them healthy tools to work through those disagreements, tools they'll use for the rest of their lives.

Every child is unique, and some siblings do have a harder time with each other. So it may surprise you to learn that the key ingredient to a healthy, fun-filled, satisfying dynamic between your children is not their behavior or temperament. These are important, of course. But the key is you.

Decades of research on siblings and families have produced fascinating findings. I'll discuss many throughout this book. But here's one of the most important, confirmed by numerous studies:

When parents have better relationships with their children, those children have happier relationships with

each other. When parents have more negative or puni-
tive relationships with each child, the children behave
more aggressively and selfishly with each other.[1]

So while you can't control your children, you *can* control someone who has a tremendous influence on how your children relate to each other. You.

Yes, your children will inevitably feel some rivalry with each other. There will be times in every family when siblings seem to fight about every little thing, or say they hate each other. But it is usually possible to help the love win out over the rivalry, by using a child-raising approach that I call "peaceful parenting."

1

How You Can Be a Peaceful Parent

When I am able to remain present and breathing, love often unfolds. When I am in my past or fear, then I cause an escalation that may not have even been brewing in reality.

—Staci

Peaceful doesn't mean that things aren't rambunctious or lively or hilarious at your house. It just means that *you* work toward being more peaceful and less reactive inside. That makes you a better role model for your children, and helps them build a brain and nervous system that can self-regulate.

No parent is peaceful all the time. But parents who want more peace in their families, and in their own hearts, find that three practices are invaluable:

1. **A peaceful parent regulates his or her own emotions,** even in the face of a child's strong emotions and misbehavior. That's what allows us to relate positively to our children, and to do so even when emotions run high. We can count on children behaving childishly at times. So we have the responsibility to act like grown-ups, which means not giving in to the temptation to throw tantrums ourselves. As parents, we

always have the power to calm a child's storms—or to worsen them—with our own response.

How does the parent's commitment to regulate her emotions affect the sibling relationship? Since parents are the role model, you'll hear your child speak to his sister or brother using your words and tone of voice. Children of parents who regulate their emotions learn to manage their own feelings, and therefore their behavior—including toward their siblings. They can calm themselves more easily, so they fight less. They still get jealous, but they have more internal resources to manage their mixed feelings in a healthy way, so the affection has a chance to win out over the rivalry.

2. **A peaceful parent prioritizes staying warmly connected to his or her child.** Every child needs to feel heard, understood, and valued, just for being himself, or he feels unsafe and acts out.

There's another huge benefit: Connection is what motivates children to follow our guidance. We can't really *make* anyone do something without using force, and that only lasts for as long as we have a substantial physical advantage. Our children have to *choose* to do what we say. That's why many parents experience life with their children as an endless series of bribes, threats, and power struggles just to get through the day. But when parents connect deeply with their child, the child *wants* to protect that relationship and is much more likely to follow their parents' guidance. So children who feel connected are more cooperative with parents. That's easier on the parents, of course, but also on any siblings who live in the home, because the child is more cheerful and emotionally generous.

Finally, a child who feels connected to a parent is more likely to value what the parent values and follow the parent's modeling. That means she's more likely to act as her parent acts toward the sibling, so she's more likely to be nurturing, kind, and patient.

3. **A peaceful parent coaches, instead of controlling.** What does it mean to coach instead of control? A coach teaches and supports a child to develop as his best self. A coach doesn't punish. He patiently creates opportunities for the child to grow, and celebrates every step in the right direction. Children respond to coaching by wanting to try hard and to "be like" the coach. Controlling, on the other hand, is forcing a child to behave as you'd like by threatening punishment when she doesn't.

   That means that peaceful parents don't punish their children. Of course, they set limits, but that doesn't include punishment. I know that many people think strict parenting produces better-behaved kids. It simply isn't true. Research studies on discipline consistently show that strict or authoritarian child-raising actually produces kids with lower self-esteem who behave worse than other kids—and therefore get punished more![1]

   The other problem with punishment is that if the child isn't actually choosing the behavior, he doesn't "own" it. He isn't intrinsically motivated to "do what's right." When my daughter was sixteen, I interviewed her for a blog post about how she had learned to behave without ever having been punished. She said, *"Either way—if you punish or not—the child learns not to hit. But if you're punishing to teach her, she learns not to hit so that SHE doesn't suffer. If you're using empathy to teach her, she learns not to hit because it hurts the other person. So she becomes a better person. She cares more about other people."*

So yes, it would be much more convenient if our children just obeyed us! But their need to *choose* their actions is actually a good thing. It's the beginning of taking responsibility for themselves. If you coach your child, you're helping him develop the skills and desire to be his best self more often. His motivation comes from inside. We'll talk throughout this book about how you can use empathy, teaching, and modeling to coach your child, so he *wants* to cooperate, and you'll never need to punish again.

And what about the effect of parental coaching, instead of controlling, on the sibling relationship? Research shows that parents who punish and control end up raising children who are more negative with each other, because they've observed that the way to get others to do what they want is to use threats and force.[2] They've paid attention to their parents, after all. By contrast, peaceful parents coach children to master the interpersonal skills of conflict resolution, like learning how to get their needs met while still being respectful of the other person—so they're better at navigating the inevitable bumps of living with other people.

Are peaceful parents always peaceful? Of course not! They're human. Like all humans, no parent is perfect. And regulating ourselves is the hardest emotional work we do, so it can be an uphill battle despite our positive intentions. *What distinguishes a peaceful parent is the commitment to self-regulation, connection, and coaching instead of controlling. That commitment changes our behavior, one action at a time.* Since the parent-child relationship is just a series of moments together, all those positive choices are cumulative. Two steps forward, one step back still gets your family onto a more positive path and, before you know it, into a whole new landscape.

The Parenting Skills That Help You Become More Peaceful as a Parent

If you're aspiring to evolve into a more peaceful parent, where might you start? With two essential parenting skills: Returning yourself to calm and emotion-coaching.

RETURNING YOURSELF TO CALM

I never yelled until I had two children.
  —Elaine

Most parents wish they could "stay calmer." But no one stays calm all the time, at least not when they have more than one child. We'll always be buffeted by the trials of living with children, and find ourselves off-center. Instead of trying to "stay calm," why not set yourself the goal of noticing when you're starting to get upset—and develop a repertoire of strategies to return yourself to calm?

This process is a bit like learning a musical instrument. At first, it seems impossible to tap out a simple tune. But if you keep practicing, in a year you can play a sonata. Like any practice, you'll never be perfect, but returning yourself to calm gets easier every time you do it. You're actually rewiring your brain, building the neural connections for better self-regulation.

If you can get enough sleep and keep your basic needs met—often a huge challenge for parents—you'll be more able to catch yourself before you slide onto what Dr. Daniel Siegel, coauthor of *Parenting from the Inside Out,* calls "the low road."[3] You know what the low road is. It's when you're stressed, exhausted, resentful. When you insist on being right or wringing an apology out of your children. When you're in the grip of fight-or-flight and your kids look like the enemy. When your fuse is so short that you feel justified in having your own little tantrum. You know what the high road is, too. When you're feeling really good, so you can be emotionally generous. When you respond to your children's squabbles with patience, understanding, and a sense of humor. When you enjoy being a parent.

The first step is training yourself to notice when you're starting to slide toward the low road. The second step is *not* to take any action until you've recentered yourself. That can be a short process—a few deep breaths. Or it can take twenty minutes, in which you do some physical exercise or meditate. (Can't do either with your kids there? Try putting on music and dancing with them to shift your emotional state.)

This sounds hard, and it is. But you can start small, with some easy techniques. For instance, try the simple "Take Five" practice to check in and recenter yourself. Just count five deep, slow breaths. To deepen the effect, notice what's going on in your body as you breathe. Imagine you're breathing light into any tense places in your body, and breathing out tension. This deceptively simple practice makes you more aware of your stress, so you can breathe through it and let it go. Research shows that conscious breathing like this can shift you from stressed to calm in five breaths, and it becomes more effective as you do it more often.[4] You can "Take Five" with a crying baby in your arms, while you're giving your children a bath, or at a stoplight.

But most important, you can do this when your children are fighting, before you intervene. And that's essential, because when emotions are running high between our kids, they're already in "fight, flight, or freeze." That means they think it's an emergency. So it's natural for us as parents to respond as if it really *is* an emergency. The problem with that is that no one can think straight when the brain is overwhelmed with the biochemicals that flood us during an emergency.[5] So we aren't at our best as parents.

Consider how this works. Your son pushes his toddler sister over. Is it an emergency? Actually, no. But it certainly feels like one. Without even realizing it, you're plunged into a state of "fight, flight, or freeze" and your son looks like the enemy. Before you know it, you're intervening with sirens blaring to vanquish the foe and rescue your baby.

Unfortunately, those blaring sirens can't help but escalate the tension both children are feeling. Your daughter, who was startled but not hurt, begins to wail. Your son flees behind the couch, where you pursue him, screeching and threatening. Restoring calm takes twenty minutes.

If this situation is repeated often in our home, our children's amygdalas—the part of the brain that alerts us to danger—become more active, more worried. They go more quickly from zero to sixty when they get upset. Because they feel threatened and upset more easily, they fight with each other more.

It's important for you to know that babies are born with their brains unfinished, to give the child the best chance of adapting to the specifics of their environment. *Their brains are literally taking shape depending on their interactions with us.*[6] And the more we "fly off the handle," the more our children get the message that life is often an emergency. They build a brain that's geared for self-protection, which makes the child more aggressive.

Of course, life with children is full of good reasons for parents to feel upset, overwhelmed, and angry. The baby won't stop crying, the toddler hits the baby, the preschooler flushes the toddler's teddy bear down the toilet, and the six-year-old starts repeating every insult he hears at school to reduce his little brother to tears. Especially when our children are fighting, it's natural for us to get upset. So we leap into the fray, yelling, taking sides, and saying things we regret later. We're just trying to solve the problem, but when we act from a sense of emergency, it inevitably makes things worse, both in the immediate situation and in our kids' relationship with each other. If we want to break the cycle, we need to learn to regulate ourselves.

Camille's parents grew up in loud households, and when they're frustrated, they yell. When three-year-old Camille gets out of line, naturally, they yell at her. And when Camille's little brother Marco takes one of her toys, or starts whining, Camille yells at him. In fact, when Camille is simply grumpy or out of sorts, she shouts at Marco. Now sixteen months, Marco is starting to shriek back at her.

Isabel's parents also grew up in loud households, but they've worked hard to stop yelling. Naturally, they get frustrated, especially when three-year-old Isabel acts out. So they've developed a repertoire of ways to regulate their emotions when they get upset, to minimize the number of times they raise their voices to their children. When Isabel's little brother Milo takes one of her toys, Isabel has learned to try to trade toys with him. When Milo starts whining, she echoes her parents: "Milo, you sad? . . . I help you." Now sixteen months, Milo often offers Isabel toys, and Isabel is better than her parents at cheering Milo up.

Children learn what they live. When we yell, we're modeling the behavior our kids will follow:

- To yell at each other and at us.
- To respond to the inevitable conflicts and frustrations of daily life by yelling and blaming instead of working with the other person to find a solution.
- To take it out on others when they're out of sorts.

It may sound unexpected, but learning to return yourself to calm is one of the most important actions you can take to strengthen your children's relationship with each other. Is this easy? No. Regulating our own emotions is the toughest part of parenting, and it's usually a work in progress. Any one of us will go over the edge if we're pushed too far. *But that's why it's your responsibility as the parent to stay away from the edge.* Regulating our own emotions is one of the hardest things for any of us to do, but that doesn't excuse us from tackling it. If you're a yeller, there's no time like the present to change your ways. It isn't easy, but I've seen thousands of parents do it. (For more support to stop yelling, please see Part 1 of *Peaceful Parent, Happy Kids: How to Stop Yelling and Start Connecting.*)

The good news is that when you're able to react calmly, even as emotions get hot, your children learn more productive ways of managing their emotions when they're upset. They learn:

- This situation seems like an emergency to me, but it actually isn't.
- I know I will be listened to, so I can listen to my siblings, too.

WE CAN ALWAYS WORK THINGS OUT: EMOTION-COACHING

What's emotion-coaching? It's helping your children develop emotional intelligence. Emotional intelligence is what enables us to regulate our emotions, work and play well with others, and work through conflict in any relationship so both people get their needs met in a healthy way. The term "emotion-coaching" was coined by John Gottman, the author of *Raising an Emotionally Intelligent Child.*[7] His many years of research observing families in his Love Lab in Seattle led him to the conclusion that being a loving parent, while essential, is not enough to raise children who can self-regulate. Kids also need our help with the tough emotions that challenge them: jealousy, anger, fear.

To help children with emotions, we first need to understand that once we let ourselves feel an emotion, it begins to dissipate. If, on the other hand, we try to push the emotion away, we end up stuffing it down in our unconscious, where we're no longer in control of it. That's why we get "triggered" and explode: those pent-up emotions are always jostling to come up and get healed, but since they aren't under conscious control, they pour out unregulated. So our goal in emotion-coaching children is to help them feel safe to feel their emotions, which heals upsets as they occur, and helps kids learn to manage their feelings. Once they can manage their emotions, they can manage their behavior.

Why does emotion-coaching matter for the sibling bond? "Even in families where children are given plenty of affection by both parents, young children may fail to develop prosocial relationships with their siblings if nobody teaches them how," says Laurie Kramer, a sibling expert who worked with Gottman.[8] Emotion-coaching helps kids learn to calm themselves, understand their brother or sister's point of view, and put their needs into words instead of lashing out physically during a sibling conflict—so they can come up with win/win solutions.

Emotional intelligence skills begin with the child's ability to soothe himself when he's upset. Some children are born with more innate ability to regulate themselves. But all parents have a huge influence in helping their children develop emotional regulation. Since the brain takes shape in the first few years of life in response to experience, *babies' brains build the neural pathways to soothe their upsets every time you soothe them.*[9] Simply by comforting your baby or toddler when she's upset, you prompt her body to release calming biochemicals and strengthen her future ability to soothe herself—

the most fundamental emotional intelligence skill. (You may have heard that babies learn to self-soothe by being left to comfort themselves, but recent brain research has debunked that outdated advice.[10]) As your baby gets older, you continue the process of helping him learn to self-soothe by acknowledging his hurt or frustration. This helps him accept his emotions, which is the first step in learning to manage them. If your child has a hard time soothing himself, you can help him learn this essential skill by taking him in your arms while he's sobbing, and breathing deeply yourself, making a soothing noise on the outbreath. As he begins to regain composure, you can suggest that he breathe with you.

The most important emotion-coaching skill for parents is empathizing with a child's emotions, which both soothes the child and helps her develop her own capacity for empathy. Virtually all children are born intuitively able to understand the emotions of others through their mirror neurons and limbic system. But unless children experience feeling understood, they don't learn to feel safe with emotions, so other people's upset feelings scare them. Your commitment to empathize with your child, therefore, is an important determinant of his ability to offer understanding to his sibling.

Your empathy also helps your children develop self-regulation. When a child feels understood, he feels closer to his parents, so he's more likely to accept limits and cooperate. He learns that emotions aren't dangerous, and he has a choice about whether to act on them, so he develops more self-control. This helps him handle disappointment better, so he becomes more resilient. By contrast—and this is important—a child who thinks his feelings aren't okay will stuff them down. Unfortunately, repressed emotions aren't under conscious control, and will burst out in "bad" behavior later on.

What do you actually *do* when you empathize? Empathy just means recognizing—in your heart, not only with words—what the other person is feeling. The trick here is to suspend our own agenda so we can really listen and notice what our child is feeling. Whenever children are having a hard time, empathy is the place to start.

"It's hard when you want to play, but your brother wants some time alone."

"It can make you feel left out when it's your sister's birthday, and yours is still months away."

"Oh, sweetie, I'm so sorry your sister tore your painting . . . you're so sad and mad that you want to hit. Let's go tell your sister in words."

Empathy is not automatic for most of us. That's not because we're unkind. It's because we go through daily life seeing other people through the lens of our own needs and desires. When our child is upset, we don't automatically see it from her perspective. We see it from our own. That means that we'll often see her emotions as inconvenient, overreacting, and maybe even purposely making our lives difficult.

But if we want our child to have empathy for her sibling, or anyone else, we need to offer empathy to her. That means that whatever she says or does, the goal is to acknowledge her perspective with understanding—even when you don't agree with her view.

What if you can't be empathic 24/7? That's okay. It's a goal, and like most worthwhile goals, it takes a lot of practice. Sometimes you'll be too mad, or too distracted, or too tired. Your child doesn't need you to be empathic 100 percent of the time. Just work on increasing your percentage.

Many parents fear that accepting their child's emotions will create a "drama queen," but in fact it's just the opposite. When parents truly open their hearts to allow whatever their child wants to express, the child learns:

- *"My emotions are normal, not dangerous."* Emotions can feel overwhelming, but the child learns that it's okay to feel them, and once he does, the emotions lose their charge.

- *"When I say how I feel, I don't get so mad."* The emotions stay under conscious control, so the child can better regulate his behavior, even when he's upset.

- *"Noticing what I feel helps me use words to express my feelings instead of hurting my brother."* You may not like your child yelling about how upset she is, but it's a huge step forward from physically lashing out.

- *"I thought I was mad, and I am. But mad is complicated. It's all wrapped up with feeling hurt and scared and sad. Once I notice those things, I don't feel so mad anymore."* This is the foundation of anger management. Don't you wish you'd learned this as a child?

This approach to emotions may be new to you. Remember, I'm not suggesting that you change the behavior that you allow in your home, just that all emotions can be accepted. This allows your child to "make friends" with her emotions, which in turn helps her learn to regulate them. Over time, accepting emotions will come to you more naturally, even when you're under stress. You'll notice that you don't get upset as easily when your child gets upset, and that you're able to be patient in a whole new way.

As you try this empathic approach, you'll see an immediate change in your child. He may even start offering you hugs when you're upset. A child raised by emotion-coaching parents will understand the feelings that motivate others, and ably navigate the complex emotional world of relationships with friends, classmates, and teachers. And—hallelujah!—siblings.

2

How Peaceful Discipline
Supports the Sibling
Relationship

An impressive body of research has established that a parent's relationship with each child—including the way the parent disciplines—has a strong impact on the quality of the relationships between his or her children.[1]

Gene Brody, one of the most respected and prolific researchers in the sibling field, has consistently found that when parents resist being punitive when guiding their children, their kids fight less and are nicer to each other. As we mentioned in the introduction, younger children are still likely to fight with each other even when their parents don't punish, presumably because little kids have a harder time controlling themselves. But as the children of coaching parents get older, they're more able to regulate their emotions and to be kind to their siblings than children who have been raised with conventional discipline.[2]

One study of sibling relationships found that the siblings in the study who were "compassionate and caring toward each other" (about one third of the kids) had parents who were warm and gave their children support to meet their expectations. Another third of siblings were rated as "highly rivalrous" and "sometimes aggressive" although "sometimes warm"—basically the way we often think of most sibling relationships. These children came from families in which at least one parent was either strict, permissive, or disengaged. Another 22 percent of the siblings were rated as highly aggressive and cold to each other; these children had parents who were *both* either strict or disengaged. The last 10 percent? They came from dysfunctional families in which the parents were not emotionally available to the children. These children were enmeshed, meaning their relationships were dysfunctional.[3] They took care of each other because their parents weren't able to be there for them, but siblings aren't meant to raise each other.

So parents who set reasonable expectations and give their kids support to meet those expectations raise children who are more likely to get along. Strict and permissive parents, on the other hand, raise kids who fight more.

Why Punishment and Permissiveness Cause More Sibling Fighting

Most of us know instinctively why permissiveness doesn't help our children get along. If we want them to treat each other well, we need to set clear expectations about the standard of civility in our home, and support our kids to live up to those expectations. That's why the advice that parents should ignore most sibling fighting can be counterproductive, which we'll discuss more in Part 2.

It's often harder, though, for parents to understand why punishment creates more sibling fighting. After all, we punish to enforce our limits and teach important lessons. Why would that make our children *less* likely to be nice each other?

Seeing this issue through your child's emotional eyes gives us some surprising insights. From your child's perspective, discipline isn't the way you teach her appropriate behavior. Rather, your child correctly sees discipline as the way you handle conflict when family members get upset or have conflicting desires. In other words, *the way you discipline your child becomes her model for working out interpersonal problems.* So punishment, which is the use of force, teaches her to use force against her siblings whenever there's a problem to be solved.

Want some other insights into how your child perceives punishment, and thus how it shapes your child and her relationships with her siblings?

1. **Punishment focuses kids on avoiding more punishment, which is not the same thing as caring about others.** They may learn not to hit their sibling, but only so they won't get in trouble, rather than so their brother or sister won't be hurt. Punishment delays the development of empathy, which means that children find it harder to appreciate their brother or sister's perspective.[4]

2. **Setting limits without empathy deprives kids of the opportunity to internalize self-discipline.**[5] No one likes to be controlled, so it's not surprising that kids reject limits that aren't empathic. When kids resist our limits, they see the "control" as outside themselves. As crazy as it sounds, that means *they see it as YOUR job to stop them from attacking their sibling when they get angry, rather than as THEIR job to control themselves.* When we set limits so the child feels understood, he ends up internalizing our limits—and taking responsibility for himself, even in the absence of authority figures.[6]

3. **Kids raised with punishment learn to use it against their sibling to increase their own standing and power.** When children know that their rival will be punished, they have an incentive to tattle, both to hurt their sibling and to be able to play the role of the "good child." (More on tattling in Chapter 4.)

4. **When siblings are punished for fighting with each other, they become more resentful of each other and more focused on revenge.** Often, they get into a negative cycle of inciting conflict while trying to make it look like the other child's fault.

5. **Kids raised with punitive discipline are more likely to have tendencies toward anger and depression.**[7] That's because we're teaching them that part of who they are—their emotions—isn't acceptable. Since parents aren't there to help them learn to manage those difficult feelings, they're left lonely, trying to sort out for themselves how to overcome their "lesser" impulses. This makes it harder for them to manage their anger, and more likely that they'll take it out on their siblings, who are often the closest target.

6. **Punishment teaches fear.** Kids learn what they live and what you model. If kids do what you want because they fear you, it's a small step to bullying. If you yell, they'll yell. If you use force, they'll use force. Against anyone they can, including their sibling.

It may be difficult to hear it, but the research is clear: Children end up learning some entirely unintended lessons from punishment—about wielding power, resolving disagreements, and handling upsetting emotions. So punishing children not only undermines your child's development in general, but also has a negative impact on your children's relationship with each other.[8]

Rethinking Discipline

And what about discipline? How does that relate to our discussion about punishment? The word "discipline" actually means "to guide," from the same root as the word "disciple." Punishment is more about force than guiding; it's defined as causing another person emotional or physical pain to convince them to do things our way. But in our culture, most of what we consider discipline is indeed intended to cause the child emotional (and sometimes physical) pain to get him to do things our way. So discipline as we use it, and think about it, is a form of punishment.

Since the word "discipline" is so often misinterpreted, I suggest that we stop using the word. Instead, let's consciously move "beyond discipline" and instead think of ourselves as coaching our children using loving guidance. What would that change? Well, to start, it would change our understanding of our children. Instead of seeing kids as in need of "discipline" to convince them to behave, we'd use an entirely different lens.

1. **Children are born needing to connect with an adult who will guide them.** Children will follow our guidance and protect that parent-child connection as long as it doesn't compromise their integrity. If you stay connected to your child, he will *want* to cooperate. When he doesn't, it's because he can't, and he needs your help with the emotions that are driving his inappropriate behavior.

Are you wondering if some misbehavior is simply the child doing what he wants? Of course it is! But in that case, it's a symptom that the child considers his connection to you less important than doing what he wants. So the relationship needs strengthening, or the child needs help with the emotions that are keeping him from connecting with you. *When a child trusts that we're really on his side, he's willing to give up doing what he wants, to do something he wants more—which is to stay positively connected to us.* If you think about it, that's the definition of self-discipline—giving up something you want (that piece of cake) for something you want more (your health and fitness). So every time your child chooses not to hit his sister, because what he wants more is your warm respect, he's building the neural pathways to become more self-disciplined. And that self-discipline will last for the rest of his life.

2. **Children learn what they live,** through repeated experience. Every interaction with your child models how to manage oneself and relate to others.

3. **All misbehavior is a cry for help or connection.** Respond to the need, and the behavior will change. If a child isn't meeting our expectations, she needs more support to do so, whether that's teaching, connection, or help in working through the emotions that are getting in her way. Much of what we consider "misbehavior" is normal childishness and can be "corrected" simply through loving guidance.

4. **Once children can regulate their emotions, they can regulate their behavior.** If your child feels connected to you, he wants to follow your lead—but sometimes he can't, because

his big emotions overwhelm his still-developing prefrontal cortex. As we've already discussed, you can help him learn to regulate his emotions by using the powerful tool of empathy. Sometimes that won't be enough, and stormy emotions will push your child to lash out. At those times, your child needs your help to work through those feelings so he doesn't have to act them out. As children get older, they're increasingly able to use words to express emotions and move past them, but young children usually just need a chance to cry, as described later in this chapter.

5. **The key to setting effective limits is empathy.** This is not permissive parenting. You're the leader, and you're responsible for guiding your child's behavior. So coaching doesn't mean giving your child everything she wants. She can't draw on the walls, stay up all night, or hit the baby. But even as we insist that she behave in accordance with our values, we can show her—by our listening, empathy, and willingness to find win/win solutions—that we care about what matters to her. Empathic limits defuse resistance, because the child at least feels understood, even when she doesn't get what she wants.

Guiding our child peacefully, then, means we're working to stay calm ourselves and to teach with peace instead of with force. We're modeling how to express our needs and set boundaries on another person's behavior in a respectful way. Peaceful parents know they can't control their child's behavior—only the child can do that. So we create a relationship of trust with our child so that he's open to our guidance. His healthy choices yield happy results in his life, so he sees the benefits and begins to "own" those desirable behaviors. That's why children who are coached are more likely to choose to do what's "right" as they grow up, even when you're not watching.

Setting Empathic Limits

The sweet spot between strict and permissive is giving the child support to meet our expectations. How can we give support when we need to set limits? Set the limit with empathy, by reconnecting and acknowledging the child's point of view. Let's look at some examples.

Always start with a deep breath to center yourself. Then, guide your child to the desired behavior—at the same time that you reconnect with him.

Setting a Limit While Acknowledging the Child's Feelings and Needs

Rather than: *"Don't shout at the baby! You're making her cry more!"*

Try: *"I understand that the baby's crying is so loud it hurts your ears. It hurts mine, too. Shouting at her isn't okay, though . . . It scares her and makes her cry even more."*

Setting the Limit with Empathy and Redirecting the Child's Impulse

Rather than: *"You bully! That's it, time out for you."*

Try: *"You're mad! And I won't let you hit your brother. Can you tell him in words how mad you are and what you need from him?"*

Setting the Limit with Empathy and Giving the Child Her Wish in Fantasy

Rather than: *"Don't be selfish. I've been playing tea party with you for an hour, and the baby's hungry!"*

Try: *"You wish we could keep playing tea party. I do need to get the baby when she cries, so she doesn't feel afraid and alone, just like I come to you when you cry . . . I bet sometimes you wish it was just you and me again, the way it used to be, right? Sounds like you'd love it if we could just sit here all morning and have a tea party, and you didn't have to share me at all . . ."*

Setting the Limit with Empathy and Giving the Child a Choice

Rather than: *"That's dangerous! Give me that stick!"*

Try: *"Austin, do you hear Lewis? He's saying he doesn't want that stick so near his face . . . You can either put the stick down, or come with me over here to swing it where it's away from your brother."*

Setting the Limit with Empathy and Inviting the Child to Cooperate with Playfulness

Rather than: *"If you can't stop fighting over the couch, both of you have to get off it!"*

Try: *"We'll solve this fighting over the couch! I never get the couch to myself!"* as you plop on top of your kids.

Setting the Limit with Empathy and Holding Your Boundary with Action

Rather than: *"I've told you three times to stop splashing your sister! Out of the tub now! Stop that crying, it's your own fault."*

Try: *"Peyton, look at your sister's face . . . That's too much splashing for her. And for me, it's getting me all wet, too. Can you stop splashing? No? Okay, bathtime is over for tonight . . . Out you come. You're crying, you weren't ready to get out yet . . . You love splashing, don't you? Splashing's not okay with the* *baby in the tub. How about tomorrow we set up the wading pool in the backyard and you can splash as much as you want?"*

Setting the Limit with Empathy and Inviting the Child to Work with You to Come Up With a Win/Win Solution

Rather than: *"No, you can't put the music on while the baby is napping. Find something else to do."*

Try: *"You want to put the music on loud so we can have fun dancing . . . I need it to be quiet so the baby stays asleep and you and I can play . . . Hmmm . . . How can we all be happy here? How about we play Legos together now, and when the baby wakes up, I will put her in the sling and we can all dance together to your music?"*

Rethinking Time-Outs

I tried time-outs with my four-year-old. Just like you warned, she went right to the "I'm so bad, I can't stop hitting my brother, and you don't love me anymore." She said it right after the first time I put her in her room for slapping her two-year-old brother.
    –Valerie

We've explored why setting limits without punishing will transform your children's relationship with each other. But what about time-outs? Most parents with more than one child use time-outs when their children fight, to separate their kids and, hopefully, teach them to be nicer to each other.

But time-outs are punishment. They don't actually teach kids to be nicer to each other. In fact, they tend to worsen kids' behavior, just like other punishments. Why?

- Time-outs create shame. Kids believe that if they were "good," they would be able to stop the bad feelings that are making them act so badly. Unfortunately, when we feel bad, we act badly. So shame creates a negative cycle that keeps reinforcing the child feeling like a bad person inside.

- Time-outs don't help kids learn emotional regulation. When you send him off to his room by himself, he'll calm down eventually. But because he hasn't actually expressed those feelings, he's pushed them down inside where they aren't under conscious control. That's why time-outs tend to make kids angrier and less emotionally regulated, so you'll see him walk by his sister and push her for no reason.[9]

- Time-outs don't actually solve the problem between the children that caused one or both to lash out. Parents often feel as if they've taken care of the problem by giving the child a time-out and a lecture, but he's no more prepared to navigate conflict the next time.

- Time-outs, like all punishment, weaken our bond with our child. Unfortunately, that bond is the only reason children behave to begin with. So parents who use time-outs often set their child up for a cycle of escalating misbehavior.

- Time-outs fuel power struggles between parent and child. To the degree that kids feel powerless, they take it out on someone less powerful—usually a sibling.

- Time-outs "work" through fear, as a symbolic abandonment. As Alfie Kohn points out, they're a form of "love withdrawal."[10] Since sibling rivalry stems from your child's fear that he's losing your love to his sibling, any discipline that involves love withdrawal is bound to worsen sibling rivalry.

You may have read that there's a "right" way to do time-outs that has been shown by research to be "effective." But effective at what? I've read many studies showing that time-out stops the misbehavior in the moment. But so do spankings, and we know that spankings are a risk factor for kids' emotional health.[11] I've never seen a study that examined the long-term emotional health of children who grew up being disciplined with time-outs, and compared those children with kids who have never had a time-out or other punishment. And yes, there are now hundreds of thousands of children who have been brought up with loving guidance rather than punishment, thanks to Haim Ginott (the father of the positive parenting movement), Jane Nelsen (who founded the positive discipline movement), and many other advocates for children.

We do, however, have a good deal of evidence that time-outs don't work to prevent a recurrence of misbehavior, which raises the question of whether the time-out may even be causing those recurrences. A study done by the National Institute of Mental Health concluded that time-outs are effective in getting toddlers to cooperate, but only temporarily.[12] The children misbehaved more than children who weren't disciplined with time-out, even when their mothers took the time to talk with them after the time-out. Michael Chapman and Carolyn Zahn-Wexler, the authors of the study, concluded that the children were reacting to the perceived "love withdrawal" by misbehaving more. That's in keeping with the studies on love withdrawal as a punishment technique, which show that kids subjected to it tend to exhibit more misbehavior, worse emotional health, and less developed morality.[13] These results are not surprising, given how much children need to feel connected to us to feel safe, and how likely they are to act out when they don't feel safe.

I can understand if you're feeling a bit worried right now. If you can't use time-outs, how will you keep your kids from running wild? The answer is that time-outs aren't actually helping your child behave better; they undermine her connection to you and cause more acting out. I've seen thousands of families transition to a peaceful parenting approach where they focus on regulating themselves, reconnecting with their children, and setting limits with empathy—and their children stop acting out so much. Peaceful parenting raises children who *want* to follow your family rules, so your need for punishment, including time-outs, will gradually fade into the past.

Rethinking Rewards

Surely, going positive is a good thing. Why not use rewards instead of punishment? After all, don't rewards make the desired behavior more likely?

Well, yes—the reward makes the child want more rewards. But there's cautionary research on rewards as well. Once you introduce *extrinsic* rewards like stickers, the child stops valuing the *intrinsic* rewards, like the happy look on his brother's face when he shares.[14] So the reward only works for as long as the child wants the stickers, and meanwhile he isn't learning to value that warm feeling inside that comes from engaging in the considerate behavior. In fact, many studies have shown that a reward makes a child *less* likely to share, unless you're watching.[15]

The other problem with controlling kids' behavior using rewards is that when humans feel controlled from the outside, whether by rewards or punishment, they naturally rebel. Don't you? One mother told me that her strong-willed daughter finally "behaved" well enough to earn a Barbie at Target. As she walked out of the store, she pulled the head off the Barbie and hurled it on the ground. When humans feel manipulated, they become oppositional.

Please note that I'm not saying not to encourage your child. Kids, like the rest of us, thrive on acknowledgment and encouraging words. But rewards don't give children a chance to discover that the behavior we're advocating works for them, not just for the reward, but for deeper, more satisfying reasons—beginning with the delighted look on their mother's face, but evolving into having more fun with their sister and feeling good about who they are.

The Difference Between Consequences and Limits

Many parents are confused by the difference between limits and consequences.

"Natural" consequences are the result of a child's behavior, and you have nothing to do with creating them. For instance, if he always squirts his brothers in the face when they're having water fights in the backyard, his brothers may not want to have water fights with him. Often, natural consequences teach your child more effectively than any lesson you could devise, if you can resist stepping in to "rescue" your child from the consequence.

"Limits" are boundaries you establish about what behavior is permitted in your family. If your child crosses that boundary, you lovingly redirect him. If he can't follow your limit, you remove him from the situation. That's not a punishment; you're just holding your limit. So if your rule is that water fights are fine but "no spraying anyone in the face," and your child repeatedly breaks that rule over your other children's objections, it's your job to hold that boundary.

"Dante, the rule is no spraying in the face. Your brothers are saying NO! Can you stop spraying them in the face, or do you need my help?"

If Dante says, *"Okay, I'll stop,"* he probably will. Why? Because he's making a conscious commitment. But what if he doesn't? He needs your help.

"Dante, your brothers are saying, 'Stop spraying our faces!' and you keep spraying. Come over here with me and let's do some breathing and calm down a little, so you can stop yourself when you get excited." Setting limits means you need to follow through, and sometimes you will have to use your greater physical size to move your child. Notice, though, that you're not being punitive or mean about it. Yes, you're holding a boundary, but instead of "enforcing," this is more like coaching, supporting your child to meet your expectations.

Before you let Dante rejoin the game, you'll need to ask again if he thinks he can regulate himself, help him come up with a plan, and get a commitment from him. *"Dante, why is the rule that we don't spray faces? How will you remember? What if you get excited? Great, so the plan is . . . Let's shake on it."*

You'll also want to point out the natural consequence of his previous behavior, and help him make a repair. *"Your brothers are worried that you'll spray them in the face again. How can you help them feel safe to play with you now? . . . Great, so you're going to tell them that you won't spray their faces again, that you can control yourself?"*

What if Dante "forgets" in five minutes and just can't resist blasting his brother in the face? You remove him from the game. *"It was just too hard for you today . . . We'll try again tomorrow . . . You're growing every day, and getting more able to control yourself to be a responsible playmate."* What if he cries? There are worse things than crying. His tears are part of the grieving process, and that grief is part of what will help him control himself next time.

Notice that I haven't mentioned "consequences" imposed by a parent for a child's transgression, such as time-outs or losing privileges? Those are punishment. They're not very effective in changing young children's behavior for the same reasons that other punishments aren't effective: Punishment makes a child who is already having a hard time feel even less like cooperating, and it doesn't help the child with the emotions that caused her to act out to begin with.

So, for instance, if he always squirts his brothers in the face when they have water fights, something is going on that he needs help to master. Maybe he isn't seeing the pain and fear on their faces and he needs your help to learn empathy. Or maybe he does see, and enjoys it, which suggests that he needs help with his jealousy, or that he needs to feel more powerful in his life. Or maybe he feels terrible as soon as he does it but can't stop himself before it happens, in which case he needs your help with impulse control. You can see that his behavior during the water fights is just a symptom of a larger issue that he needs your coaching to heal.

You're probably wondering if this is unnecessary coddling. Regardless of why he's doing this, wouldn't he stop if there were an unpleasant consequence? In other words, *"Dante! You're hurting your brothers! Time-out! You sit over there until you can behave!"* But what does he learn? No matter what you say to him before he goes back into the game:

- Instead of thinking of himself as someone who needs a little help because he's still learning to regulate himself, he concludes that he's someone who hurts others. He must be a bad person; after all, he couldn't stop himself and he's in time-out.

- Instead of having your help to "breathe and calm down," he's left to settle himself, which usually means he stuffs those emotions down, beyond his conscious control. That makes them more likely to pop up later, which means in ten minutes he'll be spraying his brothers in the face again. That's why kids end up in time-out over and over again some days.

- Instead of seeing you as on his side, even when you have to set a limit, he decides that you always side with his brothers—you must like them better. Just wait until he gets his hands on that hose again!

But shouldn't there be a "consequence"? Of course! Look at all the consequences of what happened here. What has your child learned, consciously and unconsciously?

- *"When Mom tells me to do something, she means it. There's no point in trying to ignore her."*
- *"When I hurt others, I have to leave the game until I can manage myself."*
- *"I make mistakes, but Mom always understands. She helps me figure out how to do better."*
- *"When I hurt someone, I can make things better."*
- *"Everyone in our family takes our family rules seriously. The most important one is treating each other with respect and kindness."*

He doesn't know it, but because he's choosing to control himself, he's also building the neural pathways for increased self-discipline and emotional regulation in the future.

The truth is, we can't make another human being do what we want. We can only help them *want* to. Empathic limits help your child *want* to follow your guidance, so those good habits become part of who he is, whether you're there or not.

What If Empathy Doesn't Work?

When parents begin using loving guidance, they're often amazed by how well empathy "works" to calm their child and help her accept their limits. In fact, empathy is so effective in reconnecting with our upset child and helping her calm down that it takes us by surprise when it "doesn't work." But empathy isn't a trick to control the other person. It's a means of connection, and of helping our child process emotion. So when empathy doesn't "work," consider whether you're really connecting, and whether you're helping your child with her emotions. Here are the problems I hear most often from parents about "using" empathy:

1. **"Empathy makes my child cry harder."** That means your empathy is actually "working" perfectly. Think about a time when you had some big feelings locked up inside—maybe something bad happened. You were holding it together. Then someone arrived with whom you felt safe, and they hugged you or said something compassionate, and you burst into tears. So when kids have big feelings and we empathize, they do get more in touch with the feelings. But that's a good thing. Because once they feel those emotions, the emotions evaporate. A good cry positively transforms our body chemistry as well as our emotional state.

2. **"Empathy doesn't stop the tantrum."** Once your child is swept into "fight or flight" mode, words don't help. So instead of labeling emotion, communicate safety so your child can show you all those feelings. The fewer words the better, just enough so she hears your compassion and knows you're standing by with a hug. Empathy won't stop the tantrum, but it will help your child show you all those feelings, which starts the healing.

3. **"I keep repeating, 'You are very sad and frustrated,' but he gets mad and tells me not to say it."** If we're merely par-

roting the words, children sense that, and it makes them irate. If you can let yourself actually feel how your precious child is so torn up inside, you'll get tears in your eyes. And he'll feel understood.

It also matters how old your child is. With an angry toddler, you might get down on his level and acknowledge, *"You're so mad!"* The toddler is often reassured: Mom doesn't think it's an emergency; there's even a name for this tidal wave that's swamping him. But as kids get older, telling them what they feel makes them angrier. Like most of us, they don't want to be analyzed or manipulated; they want to know that we see their side of things. Imagine if you were upset and your partner just kept repeating, *"You are very sad and frustrated!"*

There's no need to always label the emotion. Understanding his perspective is enough: *"I'm sorry you woke up from your nap to find that Daddy took your brother to the store without you . . . I know you wish you could have gone."*

As kids grow, a simple *"Oh, sweetie, I'm sorry it's so hard"* will get your empathy across.

And of course, while your child is in the middle of the tantrum, you need not tell them how sad and mad they are. Words of any kind will escalate their anger. The only thing they need to know is that they're safe, and you're ready with a hug when they're ready.

4. **"I empathize with the emotions, but then she's still upset about it."** Empathy helps us see our child's point of view and reconnect with her. And sometimes that's enough to defuse her emotions. But if she's reacting to what she sees as a big problem in her life, she may not be able to get past the emotions until we support her to solve the problem: *"You're upset that your little sister keeps grabbing things out of your doll-*

house. Let's find a place for you to play with it that's out of her reach."

- Sometimes she needs our support to solve it herself: *"You're so mad at your brother. I think he needs to hear how you feel. Let's go find your brother, and I will stay with you while you tell him."*

- Sometimes she simply can't have what she wants, but you can give her what she wants with a wish: *"It's hard when your big brother doesn't want to play with you. I bet you wish he'd help you build train tracks every single day, don't you?"*

Sometimes, though, there's no solving the problem. Maybe the disappointment is too great, or triggers some earlier hurt that's still lurking and waiting to be expressed, so that only tears will do. In that case, the empathy "worked" so that your child felt safe enough to show you his upset. That's how kids build resilience—they feel safe enough with you to let themselves feel their disappointment fully—and they learn they can come out on the other side feeling okay. He's crying? That's a *good* thing.

5. **"I say, 'You are mad but we don't hit,' and he hits again ten minutes later."** If your message isn't getting through, it's usually because your child needs more help with his emotions than your empathy is giving him. Sometimes when we use the word "but," kids don't feel that their feelings are really being acknowledged. It can help to use "and" as in *"You can be as mad as you want, AND we don't hit."*

But the most frequent reason that empathic reminders don't prevent hitting is that you simply can't expect "talk" of any kind to heal big emotions. Kids who hit have fear locked inside. They need to cry and shake and yawn and show you that fear. Only then does hitting usually stop. We'll talk more about how to help kids through big emotions later in this chapter.

In fact, empathy *always* works to reconnect with your child and help him with his emotions. So if your empathy doesn't seem to be "working," maybe words are getting in your way. Stop trying to come up with the right words. Instead, imagine yourself as a child feeling what your son or daughter is feeling at this moment. What do you wish your parent would do right now to love you through this? Do that.

Preventive Maintenance

Daily Special Time works absolute wonders in our home. Whenever we let it slip, I notice a degeneration in my children's relationship, and I see an immediate improvement when we get going again, even if it is just for five minutes a day. It seems to be even more effective if we add in family roughhousing and get a kids vs. grown-ups romp going; it really strengthens their bond.

—Belynda

What's preventive maintenance with children? You might think of it as refilling your children's love tank and giving them an emotional tune-up on a daily basis, so you don't end up in the breakdown lane. In life with more than one child, disconnection inevitably happens, and if you don't have connection practices built into your life, that disconnection creates problems before you know it. So once you have more than one child, preventive maintenance with each of them is critical.

In conventional parenting, you don't really do much preventive maintenance; you just intervene with discipline when things go wrong. But with peaceful parenting, you're trying to get to the root of why things go wrong and fill your children's needs so things don't go wrong as often. Sure, that takes work, but parenting is work either way, and this investment in positive prevention creates a more peaceful home, closer relationships, and more cooperative kids. It makes you and everyone else a lot happier to have a family pillow fight before you start making dinner—which leaves everyone in a better mood and more likely to get along—than to yell when kids can't get along at dinner.

The advantages of preventive maintenance:

- Your child feels treasured just for being herself, which is the best possible antidote to sibling rivalry.
- Your child feels deeply connected to you, which helps him *want* to cooperate with you, so your life is more peaceful.
- Your child feels safe, which helps him regulate himself.
- Your child gets your help with her emotions *before* she falls apart, which minimizes those crisis moments when both children urgently need you.
- Your children enjoy more frequent positive interactions with each other, which research shows leads to a closer sibling relationship, which leads to less conflict, which leads to more frequent positive interactions—a positive cycle.[16]

Here are the basic preventive maintenance habits that reliably transform every parent-child relationship—and therefore transform the sibling relationship as well:

1. **Use routines.** More organized families report better sibling relationships, although this doesn't mean there's a direct cause and effect.[17] But routines do help children feel safer, which helps them regulate themselves emotionally and thus get along better with everyone in the family. They also min-

imize your job as head cop and reduce power struggles. That's important for the sibling relationship, because one side effect of parent-child power struggles is that kids salve their egos by finding ways to feel more powerful than their siblings. This doesn't mean forcing your children into a rigid schedule, but noticing what seems to work for them and for you, and finding a routine that you can all look forward to.

2. **Make empathy your go-to way of relating to your child.** Most of the time, we as parents are just trying to move our kids through the schedule, so when they express negative emotions, we often find it inconvenient. And yet responding to our child with empathy may be the most important preventive maintenance habit we can develop, because it strengthens the parent-child relationship, and helps kids process emotions as they arise. So when your child says, *"I hate chicken! Why do we have to have chicken again?!"* you may well be tempted to lecture him about how hard you worked, how his body needs protein, and why he should be grateful to have a healthy dinner. Instead, try training yourself to respond first by acknowledging his perspective: *"You don't feel like eating chicken tonight, huh? I guess we have had a lot of chicken lately. And it isn't your favorite, I know. I bet you wish you could have pasta every night, don't you?"* Your child may or may not happily eat his chicken, but you'll end up having a more peaceful dinner, which may include some good problem-solving about nutrition and how to balance everyone's food preferences. And your child will finish the meal feeling closer to you, instead of with a chip on his shoulder.

3. **Daily roughhousing.** Children build up anxiety (mild fear) all day long, and they need a way to let it out. Luckily, nature

has designed humans with a great way to reduce anxiety and clear the stress hormones from our bodies: giggling. Laughter really is the best medicine, and the best way to get your child laughing is physical roughhousing that provokes a very mild fear response.[18] Laughing also releases oxytocin and endorphins, so every time you laugh with someone, you're building trust.[19] That means that when your children laugh with each other, they're bonding, which helps head off sibling squabbles later in the day. Figure out what gets your children laughing, and schedule in at least fifteen minutes of belly laughter daily, whether it's playing peek-a-boo, chasing them around the house, bucking bronco rides, or a kids against grown-up pillow fight. (For more on roughhousing, see Chapter 8.)

4. **Special Time.** Daily one-on-one time with each child builds trust, reconnects you, and helps your child express his emotions so he can move past them. Patty Wipfler of Hand in Hand Parenting has taken "Special Time" to a whole new level by recommending that parents leave this time completely unstructured and put the child in charge. In other words, this is not making cookies or reading together, and it isn't regular play, where you're a more equal participant. Simply let the child decide what to do and pour your loving attention into him. Resist the urge to take an active role yourself; instead, describe what you see him doing (*"Now the trucks are crashing!"*). If he insists on your participating, take on whatever role he suggests, but let him direct the action.

Most parents say that once they start daily Special Time, their problems with their child diminish dramatically, whether the problem is aggression between siblings, tantrums, or defiance. If you can't manage Special Time daily, then you'll want to find a longer stretch every weekend, but even ten minutes a day is more effective in meeting your child's needs than waiting to reconnect on weekends. Occasional overnights in which you take one child off for a special trip can also help interrupt a negative cycle and turn things around. If you're a single parent, or a parent who's often functioning solo, I urge you to trade babysitting with a friend, or even to use a sitter twice a week, to ensure that you get one-on-one time with each child.

If both parents are working outside the home, it can be daunting to find time for preventive maintenance. But I believe it will make such a positive difference in your life, and in your children's relationship with each other, that I encourage you to consider an experiment. Drop everything nonessential from your schedule, and try daily roughhousing and Special Time for three months. Be ruthless. No PTA meetings, no entertaining, no work emails in the evening. In fact, consider trying to arrange one hour less of work each day, even if you have to give up pay for those hours. I guarantee that you'll see such a dramatic shift in your children that you won't go back to your previous schedule until your children are older.

Regular use of these preventive maintenance practices will help your child *want* to follow your lead. When she doesn't, it will be because she can't manage her emotions. How can you help her? "Time-in" and "scheduled meltdowns," discussed in the next two sections.

When Your Child Is Acting Out: Time-In

The crying and screaming will go on for a few minutes but has more often than not ended with him hugging me, calming down, and even him saying sorry without me asking for it. He's about to turn three.

—Katrina

"Time-in" is what it sounds like—the opposite of "time-out." Where time-out isolates the child, time-in is a way for you to interrupt "bad" behavior, and to prevent it from escalating, by reconnecting with your child.

Let's say your daughter is acting cranky and belligerent. Finally, she throws her cup across the room. Should you send her to time-out?

If she could articulate what's going on, she might say, *"Hey, Mom, Dad, I'm having a really hard time here. I woke up feeling grumpy. We were out of my favorite cereal. I missed you so much at preschool. It took a lot for me to sit quietly for so much of the day and follow directions. My friend told me I couldn't come to her birthday party if I didn't play the game her way. And then I finally get home and I'm hungry and grumpy and that little brother you think is so cute is always on your lap, while you tell me to wait just a minute! I wonder if anyone around here even cares about me at all! Maybe you got a replacement because I'm just not good enough for you!"*

Of course, she can't say that. So she acts it out with her difficult behavior. She's been stuffing down fears and tears all day long, waiting for a safe chance to let them out. Now all those emotions are coming up, so she's "acting (the feelings) out." When children get provocative and purposely break the rules, they're asking for help with those turbulent feelings. Often, connection is enough to help them re-regulate, which we can solve with a time-in.

So you summon up all your compassion and remind yourself that she's a little person whose behavior is a cry for help. You say, *"Cups aren't for throwing. You're having a hard time, aren't you, sweetie? Let's go to our comfort spot and snuggle for a bit."* You hug her, then take her to a specially designated spot that feels safe and cozy, and snuggle up. You connect warmly, which may be all she needs to pull herself together. After the warm physical connection, get her giggling if you can, because laughter evaporates those stored-up anxieties almost as well as tears. Her sunny mood will return, and she'll be ready to help you clean up the spilled cup.

Wondering if you should punish her now, so she'll learn not to throw the cup? Unnecessary and counterproductive. She's already learned that she doesn't want to throw the cup next time, and some other crucial lessons:

- *"My parents are on my side. I don't actually need to throw my cup, even when I'm really upset. My parents are always ready to listen and help me."* (Strengthening the trust in the parent-child partnership so the child *wants* to cooperate.)

- *"When I'm upset, I feel an urgent need to show how unhappy I am, but if I take a few minutes to sit with the feelings without lashing out, they go away."* (Learning skills to regulate her emotions, and therefore her behavior.)

- *"My parents love and accept me just as I am, including when I'm feeling difficult emotions."* (The foundation of self-esteem.)

- *"After I calm down, I can always figure out a way to make things better."* (The first step in accepting that nobody's perfect, but we can always admit, and repair, our mistakes.)

Time-in is not a punishment. It's a way of giving your child the connection he needs for emotional regulation. Most children need this reconnection time daily, if they've been away from you. Often, the reconnection is enough to get your whole evening back on track.

But sometimes "attention" just isn't enough. Your child will let you know, because he won't feel and act better after your time-in. In that case, he needs more help with his emotions than simple connection can give. Usually, he's resisting your connection because feeling his love for you will also open the doors to all those tears he's holding back. If you jolly him along, he might be able to pull it together temporarily, but a meltdown is just waiting to happen. Why not invite it?

Helping Kids with Big Emotions: Scheduled Meltdowns

Quite often during the lead up to a big meltdown, my son will be in a terrible mood/belligerent/fight with his sister and do all the stuff that parents strive to help their children learn not to do. And then a huge gush of emotion explodes. Even though I've learned to stay (mostly) calm, it's still very stressful for me and it's often not until the dust settles that I realize that he had a "meltdown" and it's great that he's released some of the upset in his "emotional backpack."

—Lindsay

What's a scheduled meltdown? It's the same meltdown your child would have had at the playground or supermarket, except that you give him a chance to have it at home when you're ready to pay attention, while the baby is asleep.

It may seem odd to offer your child the chance to have a meltdown. But your child will have those feelings whether you welcome them or not. The reasoning part of the brain is still developing in young children, and they're easily overwhelmed by emotion. Sometimes, kids (like adults) just need to cry. Once you give him a chance to feel those scary feelings in the safety of your warm presence, the emotions evaporate and he's free to get on with his life. Tears actually reduce the stress hormones circulating in your child's bloodstream, so he's happier and more relaxed. So it's a huge gift if you can welcome your child's upsets and help him through the tempest. Not only will he be happier for the rest of the day (and probably for the rest of the week), but he'll also feel closer to you, and more cooperative.

I've never met a parent whose first response when her child acts out is *"Hurray! Now he can show me those upsetting emotions and feel better!"* Naturally, most of us respond to our kids' provocative behavior by becoming increasingly annoyed, until we're ready to lock them in their rooms, or worse. It isn't until later that we're able to see that when our child finally cried, everything got better. He clearly needed to work through some big emotions—but how were we supposed to know?

The answer is that when children whine, get rigid and demanding, or intentionally misbehave, it's *always* a sign that something is wrong. That something can be physical, like fighting off a cold, or emotional, like their teacher being out sick for a day, or a big developmental leap, like learning to ride a bike. But often it's nothing specific, just the accumulation of small stresses that the child hasn't gotten a chance to work through with play or words, and is lugging around in the unconscious, or what I call the "emotional backpack."

So when your child is having a hard day, that hard day is caused by something real, just as our hard days are. Luckily, we don't need to know the reason our child is unhappy to help him with his feelings. Children will always start to act out when they're stressed, and laughing or crying will usually heal whatever's wrong, unless the stressor continues. So anytime your child is especially difficult, train yourself to see that as a red flag. She isn't just being ornery. She's emotionally stressed, and she needs your help.

Your goal is to help your child show you what's going on. When children are upset, words are counterproductive, because the child has to work too hard to think and the emotions get shut down. Besides, most children can't articulate why they're upset, at least until after they've had a good cry. Fortunately, children are "designed" to heal themselves by surfacing their hurts, just like their immune system will push an infection to the surface to heal. All you have to do is support his natural process by creating safety.

First, acknowledge any irritation you're feeling, and try to shift yourself to a more empathic frame of mind, so you can be compassionate. This isn't easy when he's being provocative. It helps to use a mantra to remind yourself that *"Children need love most when they deserve it least."* What he needs most from you right now is to feel how much you still love him, no matter what.

Create safety. Start with physical affection. If he's open to it, do some mild roughhousing to get him laughing. (See Chapter 8.) This shifts his body from stress hormones to bonding hormones and makes it more likely that he'll cry instead of getting stuck in anger.

Invite the meltdown by setting a kind limit about anything. For instance, if he hasn't been getting enough one-on-one time with you, then *"I'm afraid we need to stop playing soon, sweetie"* will bring up all his grief about having lost you, and may well provoke tears. You can also set a kind limit about his behavior or something he wants.

If he gets angry, increase your compassion. Children often get angry when we empathize. That doesn't mean you're doing it wrong. He's snapping at you because when you offer understanding, it puts him in touch with his feelings, which at the moment are threatening to overwhelm him with hurt and fear. So he does what we all do when we feel threatened—he lashes out. In other words, his anger is a defense against more vulnerable feelings. Your goal is to help him feel safe enough to go beneath the anger. *"Oh, sweetie, I see how upset you are . . . I'm sorry this is so hard."* If you can stay compassionate enough—which is the challenge for most of us—he'll cry. That's what's therapeutic, not the anger.

What if he doesn't cry? Back off, and build safety and connection for a few days, using the preventive maintenance tools like empathy, roughhousing, and Special Time. Then summon up as much compassion as you can, and try again.

Welcome the upset. If you can respond to your child's anger with compassion and a softening of your heart, he's likely to cry. The more he cries, the better. The fear is locked in his body. He may thrash and sweat and want to push against something; that all helps his body let go of the fear. If he lashes out, move back so he can't hurt you. Remember, the anger isn't the healing part. Your job is to help him feel safe enough to get past the anger to the more vulnerable fear, grief, and powerlessness beneath.

What if he yells at you to shut up? Stop talking. The deepest healing is always beyond words, so don't ask questions once he's upset, and don't say much yourself. Just help him feel safe enough to cry. *"You're safe . . . I'm here . . . Everybody needs to cry sometimes."* There will be plenty of time to teach later.

What if he won't let you hold him? Stay close. Say, *"I'm right here when you're ready for a hug."* Then try to stay present with his pain. Don't start thinking about your shopping list. Soon he'll be back in your arms, sobbing.

What if he yells at you to go away? He's trying to regulate the intensity of the emotion. Because he feels safe with you, his feelings come up more intensely in your presence. So he's trying to send you away so that he won't feel those unbearable emotions. But he doesn't really want you to leave, because he needs you to see him safely through. Sure, he'll calm down if you leave him alone—but that just means he'll stuff the feelings down again and they'll pop out later. To work through emotions, we need to allow ourselves to feel them, and young children don't feel safe enough to face those scary feelings by themselves. Say, *"I'll move back to here . . . I won't leave you alone with these big feelings. I'll be right here when you're ready for a hug."*

Once he stops crying, he'll probably want to cuddle. He might change the subject, but he still wants to know it was okay to have those feelings, and that you still love him. You can just say, *"Those were some big feelings. That was hard work. I think we need a big hug."* Then, help him reflect by telling him what happened in the form of a story: *"You were so mad and sad . . . You yelled at Mommy and tried to hit me . . . Mommy said, 'No hitting! Hitting hurts!' and Mommy held you so you couldn't hit. Mommy will always keep everyone safe. You were so upset. You cried and cried. Everybody needs to cry sometimes. Then you were done crying, and Mommy hugged you and held you and we snuggled. Then we both felt better."*

What if it's hard for you to tolerate your child crying? This is the hardest part for most of us. Keep breathing and reassuring yourself that it isn't an emergency. What's healing for your child is your acceptance. You don't have to *do* or say anything, except stay as calm and compassionate as you can. When we're able to breathe through our own fear in the face of our child's pain, we heal something in ourselves, too.

Does this teach kids to be "drama queens"? Just the opposite. It teaches the child to accept her feelings so she can work through them, which is how children learn to regulate themselves. Some sensitive children may need to cry every day, many cry once a week, but all of them will cry less over time as they let themselves feel all those emotions they've been storing up.

Most encouraging, you'll see a big difference between meltdowns. Once your child has shown you all that raw pain and felt understood—even though nothing changes outside—he'll feel closer to you and more emotionally generous toward his sibling. He'll become increasingly happier and more able to manage himself. Often, parents say "He's back to his old self," or even, about children who have struggled for years, "He's a different child."

And since you're inviting the meltdowns at a time when you can really listen, you're dodging the tantrums that would otherwise have happened—yes, you guessed it—exactly when the baby next needs you.

How to Help Each Child with Big Emotions When You Have More Than One Upset Child

I have found when another child is witnessing the process of helping kids with emotions, they become aware and able to help. Mine often imitate what they've seen me do and can even help each other through upsets on their own with empathy and understanding.
—Seasyn

The hardest part of having more than one child is those times when they both need you at once. After all, your love may be unlimited, but you only have two hands.

That's why preventive maintenance is so important—children don't fall apart as often.

But there will inevitably be times when you're the only adult present, you have more than one child in your care, and both children really need you at once, or one child needs your full attention for ten minutes but you can't focus on him because the other child is there. What can you do?

1. **When both children need you at once, try to tend to them both.** (If you pick one, your children will perceive you as picking a favorite or taking sides.) Announce what's happening. *"I have two upset children who are both hurting right now! You both need your papa right now, don't you . . . Come here, my sweethearts, there is always plenty of room in my arms . . . You on my right, and you on my left, both of you in my arms . . . That's right, you can cry as much as you want . . . then we will sort this out and make everything better . . . whatever happens, we always work it out."* This isn't easy, but it is possible. Just keep one on each side so they're out of reach of each other physically.

2. **If you need to go to one child over the other, speak to the child you aren't going to.** So, for instance, when one child (Brian) is hurt physically, while the other child (Kaylee) is hurt emotionally, you might scoop Brian up while saying, *"Kaylee, I hear you're hurting and you need me, and I will be right there. I am just helping Brian with his owie, and then I will help you with your feelings."*

3. **Keep the less needy child busy while you tend to the one who is more upset.** If one child doesn't seem particularly upset, connect with her briefly to make sure she's okay. Give her a big hug and tell her, *"I have something special for you to do for a few minutes while I help your sister with her feelings."* Then pull out an activity you know she loves, like an audiobook or the activity box that you set up to keep your child busy while you fed the baby (see Chapter 9). Worried that your 16-month-old can't be safely occupied? Look online for sensory bags for young toddlers and use a lot of duct tape so there's no chance he'll tear it open. Keep him visible across

the room while you help the child who's upset through her meltdown.

4. **When your other child is concerned about the crying sibling, acknowledge her feelings and reassure her.** *"Your sister is sad and mad... I'm helping her with her feelings... She'll feel better soon."*

5. **If the other child insists on coming close,** sit on the floor and keep them on opposite sides of you. You'll have to shift attention from one to the other, but you can acknowledge the feelings of both.

6. **The child having the meltdown will often get angry that the other sibling is intruding.** Just acknowledge his unhappiness: *"You don't want your sister here... You're having a hard enough time without her... Sometimes it's hard to have another person around."* Then, restore safety: *"Your sister is just worried about you... She will stay over here, away from you. I am right here for you."*

7. **Keep your sense of humor.** Two crying children will feel like an emergency. But if you can stay calm, you'll help them shift their energy, too. When children are overwrought, they need you to understand why they're upset. *("You're mad and sad... your brother bumped your tower and it fell down.")* But just as important, they need your nonverbal communication that they're safe; it really isn't the end of the world even though they feel like it is. So take a deep breath and shift yourself out of "fight or flight." Just keep breathing and reminding yourself that they'll feel (and act) better after a good cry.

8. **Don't try to teach.** When we get anxious, we often try to solve problems by looking for blame. (*"If you hadn't done that to your sister, everything would be fine. Next time, listen when I tell you . . ."*) But when emotions run high, the learning centers in the brain shut down, so your child can't learn. Not to mention, when we're upset, we often say exactly the wrong thing because it comes from our own fear. Just resist talking except to connect with compassion. *"I'm sorry this is so hard, honey."*

9. **What if you need to cry, too?** Go ahead! Just explain that it's not her fault you're crying and she doesn't have to make it better; that everyone needs to cry sometimes and you'll feel better after you cry for a bit. You're modeling that emotions aren't an emergency, which is the first step toward healthy self-regulation. (Of course, if you're weeping every time your kids get upset, then you can't be helpful to them, so it's time to get some support for your own healing.)

There aren't any easy answers when everyone needs you at once. That's why preventive maintenance is so essential; it really reduces unpredictable meltdowns. And helping kids with big emotions is hard work, because you have to regulate your own. But when your child watches you help his sibling through a big upset, he learns how to empathize and help someone who's in pain, a lesson that will last his whole life. Not bad for half an hour's very hard work!

3

What Causes Sibling Rivalry—And How Parents Can Make It Better

From the parents' perspective, a new sibling is a gift beyond measure: a friend for life. But from a child's point of view, at least in the beginning, another baby in the family may look more like a gift for the parents and a disaster for the dislodged older sibling. At the very least, being forced to share parents with a new sister or brother brings up the worry for older children that they'll receive less of what they want and need. And if we're honest, we have to admit that there's some truth in our child's fear. As parents, we've all felt how hard it can be to meet the needs of one child, let alone two or more.

So all siblings will feel some rivalry, and some factors beyond our control can put strain on the sibling relationship. But sibling love is just as natural as the rivalry, and we as parents can help it win out over the inevitable jealousies. In fact, the most important factors influencing the sibling relationship are arguably within the parents' control. This chapter outlines some factors that can impact the sibling relationship, for better and for worse. The rest of the book gives you the blueprint for how you can support your children in developing a close, rewarding sibling relationship.

Your Child's Point of View: That's Not a Friend, It's a Replacement!

I was six when my sister was born. I'm thirty-four now, but I still remember worrying that my parents must not love me anymore, and being afraid they would leave me behind when they moved.

—Deidre

Authors Adele Faber and Elaine Mazlish, in their classic book *Siblings Without Rivalry*, tell an oft-repeated story about a man who brings home a second wife.[1] He says, *"I love you so much that I wanted another wife... Isn't she adorable?... We're going to be a family now... You'll have so much fun with her..."* Then, every stranger in the street stops the family to admire the darling new wife, while the first wife stands watching. She could be forgiven for developing some hostility. The story is a joke, but there is always truth in a good joke.

And the truth is, it's very hard for children to share parents. After all, you only have two hands, and if they're busy with the baby, your older child has to wait. But sibling rivalry springs from an even deeper anxiety. If he has to share scarce resources with a rival, your child's chances of survival statistically decrease. Sure, we know there's still enough love, food, and protection to go around. But his experience is that he's no longer first in line to get what he needs, and that can trigger some primal terror. After all, his genes evolved in the Stone Age. On some unconscious level, he can't help but worry. If a tiger jumps out of the bushes, which child will you save?

As parents, we know we adore our first child. That's one of the reasons we decide to add more children to our family. But our sons and daughters can't truly fathom our commitment to them, no matter what we say. Although they can't articulate their fears, and they often feel genuinely nurturing toward the new baby, most older siblings worry from time to time that they're no longer truly valued. They may even fear that, like Hansel and Gretel, they'll be forgotten in the forest, now that you have a "replacement." And of course, younger children have their own anxieties. How could you possibly value them as much as their older sibling, who is so much better at everything, and who got to the party first?

Being aware of this primal competition clues us in to the single most important antidote to sibling rivalry. *Each child must be convinced from her daily experience, that no matter what her sibling gets, there is more than enough love, attention, and appreciation for her— and that you could never love anyone more.* Once children live and believe this, sibling rivalry softens, and sibling love has a chance to bloom.

Factors That Can Exacerbate Rivalry

Researchers have identified some specific factors that can exacerbate sibling rivalry: temperament, spacing, and gender.

TEMPERAMENT

As every parent of more than one child knows, each child is born with a distinct temperament. Your children's temperaments can affect the sibling relationship in three ways:

1. **Temperament matches or mismatches.**[2] Like adults, some children will just find it challenging to live together. We all know siblings who get on each other's nerves because they're

so different. A quiet, sensitive child who experiences sensory overload in the face of too much activity and noise may feel overwhelmed and resentful living with an exuberant sibling who's constantly in motion. This can also work in your favor, though, if you happen to have two rambunctious kids who can't get enough roughhousing together, or two dramatic kids who love playing "pretend" together.

2. **Adjustment to the new baby.**[3] Not surprisingly, research shows that children who are rated as "easier" by their parents adjust more gracefully to the birth of a sibling. While they'll still need your reassurance and one-on-one time, their panic isn't as severe about losing so much of your attention. By contrast, children with more challenging temperaments may well become clingier, more difficult, or experience more sleep problems following the birth of a sibling.[4]

   What's a "difficult" temperament? This is rated by the parents, so presumably any child who takes more patience on the part of the parent might be considered to have a difficult temperament. All young children need a great deal from their parents, but kids who consistently seem to need "more" will feel the change in the parent-child relationship most acutely. So they feel more resentment toward their sibling, and they act out more. Luckily, attention from you will go a long way to reduce this tension. Just remember that if you have a child who tends to be more challenging, you can expect her to need lots of extra closeness with her parents to help her adapt to a new baby.

3. **Sibling conflict.** Children who are temperamentally more challenging for parents also find it harder to develop a positive relationship with their sibling.[5] For example, research

repeatedly shows that kids who are rated by their parents as more emotionally intense or more physically active are more likely to be aggressive with their younger siblings.[6] In fact, children rated as highly active were found in one study to experience four times as much sibling conflict as other children.[7] We can easily imagine that little Nicolas, who is always in motion, would be louder and rougher with the baby and more likely to be on the receiving end of parental frustration than his sister, Valentina, who's naturally more quiet and gentle.

When the older child is the one with the easier temperament, research shows that he or she sets the tone and helps the younger child regulate, so the sibling relationship is smoother.[8] So while a challenging child can be hard on parents regardless of birth order, the sibling relationship will be easier if the challenging child is the younger child.

The *very* good news is that you can make all the difference here. Researchers have found that parents who are able to keep a strong bond with their emotionally or physically intense child create "a protective factor to ameliorate the effect of difficult temperament on the sibling relationship."[9] That means that if you have a challenging child and you're adding another child to your family, the most important thing you can do to encourage a positive sibling relationship is for both parents to maintain a deep, nurturing, positive relationship with your older child, both before and after the baby is born. This book will give you the support to do exactly that.

CHILD SPACING

Annie has a hard time sharing me. She craves more attention and I literally can't give it to her. They will both be crying for me several times a day

and I just sit and hold both of them while they push at each other. I wanted kids close in age so they could be best friends. Now it is just a disaster.
—Sarah

How closely to space our children is a relatively new question for humans, simply because until babies began using bottles, and a surplus of food for their mothers became available, women's bodies were unlikely to conceive again soon after a birth. So where at least three years between births seems to be the historical human norm, mothers can now conceive again quickly.

Studies on child spacing show that children who are closer in age exhibit more sibling rivalry in the form of aggressiveness and competitiveness, but they're also more intimate.[10] It makes sense that children who are closer in age will play together more, which can give them more opportunities to fight—but also to build a closer relationship. As sibling researcher Judy Dunn says, "Siblings who quarrel a lot and are very competitive are often quite friendly and cooperative in other ways. When they're not fighting and arguing, these siblings play great games together and enjoy each other's company. Could it be that they're learning through the competitive arguments—learning something that helps them manage to play together?"[11] If parents can support closely spaced siblings to resolve the fighting constructively, this closeness can set the tone for a lifetime of deep connection.

But before you set out to space your babies closely, there are some important variables to consider, factors that might compromise your ability to give your children that support to create a close sibling bond. After all, fighting doesn't always work itself out positively, and constant competition can also set a tone for life.

What other factors should you consider? It's an obvious fact of life that parents only have two hands and twenty-four hours in a day to divide between their children and everything else they have to do. The more children they have, the more of a challenge it is to tend to everyone's needs. And the younger the children, the more urgent their needs. An eighteen-month-old may look a lot bigger than your newborn, but she's still a baby herself.

Most of us assume that since our little one won't remember the time before the baby, she'll adapt more easily. Unfortunately, researchers now believe that experience before conscious memories are formed actually has *more* impact on us because those implicit memories are less subject to conscious review. As Daniel Siegel says in *The Developing Mind*, "These implicit elements form part of the foundation for our subjective sense of ourselves."[12] So the issue isn't what she can remember. The issue is how long she can tolerate waiting to have her needs met, and what unconscious conclusions she draws about her own worth and the trustworthiness of others while she waits.

Isn't it good for children to learn to wait, to delay gratification? Absolutely. The question is how they learn that. When a child trusts that indeed her need will be met, she can delay gratification a bit longer. So it's true that small delays in having needs met can help a child develop trust, but that's only true as long as her needs are then met fairly quickly. How quickly? That depends on the age of the child, and on her temperament: How fast does she move into a state of emergency when she gets upset? She may well conclude that she won't get what she needs unless she becomes very demanding, which can create an enduring pattern. So not surprisingly, research shows that younger toddlers, compared to older toddlers, have more difficulty adjusting when new siblings are introduced to the family.[13]

Can you space your children close together, and still meet their needs so they flourish? Of course, and many families do. But it obviously means there will be more pressure on you to meet the needs of both children. So if you have the luxury to decide how to space your children, ask yourself some tough questions:

- How much support do you have from your partner and extended family?
- How much energy and patience do you have? Imagine the exhaustion you felt with your firstborn, except this time you'll have another child who also needs you a great deal.
- How easy, or how challenging, is your child?
- Do you have health issues? The physical health of a baby is better if his conception is at least eighteen months after the previous baby's birth, which is a small risk factor best not combined with other physical risk factors.[14]
- Are there any other significant stresses on the family? Stress has a tangible physical and emotional impact, even if we can't quantify that impact, and close child spacing creates stress for everyone involved—both parents and kids. Too much stress makes it tough to create the close parent-child bonds you want with both children.[15]

What If You Already Have Closely Spaced Children?

Sometimes the stars line up just right and we have the luxury of making a decision about spacing our children. More often, though, life intervenes, and we don't have control of when our blessings show up. So if your children are already spaced close together, please don't panic. Instead, see this factor as similar to temperament and gender, which are just givens. It simply means that there will be more pressure on you, the parent, to stay patient in the face of greater demands. Your job—and it's a big one—is to take care of yourself, so you can meet the needs of two children who are babies at the same time. That's what allows you to develop a positive relationship with each child. And that's the foundation that supports your children to develop a happy relationship with each other, regardless of their spacing.

HOW GENDER AFFECTS COMPETITION

If at least one of your children is a girl, your children may be closer than if you have two boys, who tend to be more competitive.[16] Same-sex siblings are often close, but their relationships also include more aggression, especially when they're young and particularly when they're boys.[17]

You can't control the sex of your baby, but there are ways to smooth out some of the tendency to compete. First, spacing your kids farther apart may lessen overt competition, because children are less likely to see themselves as competitors when they're at a different stage of childhood.

Second, try to minimize comparisons between your children. Even though you know logically that your two sons are different people, not necessarily any more alike than a son and daughter might be, you're more likely to compare two kids of the same sex to each other. Not surprisingly, the children themselves are also likely to see themselves as more similar—and more in competition—compared to how they would perceive their relationship with a sibling of the opposite sex.

Finally, stress each child's individuality. This reduces competition because they don't have to fight to be the "best" boy, since they're your only "Riley" and your only "Dominic." We'll discuss this more in Chapter 7, but for now, one easy rule is to refrain from referring to your kids as "the boys" or "the girls." Why not simply use their names?

The Power of Parents to Foster a Super Sibling Relationship

Worried that your family has one or more of these circumstances that may exacerbate sibling rivalry? It's true that you can't control your children's temperaments or gender, and you often have little control over spacing. Luckily, you can control what may be the most critical factor of all—you, the parent!

Why are you the most important factor? We've already considered how the three practices of peaceful parenting—regulating your own emotions, connecting with your child, and coaching instead of controlling—help you raise siblings who can get along with each other, and are motivated to do so. We've also looked in depth at how emotion coaching and loving guidance discipline practices make a huge difference in the sibling relationship. Throughout this book, we'll use this peaceful parenting approach to help you foster a close sibling bond between your children.

But the most important thing you can do to foster a good relationship between your children is to create a deep, nurturing bond with each child.[18] *Research shows that if you have a positive relationship with each of your children, they're much more likely to have a positive relationship with each other.*[19] That's true even when you have two boys (or girls) who have challenging temperaments and are very close in age. Even when one of your children has a more challenging temperament, if you can do the hard work to maintain a warm and positive relationship with your "high needs" child, you're laying the foundation for a more positive sibling relationship. In fact, you're creating a blueprint for him to use in all future relationships.[20]

But how do we create those strong bonds? By the way we respond to each child's needs, every day. Every parent-child relationship is different, depending on the contribution of both the adult and the child, who together create a "system" that tends to reinforce the same responses over and over. But no matter what your child is like, you have the choice of how to respond to him. Your responses will shape your relationship with him, and to some degree will even shape your child's brain and his way of relating to himself and to others.

Most parents think we have a good relationship with our child. After all, we know we love him. The question, though, is how close the child feels to us—especially when he's upset.

- Does he trust that, when he feels needy or frightened, we'll be there to help?
- Does he trust that when he's angry, it's safe to show us, and we'll respond with understanding, so that he can reveal the tears and fears driving his anger?
- Does he trust that we value him exactly as he is, that we aren't trying to change him, or worrying about how he reflects on us?
- Does he trust that we'll understand if he makes mistakes and coach him to do better, or does he worry that we'll see him as behaving badly and punish him?
- Does he trust that we'll manage our own anxiety so that we can coach him when he's frustrated or struggling to master something, rather than stepping in to take over?

The closer our relationship with each child, the more trust there is, and the more that child is able to use us as his safe haven. This security is what allows a child to thrive, so that he can be emotionally generous toward others, including siblings.

Throughout this book, you'll find a focus on connection, along with specific actions you can take to sweeten and deepen your relationship with each child. Your goal is both to find more opportunities for positive interactions with each child, and to minimize the negative ones that erode trust—and to repair them when they inevitably occur.

(For more support to build a closer bond with your child, please see Part 2 of *Peaceful Parent, Happy Kids*.)

PART TWO

TEACHING PEACE

What does it mean to teach peace? It doesn't work to admonish our children to "Be nice!" or "Stop fighting!" Even the motto "Be Kind"—one of the most useful for families—won't help a child who's struggling to stand up for herself. We all want our children to "be nice to others." But peace isn't the absence of conflicting needs and wants. Peace is the successful resolution of that conflict. We send a destructive message if we tell our child that how she acts is more important than how she feels, or that she should simply accept a parental resolution of a problem she's having with a sibling. Children learn to make peace when they practice encountering conflict, and then successfully resolve it—themselves—using the skills that create peaceful outcomes: identifying and expressing their own needs, listening to others, seeing multiple perspectives, and problem-solving to craft win/win solutions that serve everyone.

4

Coaching Kids to Communicate Feelings and Problem-Solve

Often one will take something and the other will cry. I say, "What are you trying to tell Jonah?" Sean will respond, "I'm still playing with that, Jonah. Can I have it back, please?" Usually, he will give it back. I've found that if I remind them to talk to each other, they are often able to resolve the situation themselves, now that I have taught them how.

—Emily

Emotional intelligence begins with understanding our emotions so that we can regulate them to reach our goals. The second half of emotional intelligence is about getting along with others: understanding the other person's feelings and expressing what we want while respecting the other person. So an emotionally intelligent child won't just cry when his brother takes his toy. But he won't hit either. He'll say, *"I'm still playing with that, Jonah, can I have it back, please?"*

If you think that's an unusually sophisticated interaction for two- and four-year-olds, you're right. Most siblings don't relate this way. According to parents' reports, young siblings fight about seven times every hour and only about 10 percent of those conflicts end happily, in "reconciliation" or even "compromise."[1] About 90 percent of the time, the more powerful child gets his way or both children withdraw from the skirmish, usually after some attempts at intimidation or force.[2] Most parents try not to intervene, reassuring ourselves that over time, our children will learn how to get along. After all, they're getting plenty of practice in resolving conflict.

And yet many studies show that the social skills of siblings aren't any better than those of only children, and most siblings keep fighting for years. Puzzling, right? Po Bronson and Ashley Merryman, in their book *NurtureShock*, offer a disconcerting explanation. "Maybe the mistake here was assuming that those thousands upon thousands of interactions with siblings amount to a single positive. Perhaps the opposite is true—that children learn poor social skills from those interactions as often as they learn good ones."[3]

In other words, left to their own devices, children may well be learning from their interactions with their siblings that bullies usually win.

So should parents jump in and try to make peace? If our intervention sounds like this: *"Give your sister the doll!"* we're just teaching our kids to lobby a higher authority to get their way, by painting themselves as the victim. They're still not learning to work out the dispute constructively with their sibling.

By contrast, children do learn the give and take of social skills when they interact with peers.[4] Why? Probably because they have to listen to the other person's perspective and look for win/win solutions if they want to keep playing. Peers, after all, have the threat of exit. With siblings, there may not be as much incentive to resolve differences so that both parties are happy. Children in our culture also have more limited exposure to cultural models of how people can constructively resolve differences, at least compared to past eras when village children were less age-segregated and little children followed older kids around. Children who are lucky enough to have a close friend with whom they learn reciprocity have notably more positive sibling relationships, and kids do sometimes learn "prosocial" skills at school or daycare.[5] Otherwise, our children may not learn constructive social skills unless we coach them.

That doesn't mean we need to be involved in every interaction between our children. They'd never get a chance to practice making peace themselves. But it does mean that if we want them to be able to say, *"I'm still playing with that, Jonah, can I have it back, please?"* instead of hitting, we need to explicitly give them guidance so they learn how to do it.

Coaching Essential Emotional Intelligence Skills

We've already talked about emotion-coaching and empathizing in Chapter 1, which give children the foundation to understand their own emotions and those of others. What else can parents do to help their children develop emotional and social intelligence, so they can get along well with each other?

1. **Talk about feelings.** When parents talk to their children on a daily basis about what everyone in the family feels and needs, siblings become more sensitive and emotionally generous to each other, as well as more likely to understand each other's point of view. This is true even when children are very young; when mothers talk to their toddlers about what the baby might be feeling, the toddler develops more empathy for the baby and is less jealous.[6]

2. **Ask questions about feelings, needs, wants, and choices.**

   - *"How did you feel?"*

   - *"What did you want?"*

- *"What did you do?"*

- *"How did that work out?"*

- *"Did you get what you wanted?"*

- *"Did your brother get what he wanted?"*

- *"How do you think he felt?"*

- *"Would you do the same thing next time, or do you think you might try something different?"*

- *"What do you think you might try?"*

- *"What do you think might happen then?"*

Listen, nod, repeat to be sure you understand. Stay warm and nonjudgmental. Keep your sense of humor, so when your child says, *"Next time I'll smash him!"* you can simply answer, *"Hmmm . . . what might happen then?"* Try not to jump in to evaluate or lecture. Reflection is how children develop judgment. Good judgment often develops from bad experience.

3. **Explain and model.** Expect to repeat yourself.

When they were fighting over ownership of something, I would say, "Jacob, say . . . 'Excuse me, Sarah, when you're finished, may I have a turn, please?' and then wait for him to repeat my words. And then I would turn to Sarah and say, "Sarah, say . . . 'Sure, Jacob.'" I did this many, many, many times, and then one day to my delight I was cooking dinner and overheard them use these exact words unprompted to resolve an issue . . . It was a proud moment. :)
    —Deanne

4. **Practice finding win/win solutions.** There are daily opportunities in every family to point out differences in needs and consider solutions that might work for everyone. *"Hmmm . . . You want to go to the pool and your sister wants to go to the park . . . How can we find a win/win solution?"*

5. **Model "I" statements,** which means expressing what you need, rather than judging or attacking someone else. So, for instance, when your daughter yells, *"Well, you're stupid, too!"* you might teach her, instead, to say, *"I don't like it when you call me names."*

   One formula for "I" statements is to describe what you feel, what you need, and how you see the situation. You might follow that up with a request that your child take a specific action. "I feel _____ because I want (or need) _____ and I observe that _____." So, for instance, *"I feel worried because I want to get there on time and I see that you aren't ready to leave yet . . . Please put on your shoes."*

6. **Model prosocial behavior.** The way the adults in the home relate to each other sets a powerful example for the children. Use that to your advantage by role-playing how you'd like your children to treat each other. For instance, you might say to your partner, *"There's only one banana left, shall we split it?"* Or model how to set limits respectfully, by saying things like, *"Excuse me, I was using that. You can have it as soon as I'm done,"* with a smile and a hug.

Your New Role: Interpreter

To teach kids communication skills, you might think of yourself as an interpreter between two people who don't speak the same language. Of course, both of your children are learning to speak the same language. But when kids get anxious and tempers flare, they don't think well, and they don't listen well. Our job is to interface between our children to help each of them give voice to his own needs and feelings, and to help each child hear what the other one is expressing. Once you help your kids build that communication bridge, they'll be increasingly able to work together to solve the problems that inevitably come up—without your help!

> *"When you picked her up, Baby Giovanna started fussing. Do you hear her? It sounds like she wants you to put her down."*

> *"Zack said stop. He doesn't want you to pull on him."*

> *"Amelia says she had the toy first, and Amber says she had the toy first . . . You both think you had it first!"*

Successful interpretation requires us to use our empathy to understand the perspective of both children. It also requires us to stay calm, so we can resist leaping to judgment, even while we set limits to keep everyone safe. If we take one child's side, the other one becomes defensive and can't listen. Imagine the child's reactions to these interventions, instead of the ones above.

> *"You're hurting the baby! Put her down right now!"*

> *"Stop that pulling! You're always manhandling your brother!"*

"Amelia, you're older, you should know better. Stop grabbing from your sister."

These comments don't create a bridge, because the child feels criticized. Even if she cooperates—and she's not likely to—there will be lingering resentment, and more antagonism later.

Interpreting is an invaluable teaching tool to help kids understand social dynamics. If you can do it with empathy and as little judgment as possible, it helps both children feel heard, which calms upset feelings and helps them hear each other.

Coaching Kids to Identify and Communicate Their Needs and Feelings

As we've seen, parents can minimize sibling rivalry by helping each child feel that he couldn't possibly be loved more than he is. But no matter how responsive your parenting, there will be times when your children's needs conflict. If your child can't express what he wants with words, he'll use his body. So our job as parents is to help our children learn to identify and voice their needs and feelings, and to help the other sibling hear and respond to that expression.

Every day that you live with more than one child, you'll have multiple opportunities to coach your children to identify and communicate their feelings to each other. Let's look at some examples.

Three-year-old James is playing with his garbage truck. Violet, fifteen months, comes up behind him and tugs on the back of his shirt. James looks over his shoulder in annoyance. As he turns to shove her away, Mom says, *"James, Violet is tugging on your shirt. It looks like you don't like that. Can you tell your sister in words? Pushing hurts."*

> **James:** No, Violet!
> **Mom:** James, I hear you saying no! Can you tell Violet what you don't want?
> **James:** Don't pull my shirt!
> *Violet has been staring from Mom to James as they talk, eyes wide.*
> **Mom:** Violet, James says don't pull his shirt. Are you trying to get James's attention? Do you want to play with him?
> *Violet smiles and claps.*
> **Mom:** James, do you see how much Violet wants to play with you? That's why she was pulling your shirt; she was trying to tell you she wants to play. I see you're playing with your garbage truck. Is there something Violet could do in your game?
> **James:** Here, Vi . . . you can have the dump truck. Go pick up blocks in it and bring them to the garbage truck.

Johnny, four, comes into the room where five-year-old Christian is flying a toy airplane. Johnny grabs at the plane.

> **Johnny:** My turn!
> **Christian:** No, it's still my turn . . . I'm having a long turn.
> *He swoops the plane past Johnny, making zooming noises.*
> *Johnny begins to cry, reaching for the plane.*
> **Dad:** I hear Johnny crying . . . are you two doing okay?
> **Johnny:** Meany!
> **Dad:** Johnny, I see that you're upset . . . Can you tell your brother want you want, instead of calling him names?

Johnny: He's teasing me! I want a turn, too!

Christian: But it's my turn now.

Dad: Johnny is saying he wants a turn with the airplane. Christian is saying he's not ready for his turn to be over . . . Hmm . . . That's a tough situation . . . I know it can be hard to wait, Johnny.

Johnny: I don't want to wait . . . I want to fly it now! I want to refuel it with the truck.

Dad: Johnny, I hear you want the plane now, and you know just what you'll do when you get it. You can ask Christian if he'll you give you the airplane when he's done.

Johnny: Will you give me a turn when you're done, Christian?

Christian: Okay. But I'm having a long turn.

Dad: Okay . . . our family rule is that you can have a long turn . . . can you tell Johnny when you think you'll be ready to give him the airplane?

Christian: I need it until bath time.

Johnny: Then I get to have it next to my bed, so I get first turn with it tomorrow.

Dad: So Christian will have his turn with the airplane until bath time, and then the airplane will sleep next to Johnny's bed and Johnny gets first turn tomorrow? Is that your agreement?

Christian: That's good. Watch me fly it, Dad!

Johnny: Okay . . . But can I be the ground crew to refuel the plane when you need to land, Christian?

What if Johnny just can't tolerate waiting and falls apart? Help him wait for his turn. (See "Coaching Kids as They Wait for Their Turn" on page 155.) You'll probably end up with a meltdown on your hands, but there are worse things, like having Johnny feel out of sorts all evening. After the meltdown, he'll find a positive way to engage with Christian and the plane, or he'll find something else to do—and everyone will have a much better evening. (See "Helping Kids with Big Emotions: Scheduled Meltdowns" on page 43.)

Five-year-old Sebastian is playing school with his seven-year-old sister, Claire, who is acting as the teacher.

> **Sebastian:** I don't want to play anymore.
>
> **Claire:** You have to play. I'm the teacher and I'm in charge.
>
> **Sebastian:** Dad, do I have to play with Claire anymore?
>
> **Dad:** Everyone gets to decide who they play with. Do you not want to play anymore?
>
> **Sebastian** *(whispering to Dad)*: She's too bossy.
>
> **Dad:** I hear you, but your sister needs to hear you.
>
> **Sebastian** *(whispering to Dad again)*: You tell her.
>
> **Dad:** It sounds like you're worried about telling Claire . . . Can you tell her how you feel?
>
> **Sebastian** *(to Claire)*: You're too bossy.
>
> **Claire:** I am not!
>
> **Dad:** Sebastian, can you tell your sister how you're feeling, instead of what you think she's doing?
>
> **Sebastian:** I don't like this. I don't get to decide anything.
>
> **Claire:** Okay . . . do you want to be the teacher for a while? I could be the bad kid!

Do you notice what all these parents are doing? Helping their kids to identify and express their emotions without attacking the other child. They do this by:

- Describing what's happening.
- Empathizing with each child.
- Coaching the children to put their feelings into words without attacking the other child.

Once children hear each other's needs, they're more able to come up with solutions that work for both of them.

Some parents respond to this by saying, *"Great, but I have to be involved every single time. When will they learn to work things out for themselves?"* The answer is that like any other interpersonal skill—asking for more mashed potatoes, holding their place in line at the slide, purchasing an ice cream cone—children naturally learn these skills through coaching and practice. But just saying, *"Use your words!"* doesn't help. We need to teach them *what* to say.

You'll be surprised at how quickly your children will learn to work things out with each other, once you start coaching like this. Even toddlers love to problem-solve and restore harmony with their loved ones. They just need us to show them how.

Coaching Kids to Set Limits with Each Other

When humans feel threatened, it's natural to attack. So young humans need our help to learn how to express their needs and emotions, including anger, to their siblings in a respectful way. The same interpretation skills work here:

- Describe.
- Empathize.
- Coach kids to identify and express their needs and emotions without attacking the other child.

If necessary, you'll also need to:

- Back your child up, if one child is ignoring the limits set by the other.
- Restate family rules if one child is ignoring them.
- Help kids problem-solve.

Eva, age five, is dancing around the room in her fairy wings, waving her magic wand to the music. She crashes into the dollhouse, where MacKenzie, age seven, is playing.

> **MacKenzie:** Oh, no! You ruined everything! I hate you, Eva!
>
> **Mom:** You sound pretty mad, MacKenzie. Can you tell your sister how you feel without attacking her?
>
> **MacKenzie:** I feel mad, that's how I feel! Eva, I just got it all set up and now you knocked everything down!
>
> **Mom:** Oh, MacKenzie, no wonder you're upset. That was a lot of work... I'm sorry you have to start over...
>
> **Eva:** I didn't mean to, MacKenzie... I was just flying... Want me to help you put the furniture back where it goes?
>
> **MacKenzie:** Hmmph! It's not that easy. I had everything just right.
>
> **Eva:** I'm sorry, MacKenzie. I could help, though... I could just stand the furniture up again where it is.
>
> **MacKenzie:** Okay... I guess you can do the bedrooms... But be careful!

Jason, age four, is shoving Nicholas, age two, aside. Nicholas is crying, trying to stand his ground.

Dad: Is everyone having fun with this game? I see Nicholas crying.

Jason looks up, wary.

Nicholas tearfully shakes his head no.

Dad: Nicholas, you can tell your brother what you don't like.

Nicholas: Don't like!

Dad: Nicholas, what don't you like? Can you tell your brother?

Nicholas: Nicholas don't like pushing!

Dad *(interpreting and getting agreement)*: Jason, Nicholas says he doesn't like being pushed. Will you stop pushing?

Jason nods and steps aside.

Jason's nod makes it likely that he'll respect the agreement he's just made. What if Jason doesn't nod? He hasn't committed himself, and he isn't likely to stop pushing. In that case, Dad needs to continue his intervention.

Dad: Jason, it looks like you're not ready to stop pushing. Nicholas is saying he doesn't like the pushing. He needs you to agree, so he feels safe. Will you stop pushing?

Jason shakes his head no.

Dad: Okay, it looks like you need to push right now, and Nicholas is not for pushing. What else could you push? Your Bobo doll? Here, let's pull it out for you, so you can push it as much as you want. Can you show me how you much you feel like pushing with your Bobo doll? Wow! That is some strong pushing, Jason! Look at you push! . . . Now I need to clean up the kitchen. Nicholas, do you want to come with me and help me make bubbles to wash the dishes?

Fifteen-month-old Kahlil hits three-year-old Ava.

> **Ava** *(not moving)*: Ouch!
> *Kahlil giggles and hits her again.*
> **Ava** *(giggling)*: Ouch!
> **Kahlil:** Ouch!
> *He hits Ava again, giggling.*
> **Mom:** Hey, I hear Ava saying *ouch* but I also hear you both
> giggling. Are you both having fun?
> **Ava:** I don't want him to hit me, but it isn't hard . . .
> **Mom:** It sounds like you want to have fun together
> but you aren't sure you like the hitting . . . Ava,
> you can play with him another way. What else
> could you do?
> **Ava:** I think he likes it when I say, "Ouch!" Here, Kahlil, hit
> the couch. That's right! *Ouch!*
> *Both Ava and Kahlil yell Ouch and hit the couch,*
> *giggling.*

Mom walks into the house after school with nine-year-old Chloe
and seven-year-old Ryan. Ryan is in constant motion, bumping into
Chloe as he takes off his shoes.

> **Chloe:** Ryan, you stupid, stop it!
> **Ryan:** I didn't do anything! And I'm not stupid!
> **Mom:** Chloe, name-calling hurts. What are you trying to
> tell Ryan?
> **Chloe:** Stop kicking me!
> **Ryan:** I didn't kick you!

Mom: Hmm . . . I don't know what happened, but I wonder if maybe your foot touched your sister when you were taking your shoes off . . . Chloe, is that what happened?

Chloe: I guess so . . . It sure felt like a kick.

Mom: Even an accidental kick can hurt . . . Ryan, it sounds like you didn't realize your foot touched Chloe . . . Sometimes that happens. But Chloe didn't know you didn't mean to touch her; it felt like a kick to her and she thought you did it on purpose . . . So what we have here is a big misunderstanding, that made you upset at each other. Right?

Both kids look at each other, still mad.

Mom: I wonder what you could say to each other to make things better.

Ryan: I didn't mean to kick you, Chloe. I'm sorry. But I don't like it when you call me stupid.

Chloe: I don't mean that you're actually stupid; I was just mad . . . But you bump into me a lot. I don't like getting hurt. Can you pay more attention?

Ryan: If you promise not to call me names.

Mom: That sounds like a good agreement. It's a rule in this family that we don't call names, and also that we don't touch each other's bodies without permission. I wonder if there's anything we could do to make it easier for you not to bump your sister without noticing . . . Anybody have any ideas?

Ryan: I don't have to sit on the bench with her to take my shoes off . . . I could sit on the floor.

Mom: Wow, would that work for you? What about you, Chloe?

Chloe: That would work. I like you, Ryan, I just don't like being bumped.

Coaching Kids to Listen to Each Other

Usually when children aren't listening to each other, it's because they're too upset to care about the other person at that moment. Your first goal is always to calm both children, so they're more able to listen. That means your intervention needs to be empathic to both children, regardless of whether you think one child is "at fault." If your intervention feels like an attack to your child, he's not likely to empathize with his sibling. That's an important reason to avoid taking sides. Start by taking a deep breath to calm yourself, and maybe reciting a little mantra like, *"It's not an emergency. I'm the role model so they learn to work things out with each other."* Then:

1. **Help your children move out of "fight or flight."** The first step is always to restore safety by communicating with your attitude, and if necessary with words, that the situation isn't an emergency, and can be solved. *"Looks like we have a problem . . . We can solve this."*

2. **Empower your child to stick up for herself** (as described in the last section). *"You can tell her . . ."*

3. **When one child isn't listening to the other, provide backup.** *"Your sister is saying stop . . . Do you need some help to stop?"* Or if the hurt child is nonverbal, *"Look at your brother's face . . . It doesn't look like he likes that."* Your child already knows he hurt his brother, and he already feels badly about it—he just couldn't help himself because of his own fierce feelings. Your goal is not to shame him, but to remind him that he has an obligation not to hurt his sibling regardless of how he feels, and to let him know that you're there to help him regulate himself.

4. **When one child doesn't see a need to negotiate, state your family rules and encourage the children to work out a win/win solution.** *"Your brother is saying that he wants to help water Grandma's garden with the hose. Our family rule is long turns at home, but we need to have shorter turns today since we're only at Grandma's for the day, so everyone gets a chance. What can you do to work this out so everyone's happy?"*

Coaching Kids to Problem-Solve

In an argument, instead of focusing on "who did what," I ask them what they are going to do to "fix the problem" or "make it right."
 —Tricia

The basic sequence to help kids solve problems is simple. You just state the problem, encourage the children to come up with possible solutions, and encourage them to agree on one of the solutions. But while you're learning to do this, you'll probably want to think about it with a bit more elaboration.

1. **Model calm,** so everyone can think better and be more open to solutions.

2. **Point out that there's a problem.** When kids are locked in struggle, they see the other person as the problem; this helps them not take it so personally.

3. **If the problem is a conflict over an object,** move the object (or the children) away so that nobody is holding on to the object.

4. **Describe the problem without judgment** so the children realize that both people have valid needs or desires.

5. **Get agreement from each child that this is indeed the problem.** You may not understand the problem as the children see it, or they may disagree with each other about what the problem is.

6. **Invite the children to come up with solutions.** In some cases, the solution will be a rule that already exists: *"Our family rule is that we don't have to give turns with new presents, but if you want to, you can."* If there's no rule to fall back on, say, *"What could you do to solve this problem?"*

7. **Even if your children can't read, write down the solutions they offer.** Seeing the possible solutions on a blackboard or a large piece of paper is especially effective in helping children "own" the process, but even your phone will do. You can suggest solutions if they're stumped, but it shouldn't be only your ideas, and your ideas should include some silly or outrageous ones to loosen up the brainstorming.

8. **Write down all solutions, even if someone objects to them.** This is the time for brainstorming, not evaluating. Silly ideas are great, because they get everyone laughing and reduce the tension. As the children suggest solutions, restate them as you write them down.

9. **Go through the solutions one at a time** and ask the children if they can both agree on that solution.

10. **Restate objections, compromises, and solutions as they're offered; then ask again if the new solution works.** This is

an important step. Often, the best solution emerges as the kids raise objections about the ideas on the list. This helps them articulate their desires, and see things from the other child's perspective, which allows them to craft a solution that works for both kids. In the beginning, you'll help them work out these compromises, but over time, they'll learn to do it themselves. The solution won't work if both children don't sign on.

11. **Once you have a win/win solution, monitor as it's implemented and keep problem-solving.** Most of us are tempted to skip this step, but it's essential if you want your children to stay committed to this process over time. If they're having a hard time making the agreed-upon solution work, do a shorter version of the problem-solving process to help them work through the kinks.

Notice there's a lot of "restating" suggested. This helps children hear each other and clarifies each comment. It also helps "depersonalize" the process, so the fight doesn't carry over into the problem-solving. Over time, it teaches the children how to restate, so they learn to communicate more clearly with each other and problem-solve more effectively—without you!

What does this look like in practice?

> **Mom:** I hear loud voices . . . sounds like maybe you two have a problem?
>
> **Tyler** (age five)**:** He keeps knocking over my Magna Tile tower!
>
> **Julian** (age three)**:** I was trying to help.
>
> **Tyler:** No, Julian, you did it on purpose! You *like* it when they fall down!

Julian: It goes crash!

Mom: So the problem is that Tyler wants to build his own Magna Tile tower, and Julian wants to help . . . and also likes to knock it down? Is that the problem? Tyler? Julian?

Tyler: Yes!

Julian: Yes.

Mom: So we have one brother who wants to build his own Magna Tile tower and leave it up, and one brother who wants to help, and knock it down . . . That sounds like a tough problem. What could you two do to solve this problem?

Tyler: Julian could leave me alone . . . I want to build my own tower.

Mom *(writing on paper)*: Okay, that's one possible solution. Tyler can build his tower himself without any help or anyone knocking it down. What other solutions are there?

Julian: But I want to build, too!

Tyler: You can build your own tower, Julian. Just leave my tower alone!

Mom *(writing)*: Is that another solution? Julian can build his own tower, too? Both of you build your own towers?

Julian: No, I can't. I can't build it tall like Tyler. My towers aren't good.

Mom: You don't like that solution. Okay, we'll talk about all the solutions in a minute. Are there any other solutions?

Julian *(laughing)*: Knock them all down!

Mom: Sounds to me like you're feeling a little wild, Julian. Okay, I'm writing that down. This idea is to knock down all the towers?

Tyler: I hate that solution!

Mom: I hear you, Tyler. Any other solutions?

Tyler and Julian look blank.

Mom: Okay, let's see if any of these solutions work for both of you . . . The first one is that each boy can build his own tower, and no one knocks down Tyler's tower . . . Do you both like that solution?

Tyler: Yes!

Julian still looks blank.

Mom: Julian, this solution is for you to build your own tower, and you could knock it down . . . but you couldn't knock over your brother's tower. Okay?

Julian: I don't like that . . . my towers aren't big enough.

Mom: Hmm . . . Tyler, do you hear that? It sounds like Julian likes to knock down your towers because they're bigger.

Tyler: We can make his towers bigger, too. I could help him make his towers taller.

Mom: That sounds like another solution to write down . . . So that solution is "Tyler will help Julian build his towers taller and then Julian can knock them down"?

Julian *(jumping up and down):* Yay!

Mom: Julian, you like this solution. This means that you can knock down your own tall tower that Tyler helps you build . . . but you won't knock down Tyler's tow-ers . . . Okay?

Julian: Okay . . . but Tyler, will you build my towers high as the sky with me?

Tyler: Okay, we'll build them high . . . but can I help you when you knock yours down?

Julian *(grinning):* Yes! We will be the tall tower wreckers!

Mom: Okay, you both like the solution that Tyler will help Julian build his tower tall and you will both knock it down . . . we have a win/win solution! And how will you keep Tyler's tower safe so it doesn't get knocked down in the wrecking?

Tyler: I'll just build my tower on the table so it's safe. Come on, Julian. Let's build your tower really tall so we can see what happens when we wreck it!

Problem-Solving, Step by Step

Describe the problem without judgment.	Invite children to come up with solutions (or restate rules).
"Matthew is saying he wants to wrestle . . . William is worried that someone will get hurt."	"Can you two agree on some wrestling rules so that everyone feels safe?"
"You both want to sit in the red chair."	"Two kids both want the red chair at the same time . . . How can you solve this?"
"Xavier says he doesn't want you to throw the sand, Jamie; it's getting in his eyes."	"Jamie, when Xavier says stop, you need to listen to him."
"Sonia is saying that your foot keeps tapping her leg, Diego."	"Sharing the couch means your bodies have to get along. What can the two of you do to make that work?"
"All three of you want to sit by the window, but someone has to sit in the middle."	"Hmm . . . only two windows in the backseat, and three kids. We do have two rides—to the picnic and then back home again—so maybe that helps?"

Don't forget to start your problem-solving by calming your-self. Then, connect warmly with both children with a smile or hug, so that each child feels safer and more open to finding solutions.

Once the children have offered solutions:

Get agreement on a solution from both children.	Help children implement and refine their solution.
"So you both agree that wrestling is okay but no punching or touching each other's faces?"	"Matthew, William is saying Stop. It looks like maybe we need to add one more rule. When someone says Stop, both kids stop wrestling. How does that sound?"
"So Connor gets the red chair at breakfast and Lucy gets it at lunch? Is that your deal?"	
"Jamie, will you stop throwing the sand?" (Jamie is more likely to actually stop if he agrees now.)	"Jamie, it looks like it is just too hard for you to stop throwing sand. We need to take a break from the sandbox."
"So you're putting the cushion between you as the line you agree not to cross?"	
"So the solution is that Jace sits in the middle on the way to the picnic, and Aubrey sits in the middle on the way back, and since Kingston doesn't have to sit in the middle at all, he does all the clean-up with mom and dad after the picnic while Jace and Aubrey play longer?"	"Kingston, you agreed to be on clean-up duty for all the kids. If you don't like that, you can talk to Aubrey about switching with her, so you would sit in the middle on the way back. But unless she wants to switch, I need your help now—a deal is a deal."

SOLVING PROBLEMS VERSUS BLAMING

When an argument does arise, I try not to put the blame on anyone; I never ask, "Whose fault is it?," but rather look for a solution where everyone is happy. It helps because it doesn't produce angry feelings toward a sibling, as a "blamed one" would tend to have. Also, as no one is blamed, no one "gets in trouble." My kids play together almost all day, usually getting along great.

   —Helena

There's a wonderful *New Yorker* cartoon of a family lost in the jungle. The father is saying, *"I admit we're lost, but the most important thing right now is . . . figuring out whose fault it is!"* When things go wrong, most of us automatically start blaming someone. We feel slightly better, because even though something is wrong, we're doing something about—figuring out why it happened! In many families, blame is so habitual that we don't even notice it.

   "Who made this mess?"

   "It's your own fault for teasing him."

   "Which one of you started this?"

We often think when we blame that we're doing something positive—holding someone accountable, teaching responsibility. But when kids grow up in a household where blame is a way of life, they're more defensive, more inclined to watch their back, and more inclined to blame and attack than to take responsibility. Not surprisingly, families who focus on solutions instead of blame raise children who have better sibling relationships. One study found, "When families are generally harmonious even when discussing problems, siblings are likely to develop less conflicted relationships."[7]

The solution? Commit to a no-blame household. Really. Just take blame off the table. When you automatically start to assign blame, teach yourself to ask instead, "What can we do to solve this?" You'll be amazed to see your children take more responsibility for their contribution to problems, once they aren't worried about being blamed.

Basic Negotiation Tools to Teach Kids

Most of us weren't taught negotiation skills growing up. But these skills make it much easier to navigate the inevitable conflicts of daily life, and all kids should know them. If you teach these skills to your children, you'll hear them begin to use them on their own to solve disagreements.

Trading

"I'll give you one of my blue ones if you give me one of your red ones."

Sweetening the Deal

"I really want the elephant. How about if I give you the zebra, the alligator, and the gorilla, and you give me the elephant?"

Taking Turns AND Sweetening the Deal

"How about we play my game first and your game second, but because yours is second, we play it for longer?"

Dividing a Treat

"You can divide the treat into two equal pieces . . . Try to make them really equal, because I get to pick my piece first."

Teamwork

"I'll help you with cleaning up your blocks if you help me clean up my Legos."

Making Agreements or "Rules"

"What rules do we need so everyone feels safe during rough-housing? How about when someone says Freeze!, everyone stops . . . Does everyone agree?"

Writing Agreements

"Okay, we agree that I have to take the first bath tonight, but then you have to be first for two nights after that. Let's get Dad to help us write it down."

TATTLING IS HOW KIDS ASK FOR HELP TO SOLVE A PROBLEM

I work hard on self-advocacy skills instead of "tattling." So "I don't like it when you hit me," or "Please don't take my stuff without asking" delivered directly to the sibling, rather than telling a parent about the offense. I figure assertiveness is a skill I want my kids to have as they get older. They are two and four now, and still need lots of help on this, but it works amazingly well!

—Mary

Parents hate tattling. That's partly because most of us get a bit irritated at the messenger of bad tidings. Tattling presents us with a problem to solve, which is bound to make us annoyed. But the part that really bothers us most is that here's our child, maliciously trying to get her sibling into trouble. Sure, we don't want her brother to sneak chocolate. But what our little tattler is doing seems even worse, somehow—she's taking pleasure in getting her brother in trouble.

Loving guidance dramatically diminishes tattling, because no one "gets in trouble" anymore. You might intervene, but you're looking for a solution, not blame. If you've stopped punishing altogether, then your children have much less incentive to tattle.

Of course, kids will still come to you when they don't know how to handle a situation with their sibling. You want your children to know that they can always tell you about anything that bothers them. It's a *good* thing that your child is asking for your guidance if she doesn't know how to handle the situation. Instead of shutting her down, you help. But not by jumping in as the avenging angel. First, you don't have the whole story. Second, solving the problem doesn't allow your children to solve it themselves. Finally, if you impose a solution, it won't be accepted by both children. So when your child comes to you "tattling" about how her sibling acted toward her:

1. Take a deep breath and remind yourself that your child is trying to make things better in the only way she knows how.

2. Restate the situation to be sure you understand. Of course, you know that your child may not always be a reliable reporter. But you're acknowledging her perception. *"Let me see if I have this straight. Your brother said you can't come to his birthday party if you don't play the game his way?"*

3. If the "offense" was against the child who has come to you, empathize, then support her to look for solutions. *"That can hurt, to have your brother say that . . . It sounds like the two of you are pretty upset at each other, so your brother said the meanest thing he could think of . . . I wonder what you could do now, to work things out with him? What could you tell your brother?"*

4. Ask her if she wants you to do something about the situation, or just needed to talk about it. *"Sounds like you know what you want to say to your brother . . . Let me know if you want company while you talk with him."*

5. If your child comes to you about her sibling when she's not involved in the situation, empathize, say thank you if that's appropriate, and take action.

"Christopher's climbing out the window!"

"Fatima is drawing on the wall!"

"José was playing computer games while you were putting the baby to bed!"

Christopher is engaging in a dangerous activity. Fatima is damaging property. And José was breaking a family rule about screen time. The truth is, you're glad to know this information, but annoyed at your child for trying to get her sibling in trouble. How do you respond?

Consider that your child is actually concerned about the danger to people or property, or about the family rule being broken. When he comes to you, he's worried. Do the family rules matter? Will you keep everyone safe?

Empathize with your child's concern and assure him that you'll handle it. *"Let me see if I have this straight. José was playing computer games and that's against the rules . . . You sound worried . . . Don't worry, honey, I'll handle this with your brother."*

If it's happening in real time, take action. *"My goodness, Fatima is drawing on the wall? Thank you! Let's go rescue that wall!"*

Then talk to the rule breaker in private, just as you always would when a child breaks the rules.

5

When Problem-Solving Fails: Teaching Conflict Resolution

Siblings are the people we practice on, the people who teach us about fairness and cooperation and kindness and caring, quite often the hard way.
—Pamela Dugdale

In the last chapter, we looked at how you can teach your children to communicate their needs and work together to solve problems. What about those times—inevitable in every family—when those skills don't work and it all blows up in conflict?

What About "We Get Along" Shirts?

Your children are squabbling—again!—and it's driving you over the edge. What do you do?

1. Send them to their rooms.
2. Find an extra large adult T-shirt, use a black marker to write "We Get Along" on it, and put it on your children so they're both in it at once, forced into complete bodily contact. Now they *have* to "get along" with each other!

3. Sit down with your children. Help each one express to the other what they're upset about so they feel heard. Help each one see the other's side so they develop empathy. Help them brainstorm so they find a win/win solution.

If you think number 3 sounds like a lot of work, and number 2 sounds like a creative solution, you're not alone. Pictures of "We Get Along" shirts routinely make the rounds online, complete with photos of mortified, sullen, or crying children. Comments always include parents who say the photo made them crack up and they can't wait to try it.

I can understand why parents will do anything to get their kids to stop fighting. Sibling fights are a constant in many households, and it's not surprising that they drive parents crazy. But this approach doesn't teach kids not to fight. What does it teach?

1. It suggests that the parents don't know how to help the kids work through disagreements in a respectful way.
2. It teaches the smaller child to "go along"—in other words, to submit to the will of the bigger child, so as not to arouse further ire from the parents.
3. It teaches the bigger child to "bully"—in other words, to use his power to force the smaller child to go where he wants and do what he wants.
4. It teaches both kids that they don't have the right to decide how their body is touched.
5. It humiliates both kids, so it teaches them that people with power get their way by using force to humiliate and subdue smaller people.
6. It teaches the kids that their parents will get mad if they express their emotions and disagreements openly, so they should make their attacks on each other more sneaky.

7. It makes each child more upset and angry, for which they—naturally—blame their sibling. This is the opposite of teaching the child to have empathy for their sibling's perspective, and it pretty much ensures that their relationship will get worse.

8. It makes it pretty clear to the children that the parents don't actually care if the kids have a good relationship, but just want them not to make a fuss.

Of course, it takes time to help your kids settle their conflicts peaceably. It's pretty tempting to just believe that if kids have no choice, they'll find ways to get along. But that's like saying, "They'll put themselves to bed if they get tired enough . . . I'm going to bed." It's reneging on our responsibility as parents.

By contrast, once you begin using a conflict resolution approach regularly, your children learn how to express their feelings, listen with empathy, and look for win/win solutions. They begin to work out disagreements before they escalate into conflicts, and there's a lot less fighting—and a lot less involvement from you. And your children learn that in every human relationship, people will sometimes disagree, but can always work things out respectfully. Without having to stuff their feelings to "get along."

Why Fighting Is Essential to Teach Children Relationship Skills

Conflict is part of every human relationship. Experts in the field of moral development, beginning with Piaget, have pointed out that children learn morality by being faced with the conflict between their needs and the needs of others.[1] Fighting over the rules and what's fair is a time-honored tradition that's essential to the development of ethics and an inner compass about what's right and wrong. So a certain amount of sibling squabbling is not only normal, but very useful to our children.

In fact, if "peace" depends on kids being forced to swallow their needs to accommodate siblings on a regular basis, it isn't good for either child. Children need to develop their voices, learn how to express their needs, and try out strategies to meet their goals.

And, of course, children also need to learn to listen to each other, empathize, and regulate their anger rather than intimidating others. They need to learn how to maintain connection while meeting the goals of both people.

So conflict is essential, but what's valuable to our children isn't really the conflict itself. It's the practice that conflict gives children in successfully working out a mutually satisfying solution with another person. That's why our goal as parents isn't to keep things peaceful by settling our children's differences for them. It's to use the many daily conflicts that naturally arise between our children as opportunities to help *them* create successful resolutions to their conflicts. While our modeling is essential to help children see these skills in action, kids also need experience in putting those skills to use themselves. Repeatedly working things out with a sibling gives them confidence that even when emotions are running hot, they can rely on problem-solving to find win/win solutions. That's what keeps them from resorting to fists.

So the next time your children fight, remind yourself that it's a teachable moment. As with all teachable moments, the biggest learning happens when children are able to discover the lesson experientially.

How to Help Children Learn to Work It Out Themselves

Theodore Dreikurs, one of the fathers of positive parenting, theorized fifty years ago that children fight with each other to get their parents' attention. The worst thing parents can do, he argued, is to get involved. A flurry of studies followed that confirmed that when parents stay out of children's fights, children indeed fight less.

But over the years, subsequent research has added more complexity to that straightforward picture. Yes, siblings fight less without parental intervention. But, it's now clear, that's because the less powerful child is less likely to stand up for himself if he knows he has no leverage to convince his sibling to take his needs into account. Without parental intervention, the majority of disputes end with the less powerful sibling submitting to the will of the more powerful sibling.[2] In fact, the presence of an adult within earshot who doesn't intervene is associated with increased rates of aggression between the children, even when that adult pretends to be completely oblivious to the children's fight.[3] Apparently, as one researcher observed, "Children . . . understand [parental] nonintervention as an implicit endorsement of their behavior, which may lead to more frequent or more aggressive conflict."[4]

It's certainly true that parental intervention in which the parent decides who's right and tells the children how to resolve the issue *increases* the number of fights. But that's at least partly because it increases the feeling of rivalry between siblings. When one child "wins" the argument because of parental intervention—and make no mistake, both children do see the parent siding with one child as that child winning—the "losing" child becomes resentful and more likely to initiate another fight.

But there is another, more helpful, way for parents to intervene. When parents restate house rules, help children express themselves to their sibling, and express confidence that the children can solve the problem by meeting the needs of both siblings, children develop better problem-solving skills. The less powerful sibling is more willing to stand up for his needs. The children are more likely to come up with equitable solutions. And they fight less. Even when they do fight, the parental intervention has made a difference: less physical aggression, and more sibling references to their feelings and to social rules (as opposed to simply attacking each other).[5]

So while I don't think adults should automatically jump in to solve disputes for children—because, as we've discussed, how will kids learn?—I also can't agree fully with the common advice that parents should simply "let children work it out for themselves." While children often do figure out how to work things out so they're both happy, it's just as common that destructive patterns can develop, where one child is repeatedly victimized, or where kids become entrenched in resentments. Why would we leave our children without guidance in such a critical area of human relationships?

I suspect the reason parents are advised to let kids work out their own conflicts is that we adults so often make things worse when we do step in. That's not because we're clueless. It's because we have a hard time regulating our own emotions. When our children are upset, we feel an intense urge to solve the problem, right now. So we size up the situation, decide who's right and who's wrong, and impose a solution. Whew! Fixed that one, thank goodness.

Except we didn't. Siding with either child almost guarantees smoldering resentments that will burst out regularly and worsen over time. Why? Because you can't actually be sure you're acting fairly if you take sides. Even when one child is perpetually the victim, that child often needles the other child or in some other way initiates the conflict. This particular conflict is just one chapter of a much larger story that you can't fully perceive.

But there's an even more important reason. Siding with either child pushes the other child away from you. After all, she thinks she's right. Even if she's four and she's yelling at her eleven-month-old sister for looking at her toy. When you side with her sister, it convinces her that you love her sibling more, which intensifies the feelings that triggered her aggression to begin with. When you take sides in any way—even if you're objectively right—one child feels like she's won and one feels like she's lost, which feeds the rivalry.

By contrast, parents who listen to both sides—not so they can make a ruling about who is right, but so both children feel heard—and then help kids sort through win/win solutions, empower their children to solve their own problems. Even better, they gradually clear up the feeling each child has of being unfairly treated, so sibling rivalry diminishes over time.

So it's not parental intervention that's the problem. It's taking sides. The trick is regulating our own emotions so that we can stay calm, empathize with both children, and resist our impulse to decide who's right. That creates the foundation for children to learn how to work things out with each other without hurt or resentment.

Just as we're very involved as kids start using the potty and eventually not involved at all, we're very involved as kids start learning conflict resolution skills and eventually not involved at all. Eventually, you'll find yourself listening proudly from another room as your children work together to find their own solutions to a disagreement.

You're not alone if you're thinking that *by now* your children should know how to get along. After all, every day you repeat yourself hoarse trying to teach them. But consider what they actually hear. Does it sound anything like this?

"Don't grab from the baby! Give that back!"

"You have to share. You've had it long enough."

"You're older, you should know better!"

"Can't you just be nice to each other?"

"How would you feel if I shoved YOU?"

"Stop fighting or you'll have to go to your rooms."

While these admonitions are all completely understandable, they don't actually help children learn how to get their needs met while respecting the needs of others. If we want them to get along, we need to teach them how, specifically. That means we need to teach them what words to say, and how to calm themselves enough to listen to the other person. And it means that we have to resist solving the problem for them, which requires us to resist our own anxious desire to smooth things over between our children. As Janet Lansbury, author of *No Bad Kids*, says, "It's a big challenge to let go of our adult wish to tie a neat bow around our children's disagreements and avoid their emotional outbursts. But our interventions can prevent children from learning much of anything other than that they are dependent on us to fix these situations, incapable of handling conflicts themselves."[6]

TEN REASONS CHILDREN BICKER, AND HOW TO RESOLVE THEM

Bickering is verbally expressing annoyance or hostility. It's not yet a full-fledged fight, but it could become one. Or it could just go on all day long until it drives you crazy.

Children "bicker" for any number of reasons, most of which fit into one of these categories:

1. There's a temporary conflict of needs.
2. There's an ongoing, unresolved conflict or built-up resentment between siblings.
3. There's a difference in temperament that's flaring up into annoyance.
4. One sibling is jealous of the other, either from a recent incident or on an ongoing basis.
5. They're bored (in this case the need is for stimulation).
6. They want your attention.
7. They're jostling for power, respect, or status.
8. They're grumpy or irritable, and the sibling is the easiest person to take it out on.
9. The child was treated cruelly by someone outside the family and is trying to work it through by treating his sibling the same way.
10. One of the siblings wants more connection than the other.

Some amount of bickering is normal, since kids are still learning how to express their needs appropriately. But bickering is always a sign that something is less than optimal. You can think of it like a light on your car dashboard saying you need an oil change. The first time it flickers, you don't have to take action. But if you ignore it repeatedly, the light will become constant, and at some point your car will break down.

How should you intervene? Use what you've learned so far in this book about coaching children to express needs, problem-solve, and set limits with each other.

- Stay calm, connect with both kids, and empathize.
- Describe the problem without judgment.
- Interpret, by coaching each child to express feelings without attacking the other.

- Restate family rules.
- Coach kids to problem-solve.

Here's how to put it all together.

A Temporary Conflict of Needs
Kids can often work this out themselves if the parent provides a little momentum.

> **Emma:** Move over! You don't own the couch!
>
> **Mason:** I was here first.
>
> **Mom:** I hear two kids who both want one couch. This is a tough situation, because we aren't getting another couch! What can you do to work this out?
>
> **Mason:** I was here first. It's still my turn.
>
> **Emma:** I don't like watching scary movies from the floor. The couch feels safer. Can we share it?
>
> **Mason:** Only if you don't touch me, and you don't scream at the scary parts.
>
> **Emma:** Okay. How about we put this pillow between us so I don't accidentally touch you?
>
> **Mason:** Okay. But don't scream!

An Ongoing, Unresolved Conflict or Built-Up Resentment
Kids usually need parental facilitation.

> **Kylie:** It's not fair that you always get the top bunk. I'm big enough now, I won't fall out.
>
> **Parker:** You don't get it because you're a girl.
>
> **Dad:** Actually, I don't think it has anything to do with her being a girl, Parker. I think you always slept there

because you were older. Now I'm hearing that Kylie really wishes she could sleep on the top bunk. How can we work this out? Let's write down all our ideas and see what we can come up with.

A Difference in Temperament That Grates on One or Both

Your children need your help to learn to live with each other, which means articulating what each one needs and helping them figure out how both kids can get their needs met.

> **Leonardo:** Shut up! I can't even think!
>
> **Sofia:** I'm just singing.
>
> **Leonardo:** You're always singing!
>
> **Mom:** I hear some loud voices. Sofia, I hear you singing with such joy. Leonardo, I hear you saying it's too loud for you. We need a solution here. What can we do?
>
> **Leonardo:** I just want some peace and quiet for once!
>
> **Sofia:** I have a right to sing!
>
> **Mom:** Sofia, you certainly do have a right to sing, and I love to hear you sing. And I hear Leonardo saying that right now he needs some quiet. What can we do so you both get what you need?
>
> **Sofia:** Leonardo can go to his room.
>
> **Leonardo:** I need to stay here to build my Legos! You could go to your room, too!
>
> **Sofia:** I want to stay here where the music is!
>
> **Mom:** Hmm . . . so one solution is that you could be in separate rooms. But it sounds like both of you want to stay in the family room with the music and Legos. Are there any other solutions?
>
> *Both kids look at her blankly.*

Mom: Well, for instance, Sofia could take the music with
her into another part of the house . . . Or Leonardo
could take the Legos somewhere else . . . Or maybe
Leonardo could wear my headphones—they block out
sound.

Leonardo: I want the headphones! I call a long turn!

Mom: You can use the headphones for as long as you need
them to have quiet.

Jealousy, Either from a Recent Incident or on an Ongoing Basis

Acknowledge the source of the jealousy. In this case, Mom sees that
it's her own behavior.

Anthony: You always get your way . . . Mom and Dad let you
get away with everything!

Chiara: You're just jealous!

Mom: Anthony, it sounds like you're feeling mad at Chiara . . . Tell me what you're upset about.

Anthony: You always say I'm older, so I should act more
grown-up. So she always gets her way.

Chiara: I do not!

Mom: Chiara, I hear you saying that you don't always get
what you want. You can tell me more in just a minute.
Right now, we're listening to Anthony. He's saying that
he's actually mad at me, not you. Anthony, I hear you
saying that you think I'm not being fair. That when you
and Chiara have a disagreement, I expect you to let her
have her way because you're older. If I really do that, it
certainly doesn't seem fair. Both of you have a right to
ask for what you want and try to find a way to get it that
works for everyone. So if I am doing that, I apologize.

Anthony, will you tell me when you think I'm doing that, so we can work on it?

Boredom

State the problem, restate family rules, and redirect.

Noah: Dad, Abigail is pestering me.

Abigail: I am not! I'm trying to tell you something!

Dad: Hmm . . . sounds to me like Abigail wants to connect with you, Noah.

Noah: Well, I don't want to connect with her!

Dad: That's okay—you don't have to play with her if you don't want to right now. But you do have to treat her with respect. Those words can hurt. Can you find a different way to tell her that you're busy right now?

Noah: Abigail, I'm busy making my paper airplane. You can play with me later.

Abigail: But I don't have anything to do! What can I do?

Dad: Abigail, I hear you're wondering what to do with yourself. And Noah is saying that he's not ready to play right now; he wants to play with you later. Why don't you come outside and help me wash the car? You always have fun with the hose.

Desire for Your Attention

When children get one-on-one time with us every day, they don't usually bicker for attention. However, when you remove your attention from your children to focus on a phone call or screen, they do tend to get anxious. After all, they need to know you'll be there for them if there's an emergency. (I know, it sounds crazy, but they're genetically programmed to keep your attention available to them because it increases their chances of survival.) Before you pick up the phone or answer that email, try to get your children engaged in something engrossing. If bickering breaks out anyway, reassure them of your presence and redirect them to separate activities.

> **Arianna:** *Nyah, nyah, nyah, nyah.* I've got your blankie.
>
> **Flynn:** Mine! Give it back!
>
> **Mom** *(to the caller on the phone)*: I'll call you right back . . . Arianna, Flynn, what's going on?
>
> **Flynn:** My blankie!
>
> **Arianna:** You baby. I was going to give it to you . . . Here.
>
> **Mom:** I need quiet when I'm on the phone. Arianna, you know the rule is no teasing.
>
> **Arianna:** I was lonely.
>
> **Mom** *(puts arm around her)*: Arianna, honey, I am right here, at my desk. Do you want to come sit right next to me and draw while I call this person back? You'll need to be quiet for a few minutes.
>
> **Arianna:** Yes, I'll draw you a beautiful picture!
>
> **Mom:** Okay. Get your crayons and some paper and bring them here.
>
> **Mom** *(hugging Flynn)*: You've got your blankie . . . What are you going to play with now, Flynn?
>
> **Flynn:** Dolly stroller!
>
> **Mom** *(walking Flynn toward the dolls)*: Great! Will you take them for a walk in the hallway?

Jostling for Power, Respect, or Status

Teach values, meet their need for respect, find healthy ways for kids to compete, and be sure you're role-modeling appropriate use of power.

> **Alexander:** I won! I got inside first!
>
> **Matias:** It's not fair! You're always first.

Alexander: That's because I'm fastest.

Matias: You are not! You're meanest. You push me out of the way.

Alexander: I can't help it if you aren't as fast and tough as me. I'm a manly man.

Matias: I'm manly, too!

Dad: Sounds to me like you two both want to be manly. Me, too! But what does it mean to be manly?

Alexander: It means you win, and you're tough, and you're fast, and nobody pushes you around.

Dad: Hmm . . . Does that mean that a manly man pushes other people around?

Alexander: Well . . . no.

Dad: Do you think a manly man cares how other people feel? Do you think a manly man takes turns being first?

Matias: Yeah! And he doesn't push people. And he doesn't do a happy dance when someone else loses.

Dad *(teaching values)***:** I think it can be confusing sometimes—what does it mean to be manly? But I know that both of you boys care about other people. I know that neither of you would put someone else down to build yourself up. That's the kind of man I try to be.

Alexander and Matias *(together)***:** Me, too!

Dad *(not taking sides, even though Alexander usually does the shoving)***:** It sounds to me like both of you like being the first one in the door. But then you end up shoving and someone always feels bad. Is there a way to solve this?

Matias: We could take turns.

Alexander: But I *like* being first!

Dad: I hear you. I think most people like being first. But do you want to be the kind of person who always has to get

what he wants, even if it makes other people feel bad . . .
even if you have to push other people out of the way?

Alexander: Well . . .

Dad *(finding healthy ways for Alexander to compete)*:
I wonder if there are other things you can compete in,
to be your personal best and be first. How about running track? Do you think you'd like to run your fastest
and try to be first in a race?

Alexander: Yeah!

Matias: But coming home isn't a race.

Dad: That's right, coming home isn't a race. So how can you
two handle coming home so it feels fair to both of you?

Alexander: All right, we'll take turns. But Dad, can we see
how I can start to run track?

Dad: We sure can. Just as soon as you and Matias come up
with an agreement about who comes in the door first
tomorrow.

Grumpiness or Irritability

Intervene to help the child who is attacking with whatever feelings
are making him so unhappy.

Luis: Your picture is ugly.

Maya: You're a meany, Luis!

Mom: I'm hearing some hurtful words. Luis, it sounds like
you're trying to hurt your sister's feelings . . . And it
sounds like it worked! Are you feeling angry with her, or
are you just having a hard time in general?

Luis: I hate everything!

Mom: Wow! You *are* having a hard time. Come be with me
on the couch, and tell me what's so rotten.

The Child Was Treated Cruelly by Someone Outside the
Family and Is Trying to Work It Through by Treating His
Sibling the Same Way

Restate family rules about civility, empathize as you set limits to
understand the source of the aggression, and help your child express
his feelings in healthy ways.

Miles: Jaxon is a poopoo head.

Jaxon: I am not!

Miles: Jaxon is a poopoo head, Jaxon is a poopoo head.

Jaxon: Stop it, Miles! You're mean!

Miles: Jaxon is a poopoo head and a crybaby . . . see, you're
ready to cry.

Dad: Miles, the rule is no name-calling and no teasing . . .
Jax, you can tell your brother what you want.

Jaxon: I want no more poopoo head calling!

Miles: You're a poopoo head, too, Papa!

Dad: Miles, now you're calling me names. What's going on?

Miles: Wyatt said I was a poopoo head and a crybaby. I'm *not*.

Dad: Miles, that must have hurt your feelings when Wyatt
called you names. I know you want to feel better, but
calling us names won't make you feel better. You know
what helps? Pretend I'm Wyatt and tell me what you
want.

Miles: Wyatt, don't call me names. And I wasn't really
crying. It just hurt my feelings when you were mean. No
more being mean or I won't be your friend. So there!

Dad: Good for you, Miles. I hear that's what you wanted to
tell Wyatt. Do you think you can tell him next time he
calls you names?

Miles: Maybe.

Dad: Okay, we can practice more later so you feel comfortable telling Wyatt what's on your mind tomorrow. Right now, do you want to roughhouse with me? That's a great way to feel better.

Miles: Yeah!

Dad: Okay, let's do it. But first, is there anything you want to say to your brother?

Miles: I'm sorry, Jax. You aren't really a poopoo head.

Jaxon: Good. Can I roughhouse, too?

Dad: Sure! It's the Miles and Jax team against Dad!

One of the Siblings Wants More Connection Than the Other

Help one child articulate his desire for closeness, and the other acknowledge her caring, even if she can't make time to connect right now.

Ethan *(jumping on Emily's back)*: I got you! You're my pony and I'm riding you!

Emily: Ethan, stop! Get off me! I have to do my homework!

Ethan clings around Emily's neck as she tries to swat him off.

Mom: Ethan, do you hear Emily? She says get off her body. When someone says Stop, it means stop.

Ethan drops off, dejected.

Mom: Ethan, are you trying to tell your sister that you want to play with her?

Ethan: I never get to play with her!

Emily: Ethan, when you get big, you'll understand homework!

Mom: I'm hearing that Ethan really wants to play right now, but Emily has to do her homework . . . Ethan feels like he doesn't get enough time to play with Emily . . .

Can we set a date for a time when you would be ready to play with Ethan?

Emily: Well, I'm pretty busy. After homework I want to play with Alexis next door.

Mom: Emily, you're in charge of your own time, and you don't have to play with Ethan if you don't want to. I think Ethan's saying he really misses you and wonders if you will ever play with him?

Emily: Don't worry, Ethan. I still love you. I will play with you soon. I am just busy today. *(She hugs Ethan, who smiles and hugs her back.)*

Mom: Ethan, were you looking for a pony to ride? I have five minutes to be a bucking bronco if you want, and then maybe we can go out and rake leaves together . . . I bet you'll love jumping in them.

Ethan: Yay!

In each of these cases, the parent could have scolded the child who was needling. But that would just have led to hard feelings and more bickering in the future. Instead, the parent responded to the bickering by realizing that the children had legitimate needs that they needed help to express. Over time, this kind of coaching helps children identify and articulate their own needs, and listen to the needs of their siblings, so they can problem-solve with each other— and you don't even need to be involved.

HOW TO PLAYFULLY DIVERT BICKERING

Making myself the target always helps things get unstuck when children are locked in conflict.

—Lawrence Cohen, author of *Playful Parenting*

Sometimes, you're out of patience with bickering. At those moments, it can just feel too hard to take your kids' concerns seriously. You both need *this* spoon, really? Neither of you can walk into the kitchen and find another spoon? You're letting *this* spoil my Sunday morning?

You feel your own tension mounting, and you know that soon you'll be raising your voice and ordering your older child into the kitchen to get his own spoon. Or maybe you'll resist siding with one child, and you'll tell them that neither one will ever touch another spoon. But you also know that won't stop the bickering, because everyone will feel bad at that point—including you! What can you do instead?

Get everyone laughing! Laughter cuts the tension. It actually transforms the body chemistry by reducing stress hormones and increasing bonding hormones. So when your children laugh together, they're bonding. Especially when they're laughing at you!

My go-to expert on getting children laughing is Dr. Lawrence Cohen, the author of *Playful Parenting* (and several other books).[7] I've been recommending the games below for years, but he inspired most of them. The basic idea is to divert your kids' animosity from each other, so they target you instead. In the process, you get them laughing, which evaporates the fight instinct. They unite against you, transforming competition into sibling teamwork. They can't help but notice that your insistence on your right to that spoon is ridiculous, and if they make the leap to realizing that their own argument was a bit silly, all the better. But you're not ridiculing them. You're presenting yourself as the object of ridicule or competition, to divert their attacks on each other, and to melt them away. For instance:

1. **It's mine!** Grab the spoon and run away with it, exclaiming with delight that it's yours. Be over-the-top silly, crooning

your infatuation and pointing out that this spoon, compared to every other spoon in the house, is the best of all spoons. *"Even working together, you two can't get this spoon . . . I won't ever share it with anyone! I will guard this spoon with my life!"*

2. **What about me?!** *"You two are always fighting over this easy chair, so I never even get a turn!"* Dissolve into mock tears. Or initiate roughhousing: *"Move over, it's my turn!"* Plop down on the chair on top of both children, starting a wrestling session in which the kids try to shove you off while you pretend to be fighting for your rights—or, in another variation, not to notice them.

3. **Pick on someone your own size.** When one child is picking on the other, you do need to step in. *"Hey, I bet you can't push ME over!"* Then look terrified and run away. You can even empower the "weaker" child and promote the sibling team by urging the children to team up against you. *"You two can't catch me . . . Even working together, you can't knock ME over!"*

4. **Would you two please fight?** When your children are in a mild stage of bickering, before tempers get too hot, say, *"Would you two please argue with each other now?"* When they begin to fight, pretend to be a TV commentator. *"We're on the scene tonight watching two sisters who can't seem to get along! Will they work things out or not? Stay with us while we observe this behavior live! Notice how big sister is bossy, but little sister is provocative! Both girls want the same cheese stick! Can they work this out? Are they smart enough to realize there are more cheese sticks in the fridge? Stay tuned . . ."* Before they know it, your kids will be giggling, teaming up to act for you, and quickly ready to cooperate to solve the source of the bickering.

WHEN CHILDREN TEASE . . .

*Instead of
Ignoring or Punishing*   *Try Setting Limits*

Kids tease siblings because they're jealous, or they need your attention, or it salves their feelings of powerlessness. Ignoring the teasing doesn't solve these motivations. Punishment worsens them.

With Empathy

Left: Acknowledge your child's perspective as you set a limit.

Right: Intervene with connection to fill your child's deeper need as you "enforce" your limit.

WHEN CHILDREN TEASE . . .

And Connection

Left: Roughhousing gets your child laughing, which eases the tension and helps your child feel reconnected to you.

Right: Now that your child feels connected to you, reinforce your family rule.

What happens when the laughter is over and they go right back to the same argument? Or your attempts at laughter fall flat? It may be that one or both of your children are just too upset. Then it isn't just bickering; it's moving toward becoming a real fight, with big emotions escalating. You'll know when that's the case, because one or both of your bickering kids won't laugh despite your best silly antics. They're too angry. Your attempts to get them laughing may even feel to them like you're not taking their feelings seriously, which will make them even angrier. Or they'll start out laughing, but quickly end up in tears. Either way, it's your signal to stop, drop (what you're doing), and breathe. Then start over, this time connecting, empathizing, and interpreting to help your children express their needs and feelings—and then coach them to a win/

win solution, as described in the previous chapter. If the feelings
are raw enough that you have a fight on your hands, keep reading
this chapter!

Empowering Kids to Stand Up to Teasing

Because most parents grew up with teasing, many parents see teasing between siblings as harmless. When it's reciprocal and
completely good-natured, it can get people laughing together and
bring them closer. In fact, some adult sibling relationships, particularly between brothers, seem to express affection almost exclusively
through the use of teasing.

But there's a certain amount of disrespect in teasing, even if it's
"all in fun." When children tease, it's usually intended to hurt—even
if the child claims he's making a joke. When a child begins taunting
about something he has that no one else has, or about another child's
limitations, teasing becomes a mild form of meanness and jockeying
for position.

"My piece is bigger than your piece!"

"Carter doesn't know how to do it right!"

If you're wondering whether to step in, look at the face of the
child being teased. That's the only person who can decide whether
the teasing feels hurtful. Empower that child to stand up for himself:
*"Carter, you look sad. Is it hurting your feelings that your brother is
saying that to you? You can tell him that it hurts when he talks to you
that way."*

It's good practice for your child to learn to stick up for himself
in situations where he feels like he's being treated badly. Usually,

that's enough to stop the teasing. If not, you might have to invoke your family rule: *"The rule in this family is that we treat each other kindly. Andrew, do you hear Carter? He's saying your comments don't feel kind to him; they're hurtful."*

Usually, coaching the teased child and reminding the teaser of the rules are sufficient to end the teasing. But what about those situations when the teased child falls apart?

Empathize, offer support, and empower: *"Ouch! That didn't feel good when your brother said that to you. It hurt . . . Do you want some help to talk to your brother about this? No? . . . You still seem pretty upset. You know, you don't have to let your brother decide how you feel . . . He can say whatever he wants, but you're the one who decides how you feel . . . You don't have to give him that power."*

If one of your children makes a habit of teasing, that's a red flag that either someone is teasing him, or he's holding in some other kind of hurt. You can use laughter to heal whatever's wrong. Just make yourself the object of the teasing: *"Hey, I hear you calling him a poopyhead. I'm the only poopyhead around here. And you know what poopyheads do? They give you poopyhugs!"* Chase him around the house threatening hugs. He'll scream with laughter, which will help dissolve those hurt feelings. You'll notice as you regularly intervene this way that he begins to come right to you to initiate laughter when he's feeling bad inside, instead of teasing his sibling.

Want a shortcut? Just grab the child doing the teasing up in a bear hug and say, *"Those words sound like they could hurt . . . You know that in our family, we're kind to each other . . . You must be out of hugs again! Let's see what we can do about that!"*

And what about the times when both children are teasing each other? Ignoring it gives kids the message that it's okay. Instead, either intervene with some roughhousing, or—if they're too mad to laugh—help them resolve the issue by intervening the same way you would with bickering, above.

Mean Words

Children need a chance to express their negative feelings about everything, including siblings. So when your child says she hates the baby, you can see that as an opportunity to help her with those feelings, rather chastising her for saying such terrible things. (See Chapter 11.) But as the baby gets bigger and understands what her sister is saying, you need to respond to the feelings of both children.

So for instance, if your child says, *"Why does she always have to be here? I wish I didn't have a sister!"* start, as usual, by empathizing: *"Sometimes you wish you had me all to yourself. It can be hard for two sisters to share their parents."*

Then add: *"Sometimes people in a family get mad, but they still love each other ... You can be mad at someone and love them at the same time ... We are all a family together. Sometimes each of you gets time with me all to yourself, and that is wonderful. And sometimes we get time all together and that is wonderful to me, too. I have more than enough love for both of you."*

What if your child expresses verbal hostility to her sibling? Allow your children to express anger as long as they aren't attacking each other. *"I hear how angry you are at your brother. You can tell your brother how mad you are without using hurtful words."*

Be clear that the expectation is kindness. *"Words like that can hurt. I hear you have some upset feelings ... Your brother is not causing these feelings, even though you're mad at him ... those are your feelings. I'm sorry it feels so bad. You can tell me why you're upset; I want to hear."*

When Your Child Says He Hates His Sibling

I hate her, Dad. I don't know why, I just do.
   –Big brother, age four

Of course I love her. She's annoying sometimes, but she's my sister.
   —Same brother, age ten

It's scary to hear our child say he hates his brother or sister. Since many of us had terrifying experiences with anger as young children, we're often frightened by our children's anger. And "hate" is a strong word. If you let this word push your buttons, though, your child is guaranteed to use it regularly.

What your child is saying is simply that he's furious. Respond to that. If you tell him the word "hate" is not allowed in your house, you can count on him using it every time he gets angry. No child can resist the power that comes from a big parental reaction.

"Hate" is not anger, or even a feeling. Hate is a "position," or a stance we assume to protect ourselves. You can't argue with a position someone is taking. You have to respond to the feelings driving it. Remember that anger is a defense against more upsetting feelings, like fear, hurt, or sadness. Helping kids recognize what's behind their anger gives them the tools to dissolve it rather than lashing out. And letting our child know that he isn't a bad person for feeling rage helps him accept his anger as normal and move through it, rather than getting stuck in it.

So how to respond?

Don't get hooked on your child's declaration of hate. Acknowledge the strength of your child's anger, but then go under it to empathize with the more vulnerable emotions (grief, loneliness, envy, fear) spurring his rage.

"You hate the new baby? I hear you. Sometimes you get really mad at her just for being here. And I see how mad you are at me, too, for spending time with the baby. You liked it better when it was just you and me. You feel sad that things are different now and I'm so busy with the baby. I wonder if you sometimes feel left out? Come snuggle with me and I will hold you and you can tell me your sad and mad feelings. When you're ready I will kiss your nose and toes and we can play baby games, just you and me, like we did when you were a baby."

This is more complicated when your child says he hates a sibling who is old enough to understand him, in front of the sibling. You respond with the same empathy, but you also acknowledge how the sibling feels, and use your interpretation skills to build a bridge.

"You're so mad right now that you're using the word 'hate.' That's a powerful word, and I hear how upset you are to use it. You can be as mad as you want, but words like that can really hurt. You can say what you're upset about without using hurtful language . . . Sometimes you and Brandon get really angry at each other, so angry that you don't even want to work things out with each other. That's what you mean by hate, right? That you don't even want to work things out. I hear how very angry you are. When we get very angry at someone, sometimes we forget we love them—but the love is still in there, hiding, like the sun behind the clouds . . . Why don't we take some time for everyone to calm down, and then I will help you and Brandon talk about what happened and why you both got so mad. No matter what, we are a family, and we will always work things out with each other."

What if your child continues to say "I hate you!" to his sibling, or to say "I hate her!" in front of his sibling? Empathize, and set a clear limit.

"I hear how very angry you are. You can always tell me what is making you angry. But your brother can understand lots of our words now, and words like that hurt. It would make him very sad to hear you

say that. You can tell me how angry you are, and you can show me by pounding your workbench with your hammer, or punching your Bobo doll, or drawing me a picture of how mad you are. I will watch you. But if you want to use words like that, you need to use them privately, where your brother can't hear you."

It's important to note that expressing the anger by acting it out with punching or pounding is not what's healing. In fact, research shows that the act of physical aggression reinforces the feeling of anger.[8] The healing comes from your child having the chance to show you how deeply he feels, and from your compassionate response. Your understanding provides enough safety so the tears and fears behind the anger come swelling up. Once he feels those, he no longer needs to take refuge in anger, or "hatred."

What about children who yell "I'll kill you!" to their sibling? He's using the worst word he knows to make sure you understand how deeply he feels—and because right now, while he's in fight or flight, both his brother and you look like the enemy. But you can expect the target of this anger to need your reassurance: *"Yes, I heard your brother say he would kill you. He's very angry right now. You don't need to worry; I won't let him hurt anyone, no matter how angry he is. You're safe. Your brother was very upset. I'll help him with his feelings as soon as I can."*

Intervening in a Sibling Fight: The Basics

When we don't intervene at the bickering stage—and sometimes even when we try to—tempers can flare into verbal or physical violence. What should you do?

1. **Get between your kids to separate them and prevent further violence.** *"Whoa! Stop!"* Hold out your hand at chest

level or put your hand on the child's belly to keep him from advancing.

2. **Help both kids feel safer so they can stop attacking.** Breathe deeply and use a calm voice. Touch each child so they feel connected to you and safer.

3. **If a child is hurt, comfort that child.** Administer comfort, bandage, ice, empathy. If the child is hurt too badly for you to even be nice to the aggressor, take the wounded child into the bathroom or another room, so you aren't tempted to shout at the aggressor. If you can matter-of-factly involve the aggressor *("Ooh, this must hurt. Quick, Lucas, get the ice pack!")*, you'll help him shift from "bad kid who hurt his sibling" to "helpful kid who repairs his mistakes and helps heal his sibling." That's an invaluable shift if you want to prevent more hitting in the future.

4. **Depending on how upset the kids are, you may need a cooling-off period.** But don't send them to their rooms, which will make them feel less safe. Your goal is to teach them some self-calming techniques so they can learn to shift out of an upset state and re-regulate themselves when life doesn't go their way. Say, *"I see how mad you both are. I want to hear what's upsetting you. Let's cool off for a few minutes so we can talk. Lucas, please sit on the couch. Charles, please come sit on this chair. Now, let's take three deep breaths together . . . Breathe deep . . . Now blow out all those angries. Again."*

5. **Bring the children together and put an arm around each** so when you listen to the one who's talking, the other still feels connected to you.

6. **Give each child a chance to speak and reflect back what you heard.** Use your skills to listen, empathize, and interpret. *"Lucas, you hit him because he broke your fire truck ladder? . . . You were so upset!" "Charles, you didn't mean to break it? . . . You just wanted to see it?"*

7. **Restate family rules.** *"No hitting! Hitting hurts."*

8. **Resist siding with either child, even when you think one is clearly right.** Really. Even if one was hurt. Your child knows that hurting his sibling was wrong, and you've just restated it.

9. **Coach each child to tell the other how she feels or what she wants.** *"Can you tell your brother, 'Don't hit me!'?" "Can you tell your brother that when he wants to use your fire truck, he needs to ask you?"*

10. **If one child attacks the other, redirect him to express how he feels, not what he thinks of the other child.** *"You stupid-head, Charles!" "Lucas, tell your brother what you want and how you feel—not what you think about him right now." "I want you to ask before you take my truck! Now the ladder is broken! I feel sad!"*

11. **Coach each child to restate how the other one feels.** *"What did you hear your brother say?"*

12. **Raise the possibility of repair.** *"You both got pretty upset. Brothers are for loving, not for hurting. What could you do to make things better?"*

When there's still a problem to be solved, coach kids to use their problem-solving skills.

1. **Validate how big the problem feels to your children.** *"Lucas's fire truck is broken. This is a tough problem."*

2. **Express confidence that the problem can be solved.** *"I know you two can work this out."*

3. **Help the children brainstorm a mutually agreeable solution, using the problem-solving process described in Chapter 4.**

4. **State the solution.** *"Okay, so Charles agrees that he will help Lucas tape the ladder with duct tape to see if it can be fixed. And also Charles will let Lucas use his dump truck for a whole week. Is that right?"*

5. **Shake hands all around as you restate the agreement and congratulate your children.** *"You really listened to each other and worked hard to come up with an agreement that feels fair to both of you. You must feel so good inside. Wow, what a team!"*

Should You Punish Your Child for Aggression?

So my three-year-old girl kicks the one-year-old, there's a bloodcurdling scream, and I'm to just sit with the three-year-old until she feels better? So, no discipline, just more attention . . . for kicking the baby?!"
　—Mother of two

Punishing children when they hit is counterproductive, because it leaves them even more frightened and resentful, and all those feelings will burst out in more aggression toward their sibling later (see

Chapter 2). But even when we know this, most parents feel an urgent need to punish when a child hits. We tell ourselves that's because the child needs to learn a lesson. But the truth? We're in "fight or flight" ourselves! Someone kicks my baby? The lion-mama in me roars. The last thing I would feel like doing is lavishing love on the perpetrator.

Except that the perp is my three-year-old, who is also my baby. And who is certainly in a state of emotional dysregulation, or she wouldn't have done such a thing. She's sending me a clear signal that she needs my help, desperately. The only way to help a child out of the abyss of fear is to regain our own composure. I know, it's a tall order. This is the hardest work there is. So practice a mantra you can use when you're triggered, like: *"No one's dying. It's not an emergency."* Train yourself to simply ignore the transgressor while you minister to your hurt child.

Now that you've calmed down, you're ready for the million-dollar question. What's the best response to prevent such incidents in the future? Conventional parenting would take a behavior-modification approach of punishment, hoping that in the future when she gets ready to lash out, she'll remember the punishment and restrain herself. At the very least, a time-out would make us feel like we took action to address the situation.

The problem is that punishment after the fact doesn't prevent crimes of passion. The defining characteristic of rage is that the thinking part of the brain isn't engaged, so we forget all the lessons we've learned. If your three-year-old saw someone else kick her sister, she'd run to her sibling's defense. But when we're in fight or flight mode, even someone we love can look like the enemy. We do things we would never do if we were thinking straight. (Yes, even adults.)

So a time-out isn't going to prevent aggression in the future. What about a more "memorable" punishment, that really causes pain? That will just make her seek more vengeance on that baby who she thinks caused her misery. If she has to sneak to do it—meaning wait until you're out of the room to kick the baby—that's what she'll do. (Not so good for the sibling relationship.)

But that doesn't ever mean we just permissively let our child wallop another person. No, we go to the source to stop the violence: our child's emotions.

We start by moving her back from the abyss of fear into a zone where she feels safer, where someone is helping her regulate her actions: *"You are VERY angry. I am right here. I will keep you both safe."* By contrast, if we yell, it would intensify her fear. Now, she's already beginning to calm down, even if we can't see it—because she knows we're there to help.

You're not soothing, at this point, which implies calming a child down. Instead, you're helping her feel safe enough to express the hurt and fear that are driving her anger. So you are *not* doing what the mom described above, *"just sitting with her until she feels better."* This isn't just a time-in during which you reconnect with your child. In fact, it's hard for kids to reconnect with us when they're so full of pain. It's like trying to fill a leaky cup.

That's also the problem with letting her calm herself down in a time-out. She doesn't get help with her emotions, and now she feels like a bad person on top of it. So at the next provocation, it's *"Take that, baby!"*

To help your child go under the anger, create safety. Stay as kind as you can while you look her in the eye, which triggers all her uncomfortable emotions. Say, *"Your sister was hurt and scared. You must be so upset to kick your sister . . . Something is making you feel so bad."*

Deep emotional healing always happens in the context of relationship, when love dissolves fear. She'll certainly start with anger: She hates the baby, she hates you, you always take her sister's side. Don't take it personally. That's just her defense against deep pain. Stay as compassionate as you can, and empathize: *"I'm so sorry, sweetie... That must hurt you so much... You can be as mad as you want at me; I will always love you no matter how mad you are... I could never love anyone more than I love you.*" If you can keep yourself calm and empathic, and keep offering safety, she'll start crying. It's your compassion that heals the hurt.

After she has the chance to sob in your arms, she'll have moved out of "fight or flight." She'll be able to reflect on her actions. But don't rush it. Give her time to regain her equilibrium. Once she can handle a little playfulness from you, you'll know she's ready to talk.

If you can resist blaming and instead be as kind as possible, she'll be more able to take responsibility for her actions, which is what will prevent her from repeating them. This is the holy grail of internalizing self-discipline, but it doesn't work when it's imposed from outside with blame and shame.

Instead of *"Kicking is bad,"* try *"You were so angry. It's okay to be angry, but it's never okay to kick a person. It hurts! What could you do instead next time you're angry?"* Help her brainstorm other options: calling a grown-up for help when the one-year-old pesters her, walking away, stomping her foot instead of kicking. Have her actually act out those scenarios, so that she develops muscle memory of them and is more likely to be able to summon them up next time before she loses control.

She's worked out her upset and feels empowered to express her needs in a more constructive way next time. Finally, she's ready to acknowledge that her kick hurt her sister, and repair their relationship. Kids actually want the chance to redeem themselves, as long as we resist punishing and shaming. *"Your sister was scared and hurt. I wonder if there's anything you could do to help her feel safe with you again."* You're helping your three-year-old learn that she can repair rifts, and strengthening the bond between your children. Both of these outcomes will make future sibling violence less likely. (We'll talk more about helping kids make repairs later in this chapter.)

Are we giving her attention for kicking the baby, which will make her kick the baby again? No. Time-outs and other punishments give the child negative attention, which actually reinforces the negative behavior. Our child learns that when he's emotionally dysregulated, he can just hit his sibling, and we'll step in and force him to re-regulate with a time-out. But that kind of re-regulation doesn't help kids with the emotions driving the hitting. It just stuffs them down in the emotional backpack. So punishment just calms the child temporarily; it doesn't prevent such occurrences in the future—and in fact, it makes them more likely. Research shows that punishment does not diminish aggression, but often increases it.[9]

We're giving our child help with her emotions that she desperately needs, so she won't ever kick the baby again. It's a lot more work than a time-out. In fact, I'd bet it's tougher than lion-taming. But it works very effectively to raise a child who *wants* to behave and can manage her emotions to do so. That makes for no more hitting and better sibling relationships. Not to mention fewer bloodcurdling screams. You'll find another detailed script that walks you through how to handle hitting (page 294) as well as an illustrated example (page 300) in Chapter 11.

When Your Toddler Is the Aggressor Against Your Older Child

My twenty-two-month-old younger daughter very aggressively scratches my older daughter, who is three and a half.
    —Tahri

So far we've been focusing on aggression from the older child. But at some point, the baby becomes a toddler and can become an aggressor, too. What then?

Toddlers don't have a fully developed frontal cortex, so their emotions routinely overcome their knowledge that "hitting hurts." And often they can't express themselves very well verbally, so they're easily frustrated. So preventing toddler aggression can be difficult.

But your older child deserves to feel safe in her own house, so you can't just sit by and "let them work it out." Obviously, you immediately get between your children to stop the hitting. You say, *"Ouch! Hitting hurts! No hitting!"*

But what if the aggression continues? As always, if you want to change your child's behavior, consider the feelings and needs driving it. Understanding the source of your toddler's aggression will help you intervene effectively to prevent the behavior. For instance:

1. **The toddler wants to connect with the older sibling.** Clumsy, yes, but he's a toddler. He wants his big sister's attention.

   Solution: Teach the toddler how to initiate a more positive interaction. Say, *"No hurting your sister! Ouch! Are you trying to get your sister's attention? Use your words! Say, 'Paola, here I am! Play with me!'"* And if you have a toddler who thinks he's a monkey, make sure your older child knows how to safely dump him on the couch in a way that gets both of them laughing.

   Of course, it isn't the older child's responsibility to play with the younger child on demand. Sometimes she won't want to. So you'll have to give her a safe place to work on her projects without toddler "help." Coach her on how to deflect the toddler gracefully by saying, *"Yes, I see you! Do you want to play with this spaceship? It goes vroom!"* But don't leave her to fend off the toddler by herself. Be available when she needs you to run interference, and offer your toddler some connection with you instead.

2. **The toddler wants what the older sibling has.**

   Solution: Teach basic social skills. Say to the toddler, *"Ouch! No hitting your brother! I see you want the giraffe he's playing with. Can you ask if he'll give you a turn? Say, 'Turn, please!'"* Siblings won't always want to give a turn right away, and you'll want to teach your toddler to offer trades. You will probably also have to "help" the toddler wait quite often (as explained in Chapter 6). It will help to explain to your other children that if the toddler trusts that she'll have a turn soon, it's a lot easier to wait. So it's up to them, but when they don't need the giraffe at that moment, letting the toddler have her turn as soon as they can manage it will help the toddler develop trust—and patience.

3. **The toddler is retaliating** for the older sibling's teasing or subtler aggression, such as grabbing toys or making mean faces.

   Solution: Put an arm around each child and say, *"I see two upset kids here . . . You are having a hard time, aren't you? . . . I'm so sorry I wasn't here to help you both."* (You're modeling taking responsibility.) *"Can you tell me about it?"* (Then, to the older child:) *"Your brother* [the toddler] *scratched you. Ouch . . . That hurts . . . I'm so sorry."* (To the toddler:) *"Scratching hurts! Ouch! No scratching . . . You must have been very mad. Were you mad at your brother? Use your words . . . Say, 'I'm MAD!' Can you say that right now? Yes, you're mad! Tell us in words, or stomp your foot—no scratching!"* (To older child:) *"I wonder why he's so mad at you? Can you think of anything that might have made him so mad? . . . Is there anything you could do differently next time?"*

4. **The toddler is unhappy and is taking it out on her sibling.**
   Parental intervention—food, a nap, a time-in to refuel, rough-

housing, a scheduled meltdown—will help the toddler feel better, so she doesn't take it out on her sibling.

Solution: Toddlers have strong feelings, but they generally have sunny personalities. If your toddler often seems unhappy and angry, consider whether there's a bigger issue. Maybe there's something physically wrong that you can pinpoint with a little detective work.

5. **The toddler is jealous of the parents' interactions with the older sibling.**

   Solution: Every child needs one-on-one time with each parent, without siblings around—ideally, daily. If your toddler seems jealous of your relationship with an older sibling, focus on connecting more with the toddler, including daily Special Time. Before you engage with your older child, for instance to help with homework, focus on the toddler for five minutes, filling his love tank and then getting him absorbed with a toy or activity. When he sees you with his sibling and demands your attention, acknowledge his jealousy: *"You see me snuggling your brother Ian, and you want some snuggles, too, huh? Everybody needs snuggles, don't they? I'm sitting with Ian right now, but I always have a hug for you, Davey . . . Come here and get a big hug . . . Do you want a hug from Ian, too? Big hug! Okay, Davey, let's find you something fun to do . . . Do you want to sit on the floor next to Ian and me, and play with this?"*

6. **The toddler just wants to be heard.** Sometimes toddlers lash out physically because they don't know how else to get their point across. Be sure to teach your toddler words to stick up for himself. Practice words like "Stop!" and "Move, please!" with your toddler, making it a fun game, to ensure that he doesn't have to hit to be heard.

Coaching Kids to Handle Aggression from Younger Siblings

Mostly, children learn from our modeling. So if you respond with calm empathy to your upset little one, your older child will learn to do that as well. Of course, he won't always be able to stay calm, particularly if he's worried about his little brother ruining his castle. And if the little one actually hurts him, you can't really expect him to master his fight or flight response without some practice.

Hopefully, though, if you've coached him and he feels close to you and thus less jealous, your older child's response will be measured. Meaning, he'll resist clobbering the nineteen-month-old, but might take his own toy and leave the room. That's not a bad natural consequence for the younger sibling to encounter. (No, I'm not recommending that parents leave the room when a nineteen-month-old is aggressive, because it triggers the child's abandonment panic. Siblings play a different role in the little one's life. And in this case, you're there to help the nineteen-month-old when big brother leaves.)

How can you coach your older child to handle the younger one's aggression?

1. **Model.** Say to the toddler: *"Ouch, that hurts! I'm going to move back from those hurting hands . . . You must be mad! Can you tell me with words what you want? Oh, you want to use the red car? Okay, here you go. I can use the blue car. See, you don't have to hit. You can just show us what you want."*

2. **Teach.** *"Your little brother hits because he gets worried about getting what he wants. He's still very little, and when he gets upset, it's hard for him to use his words. If he knows you'll try*

to help him, then he won't hit so much. So if you can tell him you understand, he won't hit as much when he gets upset."

3. **Empathize, acknowledge, and problem-solve.** *"It's hard when your brother hits, I know . . . I appreciate your trying to be patient with him . . . and I see he gets fixated on using the red car. You probably get tired of using the blue car, right? Thanks for being so flexible. If it starts really bothering you, let me know. Maybe we need a second red car, so everyone gets one."*

4. **Act out scenarios** in a fun way to help your older child remember what to do in a tense situation. Be sure to include practice saying, *"No! Don't hurt my body!"* and moving away from the younger child.

5. **Set limits.** *"Your brother's brain is still growing, so when he gets mad, he can't always stop himself from lashing out. But he's learning. And the way we teach him is, we never hit. It is never okay to hit a younger child, no matter what. Just move away so he can't hurt you, and yell for me: 'Mom, we need you!' Let's practice that."*

6. **Protect.** Be sure that your older child has a space to work on projects that the younger one can't reach. Set up a table for him so they can stay in the same room while the older one draws, builds, or does puzzles. Or move some of the little one's toys into the kitchen so your older child gets a break. There's nothing wrong with him playing with his little brother, but his main job is to grow and master his own developmental hurdles, not to provide childcare. If that need's not met, you can't expect him to be patient with younger siblings.

7. **Make sure your older child knows he always has backup.**
   Tell him, *"Do you notice that when your little brother is cranky like this, that's usually when he hits you? I think when he feels like that, he just needs to cry. So please just call me at those times, and I'll take over and help him with his feelings."* Giving your older child tools is terrific, but even adults have a tough time with an aggressive toddler.

Did you notice that none of this will work if the older child is in the grip of sibling rivalry? Older sibs need one-on-one time with parents when they feel seen and valued for who they are. They need to be reassured of their special role in the family, that the younger child looks up to them (as younger kids always do). And they need to know that they're still the apple of your eye, that you could never love anyone else more—no matter who's on your lap at the moment.

How to Stop Repeated Aggression

Within two days he became much nicer to his sister and we now feel like a family, not like before: "I was here first and she is my enemy." We constantly engage him with helping when someone is hurt (feel better hug, bring Kleenex, Band-Aid) and he's starting to talk to her, teach her, and play with her.
   —Mollie

Every child has the right to safety in her own home. If one of your children is stuck in a pattern of physically lashing out at a sibling, stopping it becomes your highest priority.

Children hit because they're feeling unsafe. Sometimes that's because a sibling is threatening them in some way, even such a mild way as looking at their toy or standing close to them. Sometimes they seem to hit for no reason at all. That stems from big upsets locked away—usually fear that you no longer love them, mixed up with grief and helplessness. Once you help your child with those feelings, she'll stop hitting. But she won't trust you to help her until you reconnect. So the most important thing you can do to stop hitting is to read the first section of this book, and use the peaceful parenting practices that create safety and help children work through emotions.

You may wonder where these big emotions are coming from. It's worth considering whether you're unwittingly contributing to the cycle of violence with your own outrage. All parents get upset when one child hits another, but when parents are so triggered by the hitting that they find themselves enraged at the hitter, the pattern of hitting often becomes entrenched. So, for instance, if you were hit by your brother, it's going to be extra challenging for you if your son hits your daughter. Understandably, you might overreact. That overreaction can fuel more aggression, because it scares your son, who's afraid that you no longer love him. So setting a limit—*"I won't let you hit . . . What's going on?"*—is essential. Exploding, shaming, or punishing creates more fear and defensiveness, swamping your child with emotions he can't handle, which will make future hitting more likely. So transforming your discipline approach into empathic limits—even when your child hits—usually helps the child stop hitting. And I've repeatedly seen children's hitting vanish almost overnight when parents worked on their own upset about it.

The other key to stopping repeated hitting is reconnecting with your child. In one family I worked with, the son was hitting his little sister virtually every day. His mother smacked him when he hit his sister, but that didn't stop the hitting. Instead, the boy became more defiant and difficult. Finally, his mother began following my preventive maintenance program and spending one-on-one time with her son every day. Instead of smacking when her son hit, she began staying connected and helping him cry, even as she set firm limits on the hitting. Within a month, the hitting had vanished.

But one day a few weeks later, the mom looked up to see her son standing behind her daughter. His hand was raised over his sister's head in a fist, poised to come down hard. The mother froze. Her eyes locked with her son's. Without breaking their gaze, his hand very slowly opened . . . and he began softly stroking his sister's hair. *"I was just petting her fuzz,"* he said proudly to his mother.

What happened here? Was the boy afraid of being punished, once he saw his mother watching? I don't think so. He had already been punished repeatedly, and it hadn't stopped the hitting. I think what happened is that this child finally had something that he wanted more than he wanted to hit his sister—a warm relationship with his mother. He didn't want to lose their newfound closeness.

Finally, if aggression is a pattern between your children, don't just hope it will stop. Instead, keep your children separated while you step up your preventive maintenance and connection with both kids. Simply don't leave them alone together until you're confident that violence is a thing of the past, and make an agreement with your child who hits about how he can protect his right to play with his sibling: *"I can't let you play with your sister if you're going to hit . . . Let's make an agreement about how you will stop yourself from hitting, even when you're really mad."* Sit with your child and coach him to brainstorm several alternatives to hitting, and help him practice them. Here's a sample agreement that Kyle, age four, dictated to his mother.

Kyle's Plan

Hitting Hurts. I won't hit Kira today, no matter what. If Kira has a toy I want, I will trade with her. Or wait my turn. If Kira is in my way, I will ask Mom or Dad for help. If I feel like hitting, I will turn

away and hug myself hard and yell "Stop!" Stop is my code word
so I remember and if Mom hears me call "Stop" she will come. If I
forget and hit, then I will need to play in the living room while Kira
plays in the kitchen.

Note that Kyle committed himself to turning away, diverting his urge to hit into hugging himself, and using a code word to call his mother for help. Because the child helps make the plan and tells you what to write, he's invested. Then, play a game to get your child laughing, which releases the tension that's built up around the whole issue of hitting, for both of you. Act out pretend situations that might make him want to hit—in a silly way, to get him laughing. The person who feels like hitting transforms the impulse by clapping his own arms around his body (hugging himself) instead of lashing out. He shouts his code word along with his action. As one mother whose son had been hitting wrote to me, *"Yesterday I took him to a very crowded bouncy house and at some point a kid pushed him. He stopped, crossed his arms around his body, and called my name. MAGIC."*

Of course, an agreement like this won't work if you do it in a punitive way. Your child has to be convinced that you're on his side, that you believe in his ability to manage himself. And it won't work without preventive maintenance. So if your child comes home from preschool every day and hits, don't let him near your other child until you've helped him to laugh or cry with roughhousing or a scheduled meltdown (see Chapter 2). Otherwise, no agreement in the world will keep him from hitting, and he'll just end up feeling like a bad kid.

Teaching Skills: Intervening in a Sibling Fight

Mom is making dinner when she hears loud voices.

> **Charley:** Jane, were you playing in my fort? You were! You messed it all up!
>
> **Jane:** I didn't hurt your stupid fort.
>
> **Charley:** It's not stupid, you're stupid!
>
> **Jane:** Get out of my room!
>
> **Charley:** You're not the boss of me!
>
> **Jane:** I'm the boss of my room! Get out!
>
> **Charley:** You messed up my fort! I'll mess up your room! *(Crash!)*
>
> **Jane:** I hate you, Charley! MOM!!

What should Mom do?

> **Mom** *(thinking)*: Hmm ... should I get involved? I'm busy cooking dinner, and sometimes, they work it out. But in this case, it sounds explosive. Maybe this is a good chance to teach them better skills ... *(She turns off the stove, takes a deep breath, and reminds herself to stay calm.)*
>
> **Mom** *(speaking as she enters Jane's bedroom)*: I hear some loud, angry voices. What's going on?
>
> **Charley:** Jane messed up my fort!
>
> **Jane:** Charley wrecked the animal zoo I built!
>
> *Mom knows better than to try to figure out who started it.*
>
> **Mom** *(empathizing with both kids)*: You two are really upset!
>
> **Jane:** I hate you, Charley!

Charley: I hate you more, Jane!

Mom *(taking a deep breath to stay calm, empathizing and setting a limit)*: I hear how angry you both are. The rule in our house is that we treat each other with kindness and respect. I hear screaming and hurtful language. Let's all sit down. Come on, Charley, sit down right here next to me. Jane, right here on my other side. Now, let's everyone take three deep breaths so we can calm down and listen to each other ... one ... two ... three. Okay, I want to hear what's upsetting each of you so much. One at a time. Last time, Charley went first. This time, Jane goes first. Jane, what happened?

Jane: Charley knocked down my animal zoo. I worked so hard on that with Autumn. We were going to play with it again tomorrow.

Mom: Charley knocked down your zoo and you're really mad, huh? I see all the blocks and animals all over ... Jane, anything else happen?

Jane: I told him to get out of my room and he wouldn't. Isn't that the rule? That he has to get out?

Mom: You want Charley to leave your room when you tell him to. That is our family rule, you're right ... Charley, can you tell us what happened from your perspective?

Charley: Jane messed up my fort! She went in my room, too! She broke the rule, too!

Mom: So you're mad that Jane went in your room and messed up your fort. And you came in her room to tell her?

Jane: But he came in and wouldn't get out, and he wrecked my zoo!

Mom: One at a time. Jane, it's Charley's turn to talk now. You'll get your turn again in a moment. Charley?

Charley: Okay, I knocked over the zoo, but that was because she called my fort stupid!

Mom: Let me see if I got this right. Charley, you were very angry that Jane went in your room and played with your fort and you think she messed it up. Then she called it stupid and hurt your feelings. Then she told you to get out of her room. Is that right?

Charley: Yes!

Mom: And you were so mad, you knocked down her zoo?

Charley: Yes!

Mom: Okay, thank you for telling us. I see how hurt and mad you are, and how hard you're working to stay calm so we can work this out. Jane, let me see if I understand. You were playing and Charley came in very angry and you told him to leave, right?

Jane: Yes.

Mom: And he was so mad, he knocked over your zoo?

Jane: Yes, and now I'm more mad! The whole elephant house is wrecked.

Why go through this?

1. So each child will feel heard.
2. So each child will get a chance to reflect and to see how acting on their anger got them into this situation. Good judgment comes from experience, but only when combined with reflection.
3. So each child will hear the other's side of the story, to develop empathy and social intelligence about the motivations of others.
4. So each child will develop more impulse control. They're both furious, but they're sitting here breathing through their rage

and putting it into words. That helps their brains process the emotions, rather than just lashing out, and builds the neural circuits to regulate their anger in the future.

Mom *(empathizing, and then helping each child to reflect on what the other child felt and how each one contributed to the problem)*: So we have two very angry kids here. Charley, I hear that you're mad that Jane went into your room, played with your fort, and messed it up. Jane, I hear that you're mad that Charley knocked down your zoo. You're both hurt that your things got messed up, right? *(The kids nod.)* Often when we're hurt, we get mad, right? *(She's teaching emotional intelligence.)* So you both got pretty mad and blamed the other one, right? . . . Now I want each of you to imagine what the other one was feeling during the fight. Jane, what do you think Charley was feeling when he came into your room?

Jane: He was mad.

Mom: Yes . . . and when he talked to you, did that make him feel better?

Jane: Well . . . I guess not.

Charley: You know you were trying to make me feel worse!

Mom: Charley, Jane is talking now, and you and I are listening and breathing so we can stay calm . . . Jane, what do you think happened inside Charley when he came into your room?

Jane: I called his fort stupid . . . and he got madder . . . and I told him to leave . . . and he got madder . . .

Mom: Hmmm . . . Do you think there was anything different you could have done?

Jane: All right, I know. I could have apologized for the fort . . . I didn't mean to mess it up. It just fell down. I guess I should have asked before I played in it . . . But he plays with my things, too.

Mom: Right now we're talking about what just happened. Is there anything you could have done to make things go differently?

Jane: Well, he's the one who knocked down my zoo!

Mom: Yes, he did. But right now I'm wondering if you see anything you could have done that would have made things unfold differently.

Jane: I could have been nicer and apologized. I didn't have to call his fort stupid.

Mom: So you think that if you had apologized when he first came in, he might not have gotten so mad? . . . Charley, if Jane had done that, would that have changed how you felt?

Charley: I still would have been mad that she messed up my fort. But I wouldn't have knocked down her zoo.

Mom: Great, thank you, Charley. Jane, do you hear that? He was mad you played with his fort, but if he thought you were sorry, and that you wanted to make things better, he would have had an easier time controlling his anger. Right?

Jane nods.

Mom: So Charley, what do you think Jane was feeling during your fight? And what could you have done differently?

You can see where Mom is going here. Next, she'll ask each child if there is anything they can do to make up with the other child. By the end of the conversation, it might even work out that Charley and Jane will work together to rebuild the zoo.

Of course, you can't do this every night. Mom is way behind on getting dinner on the table. But the good news is, you don't have to. If you do this for a couple of months, your children will begin to learn the skills you're teaching. And you'll be amazed to see them beginning to work things out without your intervention. You'll probably find that everyone in your family is calmer, and a better listener, once you get this habit going. Even you!

Helping Kids Make Repairs After a Fight, Instead of Forced Apologies

After there's been a falling-out between siblings, most parents insist that their children apologize to each other. If you ask children what they think of this practice, they'll tell you:

- *"When I'm mad, I hate apologizing. It just makes me madder at my sister."*
- *"I don't like it when my brother apologizes to me when my parents make him do it, because he acts like he doesn't even mean it. It makes me mad all over again."*
- *"It's lying to apologize when you don't mean it."*
- *"When my parents make my brother apologize, I feel like I won. That feels good, but it doesn't make me like him any better."*
- *"Later I always like my sister again. I could apologize then. But not when I'm mad."*

Doesn't it sound like forcing children to apologize is teaching the wrong lessons, and we might want to rethink the whole practice? What could we do instead?

1. **Focus on helping children communicate rather than on the ritual of apology.** If you follow the practices of helping

children express their wants and needs, listen to each other, and restate what they heard their sibling say, children will begin to heal their conflicts at a deeper level, so that apologies often become almost superfluous, just as with adults.

2. **Wait until the anger has subsided.** If she's still angry, then she needs to feel heard before she can listen to her sibling's perspective.

3. **Once the child is no longer angry, empower him to repair things with his sibling.** *"Your brother loves you and looks up to you. When you yelled at him, it looked like it really hurt his feelings. I wonder what you could do to make things better with him."*

4. **If your child suggests apologizing, listen to her voice.** If she sounds sullen or angry, acknowledge that the apology wouldn't be heartfelt, and ask her if she thinks that it would make her sibling feel any better. *"Apologizing is a wonderful way to make things better, sweetheart, but I don't want you to apologize until you mean it. I'm not asking you to say something that's untrue; I don't think that ever makes anyone feel better."*

5. **If your child asks, offer suggestions for repair:**

   - Help rebuild the tower that the fight was about.

   - Build a tower for the sibling to knock down.

   - Repair or replace the damage done, for instance a broken toy.

   - Draw a picture or make a card listing three things you love about your sibling.

- Give a big hug.

- Play a game that the sibling wants to play.

- Help the sibling with a chore.

- Make an agreement and sign it, promising not to repeat the infraction and describing how the situation will be handled in the future.

Remember, though, that you aren't assigning your child a "consequence" to pay off his debt. You're empowering him to see himself as a generous person who can make things better when he's done something hurtful. So *he* has to choose what he might do to make things better. You can give him ideas, but then say, *"I know you'll figure out the perfect thing to do . . . I can't wait to see what it is!"* Hug him and leave the room.

6. **What if your child says, *"I don't want to repair things with her!"*?**

Acknowledge that he's still very angry, and why. If you can, help him with the anger. Then set the expectation that when he feels better, a repair of some sort is in order. *"I guess you're still so mad that you don't want to make things better with her right now . . . and I know that even though you and your sister fight, you also love each other, and it makes things better if you can do something to repair things . . . Maybe you need some time before you're ready to repair things with your sister. It can take some time for the anger to melt away . . . I can't help you with your feelings any more right now, but we can talk again later . . . When you're ready, I know that you will know just the right thing to do to make things better."*

7. **Be a role model.** Children learn from us how to repair relationships. Be sure that when you and your child have a relationship rupture, you apologize and find ways to reconnect.

HELPING CHILDREN HEAL AFTER A FIGHT

Instead of Forcing an Apology

Empower Your Child to Repair the Relationship

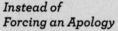

Left: Forcing kids to apologize, especially while they're still angry, teaches them to lie. Because it's meaningless, it doesn't repair the relationship. It just makes the other sibling feel like they've won.

Right: Wait until the anger has subsided and help your child think about what he could do to make things better with his sibling.

6

Why Can't They
Just Share? Why Kids
Fight Over Possessions

The triplets have taught us a bit about personal property, namely that
everyone likes to have some. Which means that each child has gravitated
toward toys which he or she perceives to be his or her own.

—John Cave Osborne,

How Three Babies Turned Our World Upside Down

One of the most common reasons children fight is that they both
want the same scarce resource—a given toy. The first child always
starts from the assumption that he "owns" all the toys—after all,
he's the one who uses them. So if you want the toys to be shared,
you'll need to create a family rule about property rights.

The idea of "private property" in a family may surprise you. We
quite reasonably want all of our children to be able to use all of the
toys, as determined by either age-appropriateness or taking turns.
Doesn't the whole idea of "ownership" contradict the meaning of
being a family?

Well, no. Not from a child's point of view. As adults, you and
your partner don't fight over who owns the toaster or the couch.
You alternate use of them, or you use them together. But to your child,
toys are prized possessions. In fact, for a young child, toys are more

than possessions—they're extensions of his sense of self. Children use toys to explore the world, and to build their relationship with it. A child may pick up a seashell or a stick and construct an entire fantasy around it. That stick is *his*; he *needs* it to be himself in the world. That's why we hear *"Mine!"* so often from young children. But what does "mine" actually mean? It's not selfishness. Rather, it means he needs to control what happens to that object. That's why, even when he hasn't touched a given baby toy in two years, he gets upset when he sees his little brother with it. His sense of well-being depends on controlling the things to which he's been deeply attached.

This gets even more complicated when you step in and force your child to share a toy with her sibling. When two children want a toy and you select one to have it, even temporarily and for a good reason, both children see you as choosing one sibling over the other. To them, you're symbolically taking your love from one child and handing it to her sibling. Naturally, she's driven to snatch things from her sibling every chance she gets. After all, her survival depends on having as much of your love as she can get!

Thankfully, this doesn't mean that a child will never be ready to pass on any toys. As he grows, he'll form new attachments, and gradually relinquish the old ones. But forcing him to give things up is likely to result in more sibling rivalry. The trick is to be thoughtful about creating family policies that are developmentally appropriate in regard to "sharing" and who owns, or controls, what. The idea of a policy may seem very formal. But, in fact, you already have a family policy on sharing; you just may not have articulated it. In most families, the policy is that the parent decides when one child has had a toy long enough, usually based on how loud the protest is from the sibling. While that seems expedient, it reinforces competition between siblings, disempowers both children, and teaches children that if they fuss, they get their way. You'll be relieved to learn that there are other ways to handle the whole concept of sharing, which teach more constructive lessons.

Let's agree that the goal is for our children to grow into generous people who are able to notice and respond to the needs of others. Of course, we also want our children to be able to meet their own needs, which include pursuing their own work and play, because that's how they develop mastery. There's an obvious tension here that parents need to recognize. We don't want our kids to feel they should interrupt what they're working on to "give" something to another child just because the other child asks. On the other hand, we do want our child to notice when another child would like a turn, and to ensure that child gets a turn. And when someone else has something that our child wants, we hope that she'll be able to control her impulses so she doesn't grab it, but instead will use her words to work out an arrangement so that she can use the object in the future. In other words, we want our child to advocate for her own needs, to respect the needs of others, and to be able to delay gratification to wait for what she wants. Right?

All of which means we need to rethink how children "learn to share."

Rethinking Sharing: A Radical Solution

When my son was two years old, he received a large ride-in car as a birthday present. He loved that car, and wanted to spend every minute in it, steering as he propelled the car up and down our driveway. Sometimes he pretended he was driving a dump truck, sometimes he was a train engineer, sometimes he was at the helm of a school bus. That car made all his fantasies come true and changed the way he saw himself.

One day shortly after the car arrived at our house, my

brother-in-law's family visited with their son, who was the same age. Naturally, my nephew wanted to drive the car. My son, however, wouldn't stop driving even long enough to negotiate. Clearly, I should have put the car away before another child visited, but this was the first time I had ever seen my son refuse to give another child a turn, so I hadn't yet learned that trick. Meanwhile, my nephew was getting more and more agitated watching his cousin drive. "If you want him to learn to share," suggested one adult, "you'll need to take him out of the car."

I wasn't afraid of my son's meltdown. But I knew, from reading the studies of Judy Dunn and other researchers in graduate school, that toddlers aren't developmentally ready to "learn to share." I knew my son well enough to know that he would feel betrayed if I took him out of his car, and would never understand why he was being asked to give up his most prized possession to another child, even temporarily. (And what does temporarily even mean to a twenty-four-month-old?) I knew instinctively that forcing a child would not help him *want* to be generous and "learn to share." But I didn't know how to begin to explain my thoughts, or how to be fair to my nephew. In fact, it took me years to articulate these ideas, as my children grew up and I worked with other parents.

How I wish that Heather Shumaker's book *It's Okay Not to Share* had been available then to help me with the ideas I was starting to formulate. (It was published the year that two-year-old turned twenty-two.) If you read only one book on how to help young children get along with their peers, this should be the book—and you'll find that Shumaker's recommendations about peers also work with siblings.

What's the radical solution that Shumaker suggests? "Sharing on demand interrupts play, erodes parent-child trust, and teaches false generosity. Take turns instead."[1] Sounds reasonable, right? But Shumaker takes this a step further, insisting that the child in possession of the toy should be the one to decide how long his turn lasts. I call this *self-regulated turns*, because the child decides how long he needs the toy, and then gives it to the other child. So in the example of my son and the car, we would have facilitated a discussion between the children in which my son would promise to give his cousin a turn with the car once he was done with it, and he would have been allowed to use the car for as long as he wanted before giving it up.

You see the issue, of course. My poor nephew would have been kicking and screaming in the driveway. A two-year-old has a very hard time waiting for his turn. That's why we as parents have gotten into the habit of setting timers and enforcing turns. I suspect it's less because we actually think it's a good way to teach sharing, and more because we can't tolerate the unhappiness of the child who's waiting for his turn.

Consider, however, what my son would have learned if I had enforced sharing by dragging him out of his car and letting his cousin have a turn. Would he have learned generosity because his cousin looked so happy? No, because he would have felt murderous, and his cousin would clearly have become the enemy. This wouldn't have helped him "learn to share." In fact, how could he experience "sharing" at that point as anything except a more powerful person taking his prized possession away from him? The problem with enforced sharing is that we're modeling grabbing. When children learn that adults will snatch a toy away once the adult's arbitrary idea of "long enough" has passed, they become more possessive. To the child, it must feel a bit like you would feel if I insisted that you give me your car, because you've had it long enough and I want a turn with it.

With self-regulated turns, by contrast, the child is free to use the toy for as long as she wants, so she can fully enjoy it, and then give it up to the other child with an open heart. She actually gets to experience that warm and wonderful emotion that comes when we give someone else something they want, and we see how happy they are. Nancy Eisenberg, a leading researcher on children's social development, says that children become more generous by having the experience of giving to others and learning how good that feels.[2] There is a catch, though, says Eisenberg. The experience must be voluntarily chosen by the child. If we force children to share, they walk away resentful, not feeling generous. Not surprisingly, they're less likely to share after that.

Self-Regulated Turns: What Children Learn

When Child A wants something that Child B has, we ask B together for the object once he is finished. Then A decides what she will do while she waits for her turn. Both kids are very proud when they "give" the object to the other "willingly" when they are all finished.
   —Erin

The self-regulated turn system works for the child who gets to decide, but what about the poor sibling who has to wait for his turn? You can expect this child to protest loudly, which is inconvenient for you and miserable for him. And beyond that, it hardly seems fair that one child has to wait while the other uses the coveted toy for as long as she pleases—does it?

Let's consider the sibling who's desperately unhappy waiting for his turn for what may well feel like forever. We have two options.

Option 1. We tell the first child he's had the toy long enough, take the toy away, and give it to the sibling. The second child learns:

- If I cry loud enough, I get what I want, even if someone else has it.

- Parents are in charge of who gets what when, and it's arbitrary, depending on their whim and how dramatically I beg for my turn.
- My sibling and I are in constant competition to get what we need. I don't like him.
- I guess I'm a greedy person, but that's what I need to be in order to get what I deserve.
- I had better "play fast" because I won't have this item for long.
- I won! But I will lose again soon. I had better protest loudly when my turn is up to get every minute I can. And then start protesting again as soon as it's my sibling's turn. If I make my parent miserable, I'll get more time with the toy.

Notice that this child's attention is barely on the toy he's won. He can't play freely. All he can do is feel the clock ticking. So the conventional approach of forced sharing undermines the ability of children to lose themselves in play, as well as undermining the sibling relationship by creating constant competition. Neither child gets to experience the generosity of having their fill and giving to the other.

Option 2. We tell the second child that he can ask the sibling when it will be his turn, and assure him that we'll help him wait until the sibling decides she's done with the toy. This time, the second child learns:

- I can ask for what I want. Sometimes I get a turn soon, and sometimes I have to wait.
- It's okay to cry, but it doesn't mean I get the toy.
- I don't get everything I want, but I get something better. My parent always understands and helps me when I'm upset.
- After I cry, I feel better.
- I can use another toy instead and really enjoy it. I'm getting better at waiting.

- I don't have to whine and cry to my parent to convince them to get me a turn. Everybody has to wait for their turn, but everybody gets a turn sooner or later.
- I like the feeling when my sibling gives me the toy. I like her.
- I can use a toy for as long as I want; nobody will make me give it to my sibling before I'm ready. When I'm done with the toy and give it to my sibling, I feel good inside—I like to give her a turn. I'm a generous person.

This child is developing impulse control and the ability to delay gratification. We're supporting deeper play by not taking away the toy in the middle of the child's use of it. We're helping both kids discover their own generosity. And we're supporting a warmer sibling relationship by reducing competition.

This can be a challenging new way of doing things, for both parents and children. But as kids learn that they'll eventually get the toy, and that their right to a toy they're using will also be protected, they get better at managing their impatience. In fact, every time you support a child through the wait, they build the brain power to delay gratification. And fairly quickly, you'll see your children start asking each other when they can have a turn, and offering the toy to their sibling when they're done with it.

That a child will offer her sibling a turn, without parental enforcement, is hard to believe for most parents. But if you adopt this policy, it will become an everyday occurrence in your home. You'll still have to buy two of the most treasured items, and you'll still have to put them away before other children visit. But rather than arbitrating sharing, you'll find yourself coaching your kids as they wait for their turn, and admiring how often they navigate taking turns without you running interference. Why not try it?

Coaching Kids as They Wait for Their Turn

The five-year-old was riding in a car and her two-year-old brother wanted a turn. He went over to hit her and grab it away, which normally would have resulted in a huge fight and a lot of yelling from me. Instead, I went over, got down on his level, and said, "You're mad because Bailey's riding in the car and you want a turn, right? It's hard to wait." He launched himself into my arms, cried, "Yeah!" and then calmly asked his sister if he could have a turn next. Then he went off to play happily until she was done. Miraculous.

—Jennifer

Even as children get used to your family rule that the person using the toy decides how long their turn lasts, they'll still always feel some longing when another person has a toy they want. You can help your child by acknowledging her feelings, helping her ask for what she wants, coaching her to make an agreement with the other child about the eventual handoff of the coveted item, and supporting her while she decides what to do while she waits. Every time you do this, you're helping your child develop the assertiveness to ask for what she wants, as well as impulse control and the ability to delay gratification. Like the five-year-old twins below, kids can often move on to another project once they're satisfied that their turn is coming.

> **Savannah:** Mom, Ella is having too long a turn on the pogo stick!
>
> **Mom:** Savannah, I hear you really want a turn with the pogo stick. Can you tell Ella that you want a turn after her turn?
>
> **Savannah:** She isn't listening to me.

Mom: It might be that she just really needs a long turn today. Do you want my help to tell her?

Savannah: Yes!

Mom and Savannah go to where Ella is hopping on the pogo stick.

Mom (*smiling at Ella, with her arm around Savannah's shoulders*): That looks like so much fun!

Ella: It is!

Mom: Savannah has something she wants to tell you.

Savannah mumbles something toward Ella.

Mom: I don't think Ella can hear that soft voice while she's jumping. Can you tell her in a louder voice?

Savannah: I want a turn, too!

Ella: But Savannah, I need a long turn today.

Mom: Hmmm . . . It doesn't sound like Ella is ready to be done with her turn yet. Savannah, do you want to ask Ella if you can have the next turn when she's ready?

Savannah: Ella, can I have the next turn?

Ella: Of course!

Savannah doesn't look any happier.

Mom: Savannah, you can ask Ella how long she thinks she needs for her long turn.

Savannah: Ella, how long before my turn?

Ella: I need a very long turn because I missed this pogo stick . . . I think I need ten whole hours.

Mom: Ella, it sounds like you want a very long turn! You know the rule at our house is that turns don't go overnight, so your turn will have to end when you come inside for dinner in an hour, and then tomorrow it will be Savannah's turn. Okay?

Ella: Okay. I am getting tired from jumping anyway.

Savannah: But then I don't get the pogo stick until tomorrow! I have to wait so long!

Mom: It's hard to wait, isn't it? Would you like to make a sign that shows it's your turn for the pogo stick tomorrow?

They get out the markers and Mom writes: "Savannah gets her long turn with the pogo stick first thing in the morning tomorrow, SUNDAY!"

Mom: Savannah, I know you can't read, but this says, "Savannah gets her long turn with the pogo stick first thing in the morning tomorrow, SUNDAY!" Okay? . . . It's hard to wait. Do you want help figuring what else to do now?

Savannah *(busy with the markers)*: No, Mom, I want to decorate my sign and then tape it on the refrigerator. I am going to be sure we all remember my turn.

But what about toddlers, who are easily overwhelmed by their emotions? Doesn't this approach guarantee a meltdown? Yes, often. But that's not all bad. In fact, if a toddler has a meltdown because he wants a toy that someone else has, it's often a sign that he really needed a chance to cry.

How do we know that? Because once he cries, he often doesn't care much about the toy that triggered the meltdown. That means it was never really about the toy to begin with. It's about his desperate attempt to regulate all those feelings spilling out of his emotional backpack. He thinks that if he can just have that one toy, things will be okay. (We've all felt that way. If we can just get those shoes, that car, that job . . .) But of course, as soon as he gets that one thing, his sibling will pick up a new toy, and he'll desperately need *that* toy to feel okay.

Supporting your child through a meltdown while he waits for a toy can be really hard on parents. Most of us would do anything to help our child feel better. We find ourselves wanting to plead with the other child to give up the toy. But I urge you to give this a chance. Rigid fixation is mostly about upsets much bigger than any toy. Those tears need to come out, and this is a perfect opportunity. You have to see this to believe it, but after "showing" you her pent-up emotions, your child probably won't even care about the toy she was waiting for.

In view of all this, what sort of agreements might a family make about property rights and sharing?

A Sample Family Agreement on Property Rights and Sharing

1. Most things in our family belong to everyone. When more than one person wants to use something, we take turns with it.
2. In our family, the person using something can decide how long their turn lasts. At the playground, we take shorter turns so that everyone gets a turn.
3. Turns start over again every morning, so no turn lasts for more than one day.
4. Each person in the family has some things that are extra precious to them, such as presents or recent acquisitions or things with special meaning to us. Others in the family must ask before using these things. They are usually kept in special places (like a special shelf, or in the child's bedroom instead of the family room) so everyone recognizes their specialness and remembers to ask before touching.
5. With visitors, we put away toys that are hard for us to share. When visitors are here, we take short turns, so everyone can enjoy playing at our home.

HELP KIDS LEARN TO TAKE TURNS

Instead of Forced Sharing

Teach Kids to Self-Regulate Turns

Kids understand the concept of "taking turns" better than they understand "sharing."

SUPPORT KIDS TO DEVELOP GENEROSITY

Help Kids Wait for Their Turn

Left: Acknowledging feelings helps children manage their emotions so they can wait their turn.

Right: Often when kids get upset, it isn't really about the toy.

Trust Kids to Take Turns When They're Ready

Left: After kids show us their big feelings, they're more relaxed and flexible.

Right: When we allow kids to *choose* to share, they develop generosity.

7

Easing the Competition

"It's Not Fair!"

It drives parents crazy. You do your best to be fair, but your children insist on competing over *everything*! Why?

- **A sense of fairness is innate.** Research shows that even babies have some concept of parity. It seems to be one of the human mind's built-in survival mechanisms to help us live in groups.

- **They desperately want to know that you love them more than anyone else, so their survival is ensured.** This is genetically programmed. Their genes want to know whom you would save if a tiger came marauding. If you love their sibling more, they're toast.

- **Children aren't so different from adults.** The entire legal profession is based on the human desire to be treated fairly.

The problem isn't that your children want fairness. It's that they think you're supposed to be Solomon and dole it out, but there's no way both children will feel fairly treated by any solution any parent can devise. That's not just because we're fallible humans, but because children in search of fairness are motivated by fear, which is always irrational. Back to the previous point: They need proof the sibling isn't being favored, to ensure their survival.

So how can you deal with the whole concept of fairness without going crazy, and in a way that helps your children feel more secure and less competitive?

1. **Empathize.** Your child has big feelings about this issue. After all, at an unconscious level this is about her survival. Trying to argue your child out of her feelings won't work. Acknowledging them will help her feel understood, which means she can stop fighting. This is the most important thing you can do to help your child with her feeling that things aren't fair.

   Instead of arguing: *"Of course you get to go first sometimes, don't exaggerate!"*

   Empathize: *"It feels like you never get to go first, huh?"*

   Instead of explaining: *"He's older, so he gets to stay up later."*

   Empathize: *"You wish you could stay up later . . . It's hard to stop playing and get ready for bed . . . I bet when you're eight like your brother, you'll love staying up later."*

   Notice you aren't agreeing. You might even be pretty sure that she went first last night. You're showing her you understand how she feels, nothing more, and nothing less. If you think back to times when you've felt understood, you will understand just how great a gift this is.

2. **Focus on what each child wants rather than getting hooked when they compare or compete.** When your children accuse you of favoring their sibling, you know intuitively that this is a serious accusation. On some level, they're saying you don't have enough love and protection for them, since you're using it up on their sister. Understandably, you can get hooked and argue about who got what. But that's a battle you'll never win. Next time:

> **Instead of arguing:** *"I did not give him more—see, you have the same amount!"*

> **Acknowledge the need your child is expressing without reference to his sibling, and reassure him that there's always more than enough for everyone:** *"It sounds like you're ready for more noodles. Show me how much you want and I'll dish them out for you."*

What if there aren't any more noodles, or you aren't about to give them seconds on dessert? In other words, your child thinks she's been treated unfairly, and you can't (or won't) make it better by giving her what she thinks she deserves to make things fair? *Address the perceived unfairness symbolically, by showering your child with love.* That's what she's actually worried about, even if she doesn't know it. So you might say something like: *"Oh, no! His piece was bigger? I can't believe it—this is terrible! Here I sat, making sure the two pieces were exactly the same, and you're telling me my splitting skills are slipping? You know what that means. If your piece was even a hundredth smaller, that means I need to make it up to you—with a hundred hugs and kisses!"* You grab her and fill her up with love. You aren't teasing her, or belittling her need. You're actually meeting her real need—to be as important to you as her brother. You're letting her know that there's always more than enough love for her, no matter what her brother gets. And the laughter helps her work through any fears that were triggered by thinking that you secretly prefer her brother.

3. **Give material possessions based on need; be sure love is limitless.** If one child has outgrown her sneakers and the other hasn't, explain to all the kids that today it's Asia's turn for new sneakers, and Amira will get hers when she outgrows her current pair. Be alert to help Amira past her envy when Asia struts in: *"It can be hard to watch your sister get something new when you didn't . . . Don't worry, when you need shoes, you'll get them, too. You know that no matter what your sister gets, there's always enough for you."* Then give her a huge hug. What she really needs is reassurance that you love her as much as her sister.

4. **Don't be afraid to treat children differently.** Interestingly, several studies in which children were interviewed about how parents treat them and their siblings have found that kids don't mind being treated differently, if they think the outcome is fair.[1] They may give you a hard time because their brother stays up later, but they do understand that an older child gets more privileges and more responsibilities. In fact, you might want to talk about this with each child before his birthday. What new responsibility does he think he's ready for?

5. **Teach your children basic "legal" skills** so they can be in charge of fairness and you don't have the impossible job of playing judge.

   • **One divides, the other chooses.** As soon as your younger child is able to point, stop being the one to divide their treat, or even dish out their ice cream. That always becomes a contest over who gets more (meaning who is more loved by you). Instead, one child does the dividing or dishing (under your supervision), and the other child chooses who gets which portion.

   • **Put it in writing!** Even before they can read, children have enormous respect for the power of the written word. Let them hammer out an agreement and help them put it in writing and sign it with their own "mark." *"Gabriel and Isaiah agree that Gabriel always gets to push the elevator button on the way up and Isaiah always gets to push the elevator button on the way down, in any elevator."*

   (For more legal skills, see "Basic Negotiation Tools to Teach Kids" on page 89.)

6. **Fill each child's cup.** The reason children compete is to ensure their survival in the face of danger and scarce resources. So your job as the parent is to love each child so he never needs to wonder if you might love his sibling more. That would be impossible, since he knows your love for him is limitless. In practice, that means:

   • You seek him out for hugs and smiles, to look at the fireflies together out the window at dusk, and just to tell him you're so glad you're his mother.

- When he needs you, you show up. If your hands are full, you apologize and tell him when you'll be able to tend to him; then keep your promise.

- You surprise him with little notes, favors, and activities. This takes some mental energy, which as a parent can be in short supply. One solution is to keep little notes on your to-do list, so that every week you do one small special thing for each child.

- You make time for Special Time and the other preventive maintenance practices. Sometimes you take each child, one at a time, for a special adventure on a Saturday afternoon. If they fight about who goes on the first Saturday, while the other kids have to wait until subsequent weeks, you can "sweeten the deal" for the ones who have to wait by giving them longer adventures.

For more on staying connected, use the ideas on connecting with your child in Part 2 of *Peaceful Parent, Happy Kids*.

Never Compare

If I can't be best at being best, I'll be best at being worst!
—Adele Faber[2]

Most of us are tempted to compare our children. It's natural, when we're irritated, to think we'll motivate our child by holding up the shining example of her sister. And when we're impressed, the first thing that comes to mind—and out of our mouths—may well be a comparison. *"Even your sister never got three goals in one game!"* The problem is that our comparisons reinforce the way we think about our children, and therefore shape the way we treat them. Maybe even worse, every comparison we make encourages our children to compare themselves.

Kids whose parents make comments comparing them to each other are more likely to compete and fight, and no wonder.[3] They know whom they have to beat; it's been made clear by hearing the comparisons: *"Can't you sit down and do your homework right away the way your brother does?"* You don't have to compare to make your point to your child. Just say: *"The rule is we do homework right after school before playtime."*

It may surprise you, but this is just as true for positive messages, which also set up competition. Your child may feel good when you say, *"You're my good boy . . . you never give me a hard time like your brother."* But not only does your son now feel enormous pressure to be "good," he's also now motivated to keep his brother in the role of "bad" kid. How else will he maintain his special place in your eyes?

This jockeying for position is one reason that kids get into the habit of tattling, teasing, and antagonizing each other. One leading researcher on siblings, Judy Dunn, drives this point home, saying that in every single study that has looked at the way mothers relate to more than one child, "Differential behavior shown by parents toward siblings is clearly implicated in conflict frequency . . . and the quality of the sibling relationship."[4]

How can you break the habit of comparing your children? Adele Faber and Elaine Mazlish, authors of *Siblings Without Rivalry*, say, "The key word is describe. Describe what you see. Or describe what you like. Or describe what you don't like. Or describe what needs to be done. The important thing is to stick with the issue of this one child's behavior. Nothing his brother is or isn't doing has anything to do with him."[5]

So instead of: *"Evan, you're not doing your share to clean up; look how much your brother has done."*

Describe what you see and what needs to be done: *"Evan, I don't see you cleaning up any of the blocks . . . they need to go into the bin. Now."*

Instead of: *"I wish your sister would practice the way you do. Your piano playing is so far ahead of hers already."*

Describe what you see and what you like: *"Madison, I've been listening to you practice your piano for half an hour. I'm really impressed at how you just kept working at that hard part. It sounds so smooth now!"*

If you pay attention, you'll find that the comparisons begin inside your own mind. It's easier to stop them there than it is when they're on the tip of your tongue. Train yourself to reframe your thoughts as if you had only one child. So, for instance, if you find yourself thinking, *"Harper just isn't the student that Alyssa is,"* discipline yourself to reframe it as, *"I'm concerned that Harper doesn't seem to like school very much."* You'll notice that as you focus more on your child as an individual, rather than in comparison with his sibling, you'll start to see more clearly what he's struggling with, and where he might need your support—instead of just seeing him as lacking something that his sibling has.

WHAT IF YOUR CHILD COMPARES?

Each child can feel she is special in the eyes of her parents. Children are constantly being compared. Most of their life they'll be rated: grades in school, the batting order on the baseball team, races and games among

themselves. The home is the only organization left that values a child for himself and not in comparison with others.
  —Dr. William Sears[6]

The human mind seems to have a tendency toward comparison, which, if we're lucky, we learn to resist, as we grow in years and wisdom. Why go there? After all, there will always be someone who compares more favorably, and less favorably, in every category.

Children, though, are still defining their identities, which they do partly by comparing themselves to others: *Yes, I am that, like her . . . No, I am not that, like him.* So they'll inevitably compare themselves to each other. When your child makes comparison comments, train yourself to respond by addressing your child's value as an individual, rather than in contrast to anyone else: *"Right now I'm interested in you, how you feel, what you want, what you do. You are my one and only Leila."*

This is especially important when children think their sibling was blessed with something they don't have and desperately want.

"Benjamin never gets in trouble at school the way I do . . . That's because he doesn't have ADHD. Nobody likes me the way they like Benjamin. Not even you!"

Most parents would respond to this by pointing out that Benjamin doesn't have ADHD, so he has things easier. But that just fuels the jealousy. (*"WHY does Benjamin get things easy, when I have to suffer?!"*) Instead, empathize and reassure your child that he's more than enough, exactly as he is—without reference to his sibling. That's what he really wants to know. *"I could never love anyone more than you, Aiden . . . I know it takes a lot of effort to control yourself at school, but every time you do it, you're training your brain and you're getting better at it. You know, even though it's hard to slow down that racecar brain and body of yours, you are very special to me and to the world, because you are the only Aiden exactly like you . . . I am so glad you're you! I feel lucky that I get to be your mom."*

Resist Labeling

Many parents think the way to let each child shine is to encourage that child's talents, while encouraging his siblings in alternate directions. That way, your musician daughter gets just as many accolades as her athletic brother. But the truth is, if one child is "the artist" and one is "the athlete," you're limiting each of them, you're undermining their self-esteem, and you're creating more sibling rivalry.

What do I mean? Think about your own life. In your family growing up, was one child the smart one? The pretty one? The other children couldn't help but suffer by comparison, and may still be trying to prove their worth in that area. But the child who gets the starring role also suffers. First, she has to protect that claim to fame from other contenders, which creates some nasty sibling rivalry. Every achievement by her siblings threatens her. Second, the pressure is enormous. What if she isn't so smart at some point? Will she still be good enough? Maybe better not take that physics class; stick to something less challenging. That's why putting kids in roles undermines self-esteem.

The other big problem, of course, is that humans aren't one-dimensional. Maybe you were the smart one and your sister was the pretty one, but really you're both smart, and you're both pretty. Why penalize one child because the other shines? Say your son is a better soccer player, but your daughter also loves the game. Or maybe she's a talented pianist, but he also really enjoys playing piano, or yearns to try violin but is afraid he won't measure up to his sister's musical prowess. Why would you deprive either child of the joy that comes from exploring all of their talents and interests?

Tragically, we tend to carry our childhood roles into adulthood.

In *Siblings Without Rivalry*, adult participants in a parenting group describe how their own parents unthinkingly cast them in various sibling roles as, for example, the "responsible" kid or the "wild" kid.[7] Every time I read their comments, I'm moved to tears by the pain these grown-up children still carry with them. Labeling is never necessary to motivate children or to make them feel special. Labeling causes pain that can last a lifetime and drive a permanent wedge between your children.

1. **Don't let one child appropriate any given strength.** Say, *"You love soccer. You don't have to be your brother. You're a different person. You're allowed to be yourself, and follow what you love. If you practice, you'll always get better."*

2. **Notice if you tend to assign roles by gender or age.** *"This is my oldest, and this is my baby."* Actually, this is Grace and this is Hannah. Focusing on their position in the family reinforces those birth order tendencies that hand Grace the role of responsible, achieving oldest, leaving Hannah to carve out an identity as the social one, or the artist, or the class clown.

   Or maybe you introduce them by gender: *"This is my girl, Leah, and this is my boy, Aaron."* What exactly does it mean to be a girl or a boy? Gender roles come with substantial loading in our culture. You don't want your kids to think that sticking to their gender roles is an important part of what makes them lovable to you, especially when Aaron turns out to be a ballet fanatic, while Leah is passionate about basketball and math.

3. **Avoid labels altogether.** Jonathan isn't your "budding scientist"; he's Jonathan, with all his many interests, strengths, and weaknesses. Let him pursue his passions as they unfold, rather than deciding his path by labeling it.

4. **Appreciate each child uniquely, not in comparison to siblings.** He's who he is, not just his brother's little brother. Instead of, *"You're throwing the ball almost as far as your brother,"* just say, *"Wow! Look how far you can throw the ball!"*

How to Celebrate Each Child Without Fueling Competition

I've noticed that the more unconditional love I give each of my children, the more they are able to mirror that with each other. And the more I concentrate on truly being present in the moment with them, and not telling them what to do or how to feel, the more relaxed and supportive they are with each other.

—Brenda

All parents naturally want to celebrate their children. And all children deserve to be celebrated. This can be tricky, though, since the achievements of a sibling can be a hot button for children who aren't feeling very good about themselves. Even for secure children, seeing how proud their parents are of their sister or brother can make them wonder if they're valued as much.

But I don't think the solution is to avoid celebrating your children. A far better answer is to make sure there's enough celebration to go around! That's because your children's relationships with each other are actually strengthened when they acknowledge each other's achievements. Research shows that one of the ways we feel connected to others is when they're able to appreciate our achievements and celebrate when things go right for us.[8] Remember the studies that found that children don't mind being treated differently if they think their parents are being fair? Kids actually like it when their sibling who worked hard is praised as long as they think they'll also be praised for working hard.[9]

So while it might take some sensitive guiding to make celebrating each person a part of your family culture, it's a great way to help your children live the truth that their siblings' accomplishments don't take anything from them—and they can take familial pride in each other's hard work and good fortune.

1. **Toast each person's achievements regularly at dinner.** Be sure there are plenty of toasts to go around.

2. **Expect kids to go to each other's performances and big events**, to wish each other "Good luck!" and to say, "Well played!" afterward. Should they go to every game and practice? Not if you can avoid it, because that can be boring and fuel resentment. But the big ones? Absolutely!

3. **Celebrate birthdays in a way that gets everyone involved.** To avoid sibling jealousy, get the other sibling(s) involved in planning the birthday celebration, so they're invested. The birthday child gets to decide what kind of cake, but the other sibling helps make it. All children spend the day, or the day or week before, making decorations. The sibling helps choose and wrap presents. And the birthday boy gets to choose a small present for his sibling, starting a wonderful lifelong tradition of giving something away on his birthday. Because much of the day is spent on family activities, everyone participates.

4. **Don't let one child "own" an interest,** as discussed above. If Alejandro always gets the lead in the school play, and Tomas finally got a bit part, be sure that Tomas gets toasted

without reference to his brother. You don't need to say, *"If you keep working at it, you'll be as good an actor as your brother."* Just say, *"And a toast to our pirate Tomas! You looked really scary on that stage, the way you were glowering at the audience!"*

5. **Be thoughtful about praise.** Imagine your child bursts into the house and yells, in front of his siblings, *"Mom, I made the winning goal!"* You'll certainly want to empathize with his excitement and acknowledge his pride: *"Wow! Tell us about it!... All your hard work is paying off!... You must be so proud of yourself... High five!"*

But stay away from superlatives: *"You're the best soccer player!"*

It might seem like *"You're following in your brother's footsteps!"* would celebrate both children, but that can be a bit tricky, because it invites comparison. You can imagine him thinking, *"Why isn't anything I do good enough on its own? Why has he always done it first?"* and feeling that he needs to outdo his brother. In general, stay away from comparison and just celebrate each child for who he is.

Even if you're really proud and can't wait to share the news, don't say, *"Let's call your dad!"* because you'll be elevating the achievement in the eyes of his siblings. The key is that you empathize with your child's excitement and pride, rather than trumpeting your *own* pride in his accomplishment. That means you don't brag to Grandma in front of the other children either. Even if you boast about all three of them, they can't help wondering if Grandma's more impressed with Miranda's straight A report card than with Camila's mastering the cartwheel.

Can you tell your child later how proud you are, in private?

Absolutely. Don't miss that opportunity. Just leave siblings out of the conversation. He doesn't need to hear that he's almost as good at spelling as his brother—*or*—that he's so much better at spelling than his brother. This is about him. And you'll want to be sure he doesn't get the message that your love is in any way dependent on his achievement. *"I'm so impressed with how hard you worked at this . . . I'm not surprised that you won the Spelling Bee, with all that work, but I know the competition was fierce and I'm very proud of you! You must be so so proud of yourself."*

Who Gets to Push the Elevator Button?

I just don't understand what's the big deal about who gets to push the elevator button!
—Jody

Maybe because it lights up. Maybe because it controls where you're headed. Maybe because it's a scarce commodity—only one button to push.

But I think such a universal childhood conflict has deeper roots. Imagine you're at a dinner party with your sister. The host asks her a question. She answers it, so gracefully and with such intelligence and passion that everyone at the table hangs on her every word. For the rest of the dinner party, your sister is the center of attention. No one looks at you. No one speaks to you. All eyes are on her. Might you be just a wee bit jealous by the end of the evening?

That's how your child feels when her sister gets to push the elevator button. I know, the two situations aren't comparable at all. But that's still how she feels.

So how should you handle it when you enter a public elevator and your children are screaming and pushing old ladies out of the way in their mission to push the button before their sibling?

1. **If one child has already pushed the button and the other child is upset, empathize.** Then ask the children to solve it. Say, *"Cooper wanted to push the button, and Calden already pushed it. What's a good solution?"* The first time you do this, you'll probably need to offer suggestions. *"How about if Cooper gets to push the Door Close button now to make the door close, and on the way down you'll trade who pushes which button?"*

2. **If you're in an elevator often and this is a recurring argument, use this as an opportunity to learn problem-solving.** *"Every time we go to my office, you two both want to push the elevator button. Every time, you fight about it. In our family, when we have disagreements, we work together to find solutions. So your assignment is to agree on a solution before we go to my office tomorrow."*

With younger children, you'll need to stay part of the discussion. As children get older and more capable of negotiating with each other, you can say: *"Please talk about this now. I'll be excited to hear the solution you've agreed on, at dinner."* Be sure the solution gets written down and posted on your family bulletin board where you can refer to it *before* you go to your office, until the agreement is a habit.

You can use this approach to solve any recurring problem. If your children squabble about who gets to choose the music in the car, coach them to find a solution, like keeping a rotation written on a clipboard in the car. Be sure to post the solutions, so the next time the issue arises, you have the agreement handy.

How to Ensure You Don't Unwittingly Foster Competition

We've talked about most of the ways parents unwittingly foster competition between their children.

1. They side with one child against the other. *"Stop picking on your sister!"*
2. They compare their children. *"Can't you let me brush your teeth with no fuss like your brother?"*
3. They label their children. *"He's the brainy one . . . She's the little devil."*
4. They let their relationship with one child deteriorate so it isn't as close.

But there's one more thing that seems so harmless—and so useful in managing life with children—that most of us have tried it. Who hasn't been tempted to motivate our kids by pitting them against each other? *"Whoever gets into pajamas first gets the first bedtime story with Mommy."* But this approach habituates your children to competing with each other for your love. And, of course, one child will always be the loser, which fosters resentment and more competition. Do you really want the soundtrack of your family life to be a never-ending chorus of *"I won!"* . . . *"No fair!"* . . . *"I'm first!"* . . . punctuated by the wails of the "loser"?

Helping Kids with Competitive Feelings

Card games, board games, tag, softball, whatever competitive effort we try ends in someone crying and melting down under the stress of losing, or even the potential for losing.
    —Nora

Most parents love the idea of a family game night. What a wonderful opportunity for sibling bonding! Then reality sets in. Most games have only one winner. That means you're guaranteed at least one meltdown, and maybe more. *All* kids have a hard time learning to deal with losing.

I think a certain amount of upset about losing is to be expected, and honored. As long as you empathize, and as long as a particular child isn't always losing, the experience of losing, and learning that life goes on and the sun comes out again, is actually a good one for kids. It builds resilience.

However, there are some ways that you can help your children with these feelings, and make games more enjoyable for everyone.

1. **Make losing more palatable.** For instance, one helpful rule for games is that the winner always has to clean up the game, which is at least some consolation for the loser. (Since the winner is glowing with victory, he won't mind at all, especially if you help.)

2. **If you have a child who often loses, play on a team with her.**

3. **Find games that require teamwork, instead of competition.** Research shows that children who play cooperative games are more cooperative and less aggressive and compet-

itive than kids who play competitive games.[10] There are wonderful cooperative games now, like Max, the Secret Door, Count Your Chickens, and Forbidden Island, that provide fun sibling bonding while they teach children cognitive skills and emotional skills. By contrast, games like Sorry! actively encourage children to undermine each other as part of the strategy.

4. **Discourage gloating.** *"It's fine to be happy that you won, but that sounds unkind... Our family rule is that we treat each other kindly... A Happy Dance when you win isn't good sportpersonship, no matter what you see professional athletes do."* Emphasize that while winning is always gratifying, your family plays to have fun and to enjoy each other.

5. **Kids need to have the experience of winning,** since so often in their lives, they feel like they're losing. With peers and siblings, and in life, a child is bound to lose often. So when you play with him, let him win. This can be hard for parents who are naturally competitive. I've had many fathers ask me how their kids will ever learn to "play fair" if we let them win. But consider that every time you as the parent win against your child using your greater size, strength, and experience, it's patently unfair. What's more, your child feels like a loser. Not surprisingly, he'll turn around and aggressively seek to make his sibling feel like a loser.

    At some point, he'll be old enough to ask if you're really trying. Say, *"You don't think I'm trying hard enough?! Okay, I'm going to try even harder! Watch this!"* And step up your game a little. Gradually, you'll move to playing full out, and eventually, your child will win against you, fair and square—and with his self-esteem intact.

6. **Help kids work together to agree on rules.** Children often get irritated at younger siblings who don't play by the rules. It helps to teach them that little ones are still learning about rules and aren't trying to "cheat." You might say to the younger child, *"Your brothers are saying they want to play by the real rules today, and you seem to want to play by rules we've never seen . . . Are those Santiago's Silly Rules? Do you want to play this game by the real rules with your brothers, or do you want to come in the kitchen with me and help me make the sandwiches?"*

7. **If your child habitually cheats, play with her one-on-one and get her laughing.** Aletha Solter, author of *Helping Young Children Flourish*, says that, "Cheating is a way that children communicate their need for assistance with feelings of incompetence."[11] Let your child cheat as she plays with you, and pretend that you don't see the cheating, but loudly lament about how badly you're doing and express bewilderment about why you're losing. Your child will laugh with delight, which is healing for all those feelings of "not being good enough" that drive her to cheat. After winning a few games like that with you, she's less likely to cheat with her siblings.

8. **When children are unevenly matched,** suggest they consider giving the younger child a head start or special bonus like the right to "do-overs" to make up for the difference in experience and age.

9. **Get kids laughing about winning and losing to defuse the tension.** Most children feel upset when they lose; it triggers the universal anxiety that they're secretly failures who will never be good enough. Laughter alleviates that anxiety. How

can you get your kids laughing? Lawrence Cohen, in his book *Playful Parenting*, suggests that you moan every time you roll the dice and don't get the number you want ... moan when one of the other players does well ... moan when you lose the game.[12] (Make sure you always lose the game.) I would add that you want to do this in a way that gets your kids laughing, not feeling guilty that you lost. Giggling about your losing doesn't make kids mean. It helps them work through their own fears and makes them more gracious when they lose.

Birth Order and Competition

Some competitive feelings come from children's awareness of their birth order. Even if parents try very hard not to give the oldest special privileges and the youngest more attention, kids often perceive themselves as having gotten the short end of the stick because they aren't the oldest, or the youngest. However, most researchers now believe that children's inherited temperament has more influence on their personality than their position in the family.[13] And—good news for parents—your child-raising style can ameliorate birth order effects. As Dr. Todd Cartmell reminds us, "Birth order effects are not the result of your child's innate temperament, but are the result of your child's *experience* as the older, middle, or youngest sibling in your family."[14] In other words, how *we* as the parents treat our children is the source of at least part of what we think of as birth order effects.

So we can lessen any negative effect from birth order by seeing and valuing each child as an individual, and by making sure that each child gets the attention he or she needs. Is that easy? No, since all parents of more than one child are short on time. But consider how your thoughtful interventions can support each of your children:

1. Oldest children tend to be more responsible, more worried, and more likely to want to please parents by following in their footsteps. Parents can support older children by empathizing with their upsets rather than expecting them to always act "grown-up," helping them laugh to reduce anxiety, encouraging them to pursue their own passions, and remembering that all children need to be babied at times.

2. Middle children often feel less valued because they don't have a specific role in the family, and they tend to receive less parental attention, so they may act out. Parents can support middle children by not getting irritated with this acting out, but instead seeing it as a cry for connection and prioritizing one-on-one time with the child.

3. Youngest children tend to carve out whatever space is left after the older children have defined themselves, so they're more likely to excel socially or in the arts. Parents can support youngest children by giving them responsibility and taking their opinions and interests seriously. Youngest children also need to experience social relationships in which they're the older or more responsible child, since they often feel they have less power in their sibling relationships.

If you'd like more ideas on how to support each of your children through the unique stresses of being the oldest, youngest, or middle child, you can find articles on birth order at AhaParenting.com.

What If You Prefer One Child?

Almost every discouragement in childhood springs from the feeling that someone else is preferred.
—Alfred Adler, one of the founders of modern psychology

Many parents find one of their children easier to appreciate. Given how much your child wants to know that you love her more than anyone else, if she's your favorite, why not just imply that?

1. Your child would feel terribly guilty toward her siblings, which isn't a good foundation for a close sibling relationship.
2. Your child might feel that she needs to undermine her siblings in order to maintain her favored position.
3. Your child would probably wonder if you're telling the other child that he's your favorite, too, which undermines her trust in your love.
4. She might tell the other children during a fight. Even if she didn't, you can assume they'd pick up on it, which would be devastating for them for the rest of their lives, and would prompt them to make her life miserable.

So this is one case where what your child wants—to know that you love him *most*—is not what's good for him. What he does need is to know that you don't love anyone else more. Remember the two things every child with siblings needs to hear? (Right, you couldn't love anyone more, and no matter how much love his sibling gets, there's more than enough for him!)

What if there's one child with whom you just don't feel as close? Maybe this is the one who's always resistant, who pushes you away, who holds a grudge. Maybe he reminds you of your ex, who was dishonest or cruel. Maybe she's simply difficult. I want to take this opportunity to make an impassioned plea to you. Every child needs unconditional love from his parents. Unconditional means just that—there are no conditions. Not, *"If only you wouldn't give me such a hard time..."* or *"If only you were a bit more like your brother."* Unconditional. Your child did not ask to be born and he did not ask for the genetic loading and environmental conditions that shaped him. Sure, he could make better choices, and I'd share your happiness if he didn't give you such a hard time. But every child deserves parents who are 110 percent in his corner, even if he has a brother who's easier in every way. He needs your unconditional love to make the most of his unique gifts. I've talked to so many adults who felt that "Mom [or Dad] always loved my sibling best" and were wounded for life. Don't let your child be one of those people.

What can you do if you notice that one of your children is coming up a bit short in your affection?

1. **Consciously look for the positives,** and tell your child what you see. *"I love to watch you play soccer!"*
2. **If you can't find anything positive at this moment, find something in the past.** *"Remember that time when you were so brave about..."*
3. **Start spending more time with the child to whom you feel less close.** Design positive, fun experiences that you can have together. Find ways to laugh together daily.
4. **When you catch yourself making a negative judgment, even in your own mind, stop and reframe,** to find the positive. *"Why doesn't he ever stop moving?!"* becomes *"He's going to accomplish a lot in life with all that energy."*

If you find you really have a hard time with one of your children, don't wait. Get professional help. Each child you have deserves your unconditional love. Each one deserves to be your favorite.

8

Tools to Prevent Rivalry and Nurture Bonding

This chapter is full of ideas that will help you build a family culture that supports sibling closeness. But they won't work by themselves. I've saved this for the end of Part 2 because these ideas are the icing on the cake. Icing may make the difference in making the cake fantastic, but you need a cake for the icing to work. Without the peaceful parenting approach outlined in Part 1, and the communication and conflict resolution skills in the earlier chapters of Part 2, the tools in this chapter won't help much.

So once you've put the rest of this book to work, and you're ready for some fine-tuning, let's consider some best practices to create a thriving family culture.

Expect Your Children to Value Each Other

The best method for preventing sibling rivalry is to work as early as possible in your children's lives to help them really value each other, so they know that the relationship with their brother or sister is special, that it will be with them their whole lives, that they really can count on each other for help.

—Professor Laurie Kramer, sibling rivalry researcher[1]

One of the most fundamental ways you influence your children's relationship is the expectation you hold about it. In her book *My Sister, My Self,* Vikki Stark interviewed more than 400 women, teens, and girls about their sister relationship. "I found over and over that sisters who were close came from families who put a lot of emphasis on the relationship," she says. "It was a family culture—you are sisters, you have each other to depend on for life and we expect you to have a close relationship."[2]

This is not forced positivity. Children cannot be expected to always be in touch with their love for each other. (Even adults can't do that!) It's completely normal for humans who live together to get angry at each other. But if we can hold the expectation that as a family we will always work things out with each other, that we deeply value our relationships with each other, that siblings have a unique bond that is to be treasured and protected, then we'll transmit that assumption to our children. How?

1. **Celebrate your family, which includes siblings.** Family traditions and rituals help children bond. A sense of family identity—*"We're the reading Ryans!"* or *"We're the exploring Zimmermans!"*—makes children feel like part of a team.

2. **Explicitly teach values,** including kindness and supportiveness. Family rules and a family motto (see the next section) that express values give children a positive framework for their relationship with each other. Talk about what family means: *"We're a family; we take care of each other . . . We sup-*

port each other ... We appreciate each other ... We always work together to work things out ... We celebrate each other."

3. **Explicitly teach emotional intelligence.** Point out that nobody's perfect, and we all depend on each other's compassion and forgiveness when we're having a hard time. Once children understand that feelings matter, and drive behavior—but we're always responsible for choosing our behavior—they become more tolerant of each other.

4. **Honor individuality and celebrate difference.** Talk often about the fact that each member of the family is unique, brings a different perspective that is to be respected, and is valuable just because they are themselves. The family needs each person for it to be whole. It's okay for kids to be different from you, and from each other. Look for those differences, talk about them, enjoy them. *"Yes, you love chocolate ice cream ... I'm more of a caramel fan myself. Isn't it great how everyone is different? That's part of what makes the world interesting."* This also helps kids see themselves as unique individuals, so they won't feel as much need to compete with each other.

5. **Create a "sibling book" to help your children see their relationship positively.** A personalized book helps your children understand that even though they may fight with their sibling, siblings always work things out. You can find an example—*Brothers Are Forever*—at AhaParenting.com, which you can download as a Word document and personalize.

6. **Talk about how lucky your children are to have each other.** Ask, *"What is your favorite thing about having a brother?"* or

"What is the coolest thing you've taught (or learned from) your sister?"

Family Routines That Foster Sibling Bonding

I step back and let them comfort each other if they get hurt. It's hard to not swoop in and grab that hurt and sobbing two-year-old but to watch the five-year-old hug her (or vice versa!) with incredible love is amazing. My children seek each other for hugs and comfort and I love to see it.
—Melinda

1. **Morning snuggles.** Make sure you get five minutes of relaxed snuggle time with each child as they wake up. I know, it sounds impossible. But if everything else is already done, you can relax for five minutes. That time connecting with your child will transform your morning. You fill your child's cup before the day starts, and you reconnect after the separation of the night, which gives your child the motivation to cooperate instead of fight with you—or his sibling. What if more than one child piles into bed with you? Snuggle with everyone!

2. **Family kindness journal.** Buy a bound book, or tie sheets of paper together with a ribbon, or just add sheets of paper to a binder. Label it "Our Family Kindness Journal" and let the kids decorate it. You might begin with a quote about kindness, such as the Dalai Lama's: *"Be kind whenever possible. It is always possible."* Then, notice acts of kindness between your children, and write them in the journal, with the date.

"Brody helped Katelyn with her fort when it kept falling down."

"Kevin shared the cookie he brought home from school with Michael."

"Natalya helped Yuri reach the light switch. Yuri was so pleased."

"At the grocery store today, Evie suggested that we buy oranges for Damian."

Soon, your children will be noticing the small kindnesses between them and asking you to record them. Before you know it, they'll be inspired to perform more acts of kindness toward each other. You might even want to explicitly encourage everyone in your family to do one kind act for each other person every day, pointing out that kindness has a way of warming the hearts of both people—the giver and the receiver.

3. **Make it a daily practice to comment on some way that each child helped another child.** Say *"I noticed that you comforted Liam when he hurt himself . . . He must have really appreciated that,"* or *"I saw you help Victoria with her pajama top. What a helpful sister!"*

4. **When it's chore time, work in teams.** All children want to feel that they're making a contribution. So instead of seeing chores as a way to get help with the household work, reframe them for yourself as a way for your children to see themselves as being of service to the family. If you're trying to teach a child to master a given chore, then the parent usually needs to work with the child. But having your children work with each other is a terrific way to foster the sibling team. Give

them a task that takes teamwork and let them figure out how to work together on it.

5. **Let siblings nurture each other.** When one child gets hurt, make it a practice for everyone in the family to stop playing and tend to the child who's hurt. Hold back a moment to see if the siblings step in to nurture each other. Send a child for the ice pack or Band-Aids, or even let them be your medical assistant and tend to their sibling. Include all the children in this, including any child who was involved in the other getting hurt. Dr. William Sears describes a lovely practice in which "if one child was either physically or emotionally hurt, the others were encouraged to offer comfort to ease the pain. We called this practice 'laying on of hands.' The sib under pressure (whether it be an upcoming test, or an emotional or physical hurt) would sit in the middle of the group while the rest of us would place a hand on him and pray for his comfort in a calming way."[3]

6. **When you take photos, always take some of your kids together and some of each child solo.** Children see the individual photos you take of them as symbols of your love. Photos of the siblings together symbolize the importance of the sibling bond.

7. **At dinner every night, let everyone share the best and the worst parts of their day.** If the best part has to do with a sibling, celebrate it. If the worst part has to do with a sibling, empathize with the person who shares. (*"It sounds like you were really upset when you and Molly argued about the rules for playing that game . . ."*) Since tempers have cooled, the sibling might actually jump in with a peace-restoring comment. If not, see if you can offer one, without taking sides:

"It's a hard thing when two people have really different ideas about how to play a game . . . Sometimes they decide they love playing together so much that both people are willing to change their ideas a little so they can still play . . . Maybe tomorrow will be like that, and you'll both have a better time." Why risk tearing the scab off a source of tension? Because this gives you a chance to heal the rift. Sometimes the kids do it themselves; sometimes you do it by "telling the story" in a positive way. If it turns out there are still hurt feelings that can't be solved at dinner, it gives you a chance to schedule a problem-solving session—*"Sounds like you two are having a problem working out the best rules for the sandbox . . . It's okay to have different ideas about that . . . We can solve this, but not right now at dinner. Let's talk about it in the morning, okay?"* You've cleared the air and given them another way to understand the situation, so they don't go to sleep feeling resentment toward their sibling.

8. **Practice gratitude.** At dinner or bedtime, start a practice where everyone in the family expresses gratitude to every other family member. This works best when each person just throws in their "gratitudes" when they're moved to, so no one is on the spot while everyone stares at them. (This is a version of "appreciations," which is described in "Family Meetings" on page 210.)

9. **Include in your bedtime routine a chance for your children to always say "good night" and "I love you" to each other.** Some families also have the older child read to the younger one before bed, which can be a lovely opportunity for bonding.

10. **Create family traditions that foster sibling bonding.** Happy families not only have treasured traditions, but evolve new

ones that help them find their way through the inevitable changes of growing up by creating warm bonds and a sense of security. Examine your family traditions through the lens of the sibling relationship. What regular events (weekly, seasonal, or annual) would promote sibling excitement and closeness? You might let the children have a sleepover in the living room on the last night of school every year, or a campout in the backyard at the end of the summer. Children will find these sibling traditions very special and will create memories together that will positively flavor their entire year.

11. **Consider an annual sibling celebration.** For instance, even if you aren't Hindi, you might decide to celebrate your own version of Raksha Bandhan, a Hindu holiday for brothers and sisters. The children give each other small presents, including homemade cards listing what they appreciate about each other, and you have a special dinner—maybe out at an Indian restaurant—where you toast to them as a team. Or simply make up your own holiday, such as a "brother birthday" every year on the day that falls exactly halfway between their birthdays.

Family Rules and Mottos That Support Sibling Closeness

If you have a child over the age of six, you know that children love rules. They love to argue about them and enforce them. And the rules they love best are the ones they help make! Many parents react with apprehension to the idea that their children might help formulate the family rules. Let me reassure you that you're still the parent, and you have the responsibility of veto. But when children are involved in the process of making rules, they're much more likely to follow them.

That said, I want to caution you against too many rules. Children won't remember them if you have too many. They'll forget that some rules are more important than others, leading them, for instance, to yank their brother roughly off the couch because he isn't supposed to be jumping on it, while forgetting the rule about being kind.

Sit down with your children and a big piece of paper and ask if your family already has any rules. Your kids will surprise you with what they say. "Go to bed when Dad says" and "Don't wake the baby" may show up, but not "Be Kind." Write down everything they say, and then ask if there are any more rules that should be added. Write down all suggestions. Then tell your kids that you want to go through the list and select the most important five rules, or maybe three rules and a family motto. Write them neatly on another piece of paper. Let the kids decorate it, and hang it up. Your rules might look like this:

1. We're kind.
2. We don't hurt people or property.
3. We ask before touching someone's body and stop when anyone says stop.
4. We always clean up our own messes.
5. We do what Mom and Dad ask.

What's a family motto? A rule so important that it becomes a guiding vision for your children. You'll find yourself using it often, so that it becomes a saying in your family. Some mottos from parents on the AhaParenting.com Facebook page:

- Choose love!
- In this house, we do loving and kindness.
- Be brave, be kind, be respectful.

- What will work? Team work!
- People are more important than things.
- Family is forever.
- There is *always* more love.

How to Create More Positive Interactions Between Your Children

I'll never forget the moment when our three-year-old erupted in the most joyous cascade of laughter I've ever heard. He was playing with his one-year-old sister, and her antics touched a funny bone within him that I didn't even know existed. His many little friends couldn't trigger it either. But his little sister, whom he loved, drew something new and wonderful out of him ... In loving, we expand not only our own capacity to love but also the richness of our own personalities.

—Mary Rice Hasson, Ethics and Public Policy Center

If your children are having a hard time with each other, it's natural that you focus on helping them learn to resolve differences peacefully. But it's important to remember that their incentive to work things out happily will depend on how much of a positive balance they've built up in their "relationship bank account" with each other. Po Bronson and Ashley Merryman in their book *NurtureShock* say, "In many sibling relationships the rate of conflict can be high, but the fun times in the backyard and the basement more than balance it out. This net-positive is what predicts a good relationship later in life. In contrast, siblings who simply ignored each other had less fighting, but their relationship stayed cold and distant long term."[4]

How do siblings build up a reservoir of good feelings to draw on? Mostly, by having a good time together. Dr. John Gottman of the Seattle Love Lab has found that couples need five to seven positive interactions to counterbalance one negative interaction.[5] This ratio has been repeated in multiple studies, from couples to workplaces. As far as I know, there hasn't been parallel research done with siblings. But that's not a bad ratio to aim for.

This might make you feel despairing—after all, if they fight six times a day, how can you help them create thirty-six positive interactions? Remember that a smile counts as a positive; these don't all have to be major interactions to have a beneficial effect. Why not simply adopt the goal of helping your children have as many positive interactions as you can?

1. **Notice and promote the activities that get your children playing together.** Research on improving sibling relationships shows that children have better relationships when they share activities they both enjoy.[6] It can be tough to identify those activities, especially if there's an age or interest gap. But if you pay attention, you can usually suggest something that will interest both children. For instance, if she wants to play store and he wants to play astronaut, why not have a store on the moon? Or maybe both enjoy the play kitchen, or doing art together, or making forts. Be sure to encourage at least one shared activity every day.

2. **Don't interrupt happy play.** You probably remember the old adage "Never wake a sleeping baby." My corollary is "Don't interrupt a happily playing child." So when siblings are playing together well, don't take it for granted. Support them in whatever they need to keep playing, and don't interrupt unless it's unavoidable.

3. **Use oxytocin to get your children bonding.** Laughing. Being outdoors. Dancing. Singing. Roughhousing. Snuggling.

Include as many oxytocin-inducing activities as you can in your daily routine.

4. **Start "special time" between your children.** Amy McCready, author of *If I Have to Tell You One More Time*, suggests something she calls Mind, Body and Soul time for siblings.[7] This is a ten-minute block of time that is designated for two children to spend together. It might be just the ticket if your children are widely spaced in age, or one is less interested in playing together than the other one, because it structures time together into the regular routine and maintains the connection. If they have a hard time in the beginning figuring out what to do together, be prepared with fun suggestions. (Screens should be off-limits.)

5. **Comment to each child about how much the others love him,** and about specific things the other children have done. *"Isn't it great that your brother shared his treat with you? You and your brother are so lucky to have each other!"* These comments usually work best when the siblings aren't around and the child feels happily connected to you.

6. **When they're having a bad day, pull out an activity they'll both love,** such as making cookies or dancing, to shift the mood.

Strategies to Create a Sibling Team

We foster teamwork by pitting the girls against Daddy—in a race, in a tackle, in a game—and he only lets them win if they work together. They

don't know that, of course. But we reflect and say, "Remember how the two of you were able to beat Daddy in the race when you worked together?"
   —Elizabeth

Children's competitive instincts are related to the drive toward mastery. All humans love the excitement of the race; we're programmed to look for those road markers that tell us how we're doing in our efforts to excel (and get that next little zap of dopamine). So competition is bound to crop up in your family, no matter how many positive interactions you facilitate. But what if your children could see each other as partners on the same team, instead of competitors?

1. **Begin creating a team feeling** by including both children in your comments, even before the baby is able to contribute much to the team: *"You two are playing with that toy together and you both seem to be having so much fun. What a terrific team!"*

2. **Instead of pitting your children against each other, find ongoing ways to unite them in the same mission.** *"Can you work together so you're both ready to leave the house at 8 a.m.? That will give us time to go the long way to school so we can see the bulldozers at the construction site again. Yes? What a team!"*

3. **Promote the idea of the sibling team** by creating family activities in which your children work together. For instance, give them a huge sheet of paper to draw on together. Ask them to write a letter to Grandma together. Design a scavenger hunt in which the kids help each other, rather than compete against each other. When you roughhouse, always team children against grown-ups.

4. **Put your kids in charge of a project together.** For instance, maybe they'll wash the car together, to earn the money you would have spent at the car wash. Or maybe they're in charge of the decorations for Father's Day, or planning a fun family outing. Let the children work together to do the planning, with you only peripherally involved to ensure safety and maximum fun.

Shifting Alliances: How to Keep Kids from Ganging Up on Each Other

If you have more than two children, you've seen it. Perhaps in your family, the girls team up against the boy, or maybe the oldest resents the second child but adores the baby. The alliances can shift like the wind, or they can solidify, leaving one child out in the cold on a regular basis. What can you do to encourage all of your children to appreciate each other?

1. **Assign them tasks as a "sibling team"** to get all of the kids working together: *"If the three of you can work together to get ready for bed, we'll have time for three books at bedtime, so each of you can choose a book."*

2. **Pit the sibling team "against" the parents:** *"Okay, pillow fight! Kids against parents!"*

3. **Shake up the current teams.** Play a board game and you decide the teams. If Jade and Alexandra are always conspiring against Levi, then put Jade on your team and Alexandra on the team with Levi. She'll have to find a way to work with him if she wants to win.

4. **Mix and match.** Be sure your children get a chance to be one-on-one with each other, rather than always hanging as a group. When you have two kids who don't naturally connect, create opportunities. Take them on a special outing or find activities they can do as a pair at home. The more it's just the two of them, the more likely they are to bond.

5. **Directly interrupt the unkindness** when they whisper or exclude. *"Excuse me, you aren't being unkind, are you? You aren't purposely excluding someone, are you? That isn't what we do in our family."*

6. **Be ready to step in.** No matter how you try to avoid it, one of your children will sometimes feel excluded. If you can invite them to spend some Special Time with you, you're making lemonade from lemons by giving them something even more valuable than time with their siblings—one-on-one time with you.

Why Roughhousing Reduces Sibling Rivalry

When my two- and four-year-olds are having a tough time playing nicely together, I turn into "mommy monster" and chase them. They laugh, run away together, and find ways to team up and get me. The kids vs. mommy game seems to work every time.

—Jennifer

Most parents get anxious when children roughhouse. Isn't the end result always tears? But play is how nature designed humans, especially small humans, to learn, to ease the tensions of daily life, and to connect. Children rely on physical play to work through the natural tensions of the relationship. Moving helps work out emotion.

Laughter is even more important, since it creates more oxytocin, the bonding hormone, and decreases anxiety by reducing stress hormones. And like other young mammals, when kids "play fight," they learn to manage aggression, which makes them less likely to lash out when they're angry. So when kids wrestle, pillow fight, and roughhouse, it's good practice. Roughhousing is so valuable that it's worth the extra energy to figure out how to make it work for your family.

1. **Help children create safety rules for play fights.** If you're worried that someone's about to get hurt, try to resist just shutting down the action out of your own anxiety. Instead, help your kids make rules to keep everyone safe: *"Play wrestling is great, as long as you have rules to stay safe. What are your rules? Oh, when someone yells 'Stop!' both people have to stop? And no hitting? Those sound like great rules! How are they working so far? Do you need any other rules?"*

2. **Set limits before you get angry.** The minute you start getting worried that someone will get hurt, it's a signal to do something. No, not yell. It's time to intervene in a positive way to make sure things are safe. Many parents try so hard to be patient that they let things get out of hand. Next thing you know, someone's crying, and you're yelling. That's not the emotional regulation you want to model. State your rule or expectation, firmly and kindly. *"This kind of play doesn't belong in this room. I'm worried that you might roll into the lamp or the TV."*

3. **Assess the danger.** Is it actually dangerous? Maybe the kids are being loud and exuberant, but having a great time, and there's no actual danger to anyone, or to your home. Or maybe a small change would make a difference, like moving the bed

closer to the dresser so they can jump onto the bed safely. Maybe your children are having a throwing contest with blocks, but you can substitute stuffed animals.

4. **Connect before you correct.** Yelling across the room will just add to the frenzy. Instead, go physically to your children. When a child is spinning out of control, you can't get through to him unless you move in close in a friendly way. Make a positive connection with your child *before* you ask him to do something different. *"You two are having lots of fun with this roughhousing, aren't you?"*

5. **Empathize as you offer an alternative, and maybe a choice.** *"I know it's hard to stop, but this kind of play belongs in the basement on the tumbling mat, or outside. Outside? Let's go!"*

6. **Check in with all participants to be sure everyone is enjoying the activity.** *"Is everyone still having fun with this?"* If one of your kids is getting into a frenzy and the other seems a bit tense, you can help them check in with each other. *"Jaden, do you see that your brother isn't laughing? Let's stop for a minute and be sure everyone feels safe . . . Henry, you can tell Jaden to stop whenever you want. Do you want to practice it right now?"*

7. **Tears aren't the end of the world.** Often, kids do begin to cry when they get a big bump while roughhousing. Sometimes those tears are appropriate to the injury, and your child is ready to get back into the action after a quick hug from you. Sometimes, they sob wildly, clearly overreacting. That's a good thing; it means all that laughter has loosened up the feelings stuffed in their emotional backpack, and they're taking advantage of this owie to share the deeper wounds they can't ver-

balize. After a good cry, your child will be so much more relaxed and happy, since those feelings will be "off his chest." So instead of feeling like a bad parent because someone got hurt, relax. Take the opportunity to help your child with his big feelings, and be glad that he got a chance to cry. Afterward, ask both kids if they think they need to add any new rules to keep everyone safer next time. You might write the rules down and post them, even if they can't read yet, so you can easily remind them next time they start getting wild.

8. **Help them wind down.** Sometimes you do need to redirect to a calmer activity. But often when kids are really wound up, they have a hard time stopping, because they're about to melt down. If you sense a meltdown brewing, test it by connecting and then setting a limit. *"Okay, darlings, time to calm down now. That's enough rowdiness."* If necessary, grab him up in a bear hug. If he calms down, great! If he bursts into tears, great! Better those feelings should come out by crying in your arms than by hurting his little brother.

9. **Make sure your kids have a safe place to be wild.** Children need to roll around, wrestle, climb, and jump. Our modern lives don't always offer them that opportunity. If you don't have a yard, or a basement with a tumbling mat, make their room safe for roughhousing, and make sure they get plenty of time to romp and tussle at the playground or park. If you don't, your couch will start to look a lot like a trampoline, and your lamps will be living dangerously.

ROUGHHOUSING GAMES FOR SIBLINGS

You can use roughhousing play to defuse brewing conflicts, deflect teasing, create a team feeling between siblings, build self-esteem with children who are smaller or less assertive, and help kids with specific issues like competition. Your goal is as much laughter as possible, so be just scary enough to get them shrieking with laughter. In every game, your job is to bumble and be incompetent and let the children win. Kids giggle and sweat and love these games, and ask for them over and over.

Here are a few games to get you started. For more ideas, I highly recommend the work of Becky Bailey (*I Love You Rituals*), Lawrence Cohen (*Playful Parenting*), Patty Wipfler (HandinHandParenting .org), and Aletha Solter (*Attachment Play*), from whom I have adapted many games over the years.

Games to Help Children Bond

1. Kids against parents—pillow fights, wrestling.
2. Chase them around the house to foster teamwork: *"I smell children! I am going to catch them both! The only way to get away from me is if you are holding hands ... That is the magic that keeps you safe!"*

(See also "Games to Help Your Children Bond with the Baby" on page 305.)

Power Games

1. Let your child push you over.
2. Race—and of course, trip so he wins.

3. Play role reversal games such as Mother May I, Simon Says, and Follow the Leader. Let her give the orders.

These games:

- Reduce kids' competitiveness with each other.
- Let children experience themselves as strong and powerful, an antidote to daily experience.
- Help strong-willed children feel less pushed around.

Games to Conquer Jealousy by Filling Your Child's Love Tank

1. **God or Goddess of Love:** When your children object that you're paying attention to a sibling and not to them, say "I'm the Goddess of Love and I have more hugs than you could ever need!" Then grab the children, one by one and in groups, and give lots and lots of hugs, being goofy to get the kids laughing.

2. **Lovesick puppy:** Follow your child around exclaiming about how sweet he smells, sitting on the floor gazing up at him in his chair, licking his arm to get him laughing. When one of the other children notices and comments, immediately turn your delighted attention to them. Get your kids competing to see who can best avoid your ridiculous adoration.

(See also "Using Games to Help Your Child with Jealousy" on page 271.)

Games to Interrupt Bickering and Teasing

See "How to Playfully Divert Bickering" on page 111.

Why Not Tickling?

Laughter is always good for kids and parents, because it helps heal emotions and create connection. But tickling, even when children giggle, can make children feel powerless. The child may seem to be having fun, but she can't *help* laughing. The adult is completely in control and the child loses the ability to stand up for herself. Many kids end up out of breath, begging for the parent to stop tickling—and not all parents stop. Many adults have unpleasant memories of being tickled past the point of it being enjoyable, and being helpless to protect themselves.

So why do kids initiate tickle games? Kids need to feel physically close to us. They love to laugh. Sometimes kids are able to articulate that this is how they get to be silly and have fun with their parents. But I've observed that when parents begin to initiate other kinds of physical play that gets children laughing, the kids usually stop being so interested in tickling.

So what do you do if a child asks to be tickled? Threaten to tickle, by moving your hand close and saying, "I'm going to get you!" The threat alone should make your child laugh. You're not provoking a physiological reflex that overwhelms him. You're dancing on the edge of your child's fear, so he can laugh it out.

When Kids Share a Room

There were some rough nights in the beginning but now both are great sleepers—they just go back to sleep when the other one wakes them. And they are now so close. Our oldest helps the baby with everything.
  —Kirk

Many adults who shared a room look back fondly on their chats and giggling before they fell asleep each night. Others remember hating the lack of privacy and resenting each other. It's true that having children share a room usually makes everything more complicated, from bedtimes to safeguarding possessions to whose responsibility it is to clean up. But if your kids share a room, either for space reasons or because that's your preference, it is possible to make it not only a good experience for both children, but a treasured one.

1. **Make sure your children each get enough personal space.** They already have to share you and so much else. If your children share a room, be sure they each have "private" space where they can withdraw from the world and not interact. Bed canopies with curtains, and play tents, are invaluable for privacy. You might even paint a line down the middle of the floor, or hang a curtain or set the furniture up to define two separate spaces. For kids who are very different in their neatness levels, this is especially important.

2. **Make a rule that the bedroom is for quiet activities.** That way, a child who wants a calm place to withdraw to always has one. The rowdy child can stay in the family space.

3. **Give each child a toy cupboard where they can put their treasures away.** If there's a big age difference, let the older child lock their cupboard to keep their treasures safe from the marauding toddler. Family toys can be kept in the family common space to keep the bedroom less cluttered and encourage sleeping, rather than playing, at night.

4. **Use white noise or nature recordings at sleep time** so small noises are less likely to wake the other child.

5. **When children are young, have separate bedtimes.** Put the younger one to bed while the older one stays up a bit later, listening to an audiobook or having Special Time with the other parent. Then read her a story in the living room (dim the lights). Give her a special flashlight of her own to use while you tuck her in quietly, to make this more special.

6. **If they won't settle at naptime, or nap at different times** and will wake each other, have one nap on the couch, in a Pack 'n Play, or in your bedroom.

7. **Don't move the baby into your older child's room until he's sleeping reliably.** And if your older child is still a toddler, it's also best to delay the move until the baby is at least eight months, given that toddlers just don't have the judgment to be left alone with a young baby.

8. **Consider letting your kids share a bed once the baby is old enough.** I've heard from countless families that their children who share sleep are closer, and more understanding of each other during daylight hours. And many children sleep better if there's another warm body with them.

9. **Explain that they can't wake their sibling in the morning** until their night light goes off, and put it on a timer. Most parents find that kids sleep longer in the morning when they aren't alone, but there's always the risk that they'll wake each other. Be sure they know what they *can* do when they wake up—come wake you? Read books in their own bed?

10. **There will be a transitional time when your kids wake each other. Don't give up.** Keep a Pack 'n Play ready, or a

sleeping bag on your rug, to relocate one child on a difficult night. Most parents find summer or another vacation is the best time for this learning process, so that if there are a few nights of spotty sleep, you won't have the pressure to get everyone out the door in the morning. Soon you'll find your children have adapted and love sharing a room with each other.

11. **Be aware that things might change as they get older.** Kids sometimes need more privacy as they hit the preteen years. If it's an option to have their own rooms at that point, help them make a graceful transition. It doesn't mean they love their sibling any less.

When One Child Has a Friend Over

In some families, everyone plays together all the time. And some parents find that their children get along much better when they play mostly with each other. But children also benefit from relationships outside the family. Children have to take a little more care with friends, and give as much as they take. That teaches them prosocial skills and habits that they then bring into the sibling relationship.[8]

When a child invites a friend over, it will give the friendship more of a chance to flourish if that time is sibling-optional. That means that it's always the child's choice whether to include her sibling.

Being excluded from a sibling's playdate can be hard, of course. Sometimes the parents can be helpful in finding a way to include the sibling, and can coach the sibling on asking to be included.

Lily: They never let me play with them.

Mom: That can hurt, to see your sister having fun with her friend when you feel left out . . . I wonder whether there's something else you could do that's fun.

Lily: I only want to play with them.

Mom: You know the rule with playdates. When someone has a friend over to play, they're allowed to play alone. You can always ask, though. Sometimes your sister says yes, and sometimes she says no. But she can't say yes if you don't ask, right?

Lily: I'm scared to ask.

Mom: Do you want some help to ask if you can play? . . . Okay, let's go talk to them.

Mom and Lily walk over to Elizabeth and her friend. Lily looks expectantly at Mom.

Mom: Elizabeth, Lily has something to ask you.

Lily *(whispering)*: I want to play, too.

Mom: Lily, they can't hear you. You need to tell Elizabeth.

Lily *(louder)*: I want to play, too . . . Can I play with you and Mia?

Elizabeth: No. We're two girls alone in the forest, gathering berries to eat. We don't need another person in our game.

Lily *(dejected)*: Oh.

Mom: I hear that Elizabeth and Mia don't need another person in their game, so Lily can't be a person . . . Elizabeth, do you think the girls in the forest could find a baby fox? Maybe Lily could be a baby fox?

Elizabeth: What do you think, Mia? Would a baby fox be good?

Mia: A baby fox would be great! But you can't talk, Lily . . . Can you act like a fox? And just make noises?

Lily *(happily)*: Sure I can!

Often, of course, things don't go this smoothly and your child refuses to let her sibling join the game. At those times, the only thing you can do as a parent is empathize and grant her wish in fantasy, if necessary setting a limit at the same time: *"I guess it hurt your feelings when your sister wouldn't let you play with her and her friend . . . And you still can't stand outside her door and scream like that, sweetie, no matter how hurt you are . . . I bet you wish she would say, 'Sure, you can always play with us . . . Do you want to be the princess or the pirate?' I'm sorry your sister wants to play with her friend alone right now and you can't join them . . . Why don't you come be with me?"*

Look at the bright side. It's a terrific opportunity for Special Time with your child, without her sibling feeling jealous.

Family Meetings: The Resource You'll Be So Glad You Discovered

Does the idea of family meetings seem stilted and artificial to you? It certainly did to me when I first heard about it. But family meetings turned out to be a blessing to our family. They create connection. They give you a way to work things out between kids when everyone's calm. They help kids learn to solve problems. They help kids feel like integral members of the family. They even help siblings appreciate each other.

Held regularly at a mutually agreed upon time, family meetings provide a forum for discussing triumphs, grievances, sibling disagreements, schedules, any topic of concern to a family member. To get resistant kids to join in, combine the get-together with incentives such as post-meeting pizza, or assign children important roles such as recording secretary or keeper of the rules.

Introducing family meetings is the hard part; after that they're so rewarding they take on a life of their own. If you start family meetings during preschool, you'll have them later when you really need them. How do you begin?

1. **Explain to your kids that you have a fun idea** to make it easier to work out problems that come up. Serve a festive snack, and keep it short and fun. Over time, as your children get older and everyone enjoys the meetings, they can get longer.

2. **Schedule it at the same time every week.** That way, even if you skip it one week, working it in the next week will be easy. For instance, make Sunday evening dinners your family meeting.

3. **Create a ritual to signal that this isn't ordinary time together.** You might start by holding hands while one parent (or child) offers a blessing or lights candles.

4. **First on the agenda is everyone's favorite thing— appreciations.** In no particular order, everyone offers appreciations, until everyone has appreciated every other family member:

   - *"I appreciate that Daddy played catch with me."*

   - *"I appreciate that Eli helped me carry in the groceries."*

   - *"I appreciate that Alice worked so hard to teach herself to tie her shoes."*

   - *"I appreciate that Mom helped me sew my costume for the school play."*

   - *"I appreciate that Eli helped me build my fort."*

Children love getting and giving appreciations, and doing this regularly is reason enough to have a family meeting. It's important to begin this way to create a positive connection before you address any problems. And if this is all you end up doing during the meeting, you've done a lot, since this is such a powerful tool to build sibling relationships.

What if one child just "can't think of anything nice to say" about another child? That's a red flag that you've got some work to do to help that child past the chip on his shoulder. At that moment, you might say, *"Hmm . . . I know sometimes you get pretty annoyed at your sister. If you were to think of one time this week when you didn't feel annoyed, what was she doing?"* Even if he answers, *"She was asleep, so you could play with me!"* you have a place to begin. You can smile and say, *"I hear Dylan saying that he really appreciates that Hadley gave him a long Special Time today with me . . . Thank you, Hadley, for being so generous!"* Hadley will smile and feel appreciated, and Dylan will see Hadley as having given him something of value. Of course, you'll use this incident as motivation for yourself, to create positive interactions between your children during the coming week. That way, next week when Dylan can't think of anything to appreciate about his sister, you can say, *"Hmm . . . sometimes it's hard to remember all the things that happened in a week . . . what about that time when you two were laughing so hard in the bathtub?"*

5. **Next, ask if anyone wants to bring up an issue.** Kids fighting, sharing household work, Dad working late a lot, kids dragging their feet on the bedtime routine—anything that involves the whole family is fair game. This is *not* the time to bring up a behavior issue that concerns only one child. In fact, most items that are important to parents will get solved out-

side of family meetings. These are primarily forums for kids to get help solving issues that aren't working for them in your home. Don't let negative issues always dominate, or kids will stop enjoying the meetings. So keep a list of pleasant topics— how to plan the family trip coming up, who's going to cook for Mom's birthday—and be sure to bring those up, too.

6. **Use ground rules for discussions.** Everyone gets a chance to talk. One person talks at a time without interruption, everyone listens, and only constructive feedback is allowed. Pass a "talking stick" if you want; see AhaParenting.com for more on talking sticks. Use your coaching skills to interpret and reflect each person's needs, so no one is made to feel wrong. Brainstorm possible solutions and help your kids write out agreements. *"Hmm ... sounds like that idea works for Jamal, but not Mom. Let's find something that works for everyone."*

7. **Finish with "looking forward to's,"** in which each person describes something they're looking forward to in the coming week. This is the time to focus on all the positive things going on in your family's life. It's fine to announce on occasion that what you're looking forward to is closing a business deal or having dinner with your close friend, especially as your kids get older; you're role-modeling, after all. But when your children are young, they'll often experience your life outside the home as in competition with them, so it promotes more of that family bonding you're after to focus your "looking forward to's" on your family life.

8. **Announcements** at the very end are a good way to reenter life as usual, to remind everyone of upcoming appointments,

trips, and rides needed, and to keep the household running smoothly. But don't let this overwhelm all the good feelings you've created; defer logistical discussions that require real work.

9. **Close the meeting with a big group hug and your family motto.** For the under-five set, resist the impulse to do much business at family meetings; you want them to be short and rewarding. For elementary schoolers, it helps to add an incentive for them to do the hard work of problem-solving: a special dessert, a special game afterward. And don't be surprised if they appropriate the meeting to explain that you're embarrassing them in front of their friends, or that they need a raise in their allowance!

PART THREE

BEFORE THE NEW BABY AND THROUGH THE FIRST YEAR

9

Before the Baby Arrives: Creating a Warm Welcome

We took our 2.5-year-old daughter to every scan and heartbeat session. She was there when we found out he was a boy; we talked about all the things she could teach him, we discussed names with her and chose a name as early as possible to make him seem more real. She adores her little brother and is so gentle. Obviously there's jealousy, like when I'm feeding him, she'll come and say, "I need a cuddle, Mama," but I'll never say not right now; we always find a way to make it work!

—Victoria

Your children's relationship with each other begins when you announce your pregnancy or adoption to your older child. What's the best way to tell her? How can you help him bond with his unborn sibling? Should you wean your child now, or aim to tandem nurse? Can you get him over his "I only want Mommy" phase before the baby comes? How can you prepare your child for the separation while you birth the baby, if she's never been away from you? Great questions! This chapter will help you formulate the best answers for your family, to give your children's relationship a healthy beginning.

Telling Your Child About the New Sibling

Forty weeks can feel like an eternity to a pregnant woman, so imagine how much longer it would seem to a three-year-old. A toddler, and even a preschooler, will expect the baby to come shortly after you tell him about your pregnancy. Waiting is frustrating, and stressful, because the child has a hard time relaxing into feeling good about something that has so much uncertainty hanging over it. For this reason, the advice most commonly given to parents is not to tell a young child until they are fairly close to the due date.

However, that doesn't take into account when you'll be telling other people. You don't want friends and family mentioning the baby before you've told your child. Since the pregnancy begins to be obvious during the second trimester, it will usually become common knowledge among the adults in your circle, and that argues for telling your child when you begin to show, even though the wait for the baby will seem terribly long to her.

Remember that once you tell your two-year-old, she's likely to announce your pregnancy loudly to everyone she meets. Of course, if you emphasize that it's a secret, she may be able to control her excitement enough to stage-whisper the news. But don't expect her to be able to stay mum.

Many parents choose not to tell their children about their pregnancy until the risk of miscarriage is largely past, at the end of the first trimester.[1] Some parents, though, say that in the event of a tragedy, they will want to be open with their child about what happened, so that he or she understands why they're grieving and can be involved in any rituals acknowledging the loss.

Finally, some parents worry that if Mom is suddenly nauseous and too exhausted to play, kids will think she's mad at them, so they want to explain about the baby as soon as possible, during the first trimester. My concern with this approach is that the child's first association with the baby will be resentment that the baby is keeping Mom from meeting his needs. I agree that children are exquisitely sensitive to us and will immediately notice that something's different. But it's my opinion that we can best protect the sibling relationship by simply saying that we aren't feeling well, and then striving to connect to our child in other ways, even when we don't feel as energetic as usual. I don't think this concern should affect when we choose to tell our child about the pregnancy.

WHAT TO SAY

1. **Start a month or so before you break the news by beginning to read books about children with siblings.** As always when you read, ask questions: Has your child noticed that some of his friends have little siblings? Would he like a sister or brother someday? Why or why not?

   If your child expresses reservations, listen carefully, reflect, and give context:

   - *"I hear you. Babies do cry a lot, like Carmen's little brother. Did you know that you cried a lot? But then you got a little bigger and a lot happier, and we've had so much fun ever since! That will happen with Carmen's brother, too. All babies cry sometimes but we can help them feel better by holding and hugging them . . . and as they get bigger, they don't cry as much."*

   - *"I hear you. Babies do crawl around and knock towers down, like Blake's little sister . . . But then they get old enough to play, and there's always someone to play with, right in your own home! Don't worry, if you ever have a little sister, I will help you so she doesn't knock down your towers. And if she did, we could build it again, right? You could even teach her to build a tower, since you build such tall ones."*

The goal of these discussions is to get your child thinking about a sibling, and to alleviate whatever concerns you can before you even announce your pregnancy. End these discussions by commenting that you would love for your child to have a brother or sister someday, because they'll be friends forever. If your child asks if that might happen, assure them that someday you think they will probably be a big sister or brother.

2. **When you decide the day has come to share the news, do it from your child's perspective.** Instead of *"We're going to have a baby,"* try *"You're going to be a big sister. The baby is growing inside Mommy right now. It takes a long time for a baby to grow, but when it gets warmer and the flowers start to bloom in the spring, the baby will come."*

3. **Answer questions but keep it simple.** Give your child limited information until she asks. *"Yes, the baby is growing inside me, in a special place called the womb. See, my belly is getting bigger, right here. In this book, we can see pictures of what the baby looks like as she grows."*

4. **If your child responds negatively, listen and reflect.** *"It sounds like maybe you're worried about having a little brother or sister . . . Sometimes children worry that there won't be enough love for everyone. Babies do need a lot of love and care. But you are my only Joshua, and there could never be another Joshua just like you. I love you because you are you, and I could never love anyone more than you, no matter what. That will*

never change, baby or no baby. And no matter how much care the baby needs, there will always be more than enough for you . . . If you ever feel worried, you can always tell me how you feel, and I will understand." Will a toddler understand this? Make it shorter, and reinforce it over time. But yes, your toddler will understand this if he hears it over and over.

5. **Don't make everything about the baby.** Remember that your child won't really understand what it means to have a sibling until the baby appears, so after the initial excitement, he may well seem disinterested. That's normal. While you can comment regularly on the fact that the baby is growing inside you and he's going to be a big brother, don't act like this is the most important thing in your lives. To him, it isn't, and shouldn't be.

Twelve Ways to Help Your Kids Begin Bonding During Your Pregnancy

We spent a lot of time talking about his new baby sister when I was pregnant. She found her way into his bedtime stories and I always talked about how much she would love him, since he's her big brother. I try to let him participate in any way he wants. He is five and has buckled and unbuckled car seats, fed her, and even saved her from wandering out into the street. We call him her hero. Witnessing their love is a joy I could not have imagined!
—Sarah

1. **Wonder aloud what the baby is doing in there and how the baby is feeling.** (Is she sucking her thumb? Hiccupping? Practicing karate kicks? Enjoying her big sister's singing?) Research shows that when parents discuss how a baby is

feeling, older siblings develop more empathy and are less aggressive toward their little sibling.[2] While the research isn't conclusive yet on what happens if we start this process while the sibling is in utero, we do know that parents begin bonding with their baby before birth. So why not big siblings? Start now to help your child think of his sibling as a real person, with needs and feelings.

2. **Make it her baby, too.** Refer to "our baby" or "your sister" or even "your baby." This isn't really about ownership, of course—your children belong to themselves. But you say "my baby" to express that special relationship. Why shouldn't the baby's big sib?

3. **Encourage your child to connect with the baby.** For instance, tell her that the baby can hear her sing and talk, and will recognize her voice once he's born. Let her kiss your bump and show it her toys. Suggest she make art to decorate his room, so he can enjoy it as soon as he's born.

4. **Be the physical and emotional conduit for your children's warmth toward each other.** When your child makes an effort to connect with the baby, stop and let yourself feel your appreciation and warmth. Since your baby feels what you feel emotionally, the baby will begin to associate your child's voice with feeling good.[3] You can get this positive association developing in the other direction as well, by telling your child how delighted the baby is by his song or kiss, so he begins to develop warm feelings toward the baby.

5. **Take him with you to the doctor to hear the baby's heartbeat.** Make sure his heartbeat gets listened to also. Talk

about when you first heard *his* heartbeat and how excited you were.

6. **Ponder potential baby names together.** The sooner you can refer to the baby by name, the sooner he'll seem like a real person to the big sibling. If you can let her "name" the baby (at least the middle name) with a name you love, all the better.

7. **Buy your child a doll that he can nurture,** put diapers on, feed, wear in a sling, etc. Let him use his doll to show you all the things he's reading with you, about what babies need and how he's going to help care for his brother. Show your child how to soothe the baby by holding her securely against his chest and breathing deeply, making a soothing noise on the outbreath. Not only does this teach your child how to calm his sibling; it is a terrific way for him to calm himself, and one you can suggest that he use once the baby is born, if her crying upsets him.

8. **Speak to your baby, in your child's presence, about how lucky he will be to have such a wonderful big brother.** Mention all the things your child can do and will show the baby how to do, all the fun they will have together once the baby grows up a little.

9. **Encourage him to play with the baby.** When the baby kicks, let him poke very gently to see if the baby will kick again.

10. **Tell him stories about when he was a baby.** Explain how he loved to be held, and loved it when you carried him around and showed him things. This will help him to feel valued, and will also help him begin to understand what the baby will be like.

11. **Let her choose any furniture, toys, and clothes** that she's ready to pass on to the baby. Let her help you arrange and paint the baby's room and get everything ready.

12. **Consider sibling birth classes,** which offer lessons on how to hold a baby, explanations of how a baby is born, and opportunities for your child to discuss his or her feelings about having a new brother or sister. If you do this education yourself, be sure your child understands that babies cry a lot at first and aren't ready to play for a long time. (Children are often shocked by the helplessness of babies. As my son said, *"She can't even play with me, and that was the whole point!"*)

Be Sure Your Child Can Rely on Both Parents

Parents often imagine an egalitarian split in child-raising before they have children, and it's my view that equal co-parenting is best for kids, both parents, and the marriage. But the reality is that it can be hard to create an equal division of labor. And even if you do, the fact that one partner carries the child in her body (unless you're adopting) means that not everything can be equal. If you're nursing, then you're the one tending to the baby most often. That means your partner will often be the one caring for your older child.

This is a big adjustment for everyone. Your child may miss Mom desperately and become angry at Dad. If Mom has her hands full with the newborn, she may feel guilty or resentful about the older child's demands. And her partner may feel incompetent or rejected as the older child insists that only Mommy will do.

It's important to recognize that your child does not see her parents as interchangeable. If she loses Mom to the new baby, she'll grieve and resent the baby—even if she gets exclusive rights to Dad. So it's important that each parent get time with each child.

That said, if the child feels equally connected to both parents, it will make this transition easier on everyone. So as soon as you know there's a baby on the way, start moving toward co-parenting your child as much as possible. When you're nursing the new baby non-stop, you want your big kid to be excited about spending time with the nonnursing partner. (If you're bottle-feeding, you can be more equal in dividing time with each child.) How?

1. **Start now to cultivate the relationship between the older child and the nonnursing partner.** Your goal is for your child to enjoy *and* feel emotionally safe with Dad. That means that Dad isn't just a fun playmate. He's an equally great comforter. When the child is sad, or whiny, Dad understands. He says, *"Everybody needs to cry sometimes . . . Let's snuggle . . . Let's fill you up with hugs."*

2. **Let the nonnursing partner take charge.** Let Dad make meals, so he learns how your child likes his sandwich cut or his eggs cooked. Mom, hug them good-bye and leave the house. Or send them on adventures. Worried that Dad won't handle things as you would? He won't. That's okay. If you overcontrol, he won't feel empowered to step in and be the grown-up. In fact, small crises (*"We forgot a spare diaper!"*) are often bonding opportunities between a parent and a child.

3. **Have the nonnursing partner take over putting your child to bed at night.** Your child will have enough to adjust to when the baby arrives without also losing her familiar bedtime routine. Bedtime, remember, is the scariest time of the day for kids because they have to disconnect from their attach-

ment figures. Start now with both parents teaming up for dinner, bath, pajamas, toothbrushing, stories, and lights out. Over time, Mom can leave for parts of the routine, until finally your child is going to sleep happily for Dad. Be sure that Mom still says good night and gives a big hug, so your child falls asleep feeling securely connected to both parents.

4. **If your child wakes up at night, have the nonnursing partner take over as the point person.** The nursing partner won't be able to respond to the child at night while nursing a newborn. Again, you can hand this off gradually by having both parents respond at night for a while, with Mom paring back her involvement over time. If one parent travels a lot for work, which will leave the other parent with a newborn and a toddler who still wakes up often at night, consider having everyone sleep in the same big bed, adjoining beds, or at least the same room. Otherwise, nighttime parenting is just too taxing, and maybe even dangerous, with one partner juggling little ones in more than one bedroom.

5. **What if your child resists one parent?** Get him laughing about his biggest fear, which is that he can't get to one of his parents, because the other is in the way. Play the "You Can't Get to Mommy Game," inspired by Dr. Lawrence Cohen, the best source I know for games that are emotionally helpful to children.[4] Let the "preferred" parent sit on the couch. Get between your child and that parent, and boast, *"You can't get to Mommy! You are all mine! I will keep you from getting to Mommy!"* As he tries to get to Mommy, grab at him, but bumble and be unsuccessful. Mommy, meanwhile, is cheering the child on. When the child reaches Mommy, she hugs him and then lets him go. Dad laments that he got

through, but continues to boast and challenge the child to repeat his feat, unsuccessfully attempting each time to grab him. If your child has a preference for one parent, he will almost certainly laugh and laugh, which means that he's releasing his fears about this issue. He will also ask for this game over and over. By the time he stops asking, you'll notice that he's much more amenable to spending time with Dad. Why? Because he's bonded with him through all the laughter. But even more important, because he's overcome his deep fear that he's being prevented from being with the person he feels he most needs. This game takes real emotional generosity from Dad, but I've heard from many families that it's transformative.

Ten Tips to Support Your Child Emotionally as He Moves Toward Becoming a Big Sibling

1. **Recognize that your pregnancy is stressful to your child.** Why? Because you aren't as energetic and patient as you used to be. Because you don't pick her up as readily. Because there's less room on your lap. Because she's worried about what it will mean to have a baby in the house. In most families, there are added stresses, such as weaning or moving to a big kid bed or even a new house. Be aware that all of this can be very hard on your child. Expect some acting out or regression.

2. **Get any big changes out of the way well in advance of the birth,** such as bed or room changes, weaning, toilet training, or moving. Your child needs time to adjust without associating these changes with the baby.

3. **Emphasize your child's uniqueness** by going through his baby pictures and talking about what a wonderful baby he was, and what a wonderful boy he is now. Tell him there is only one of him in the whole world and that no one could ever replace him in your heart.

4. **Don't overfocus on the baby.** Naturally you're excited, and hopefully he's excited, too. But to him, the baby isn't real yet, and his life now is. If you make everything about the baby, he's bound to resent it. When well-meaning friends ask your child what he thinks about becoming a big brother, and he doesn't seem to know what to say, don't hesitate to change the subject: *"We're looking forward to the baby, but we don't really know what it will be like. Right now, Jason has his hands full building train tracks. Do you know how a switch track works?"*

5. **Let your child express his full range of feelings** throughout the pregnancy and birth. Expect him to veer from excitement to impatience to worry. Respond with empathy to all of it. *"It sounds like . . ."*

   - *"You're excited that you'll get to show your sister how to go sledding."*

   - *"You're tired of people asking all the time how you feel about becoming a big brother."*

   - *"You wish my back didn't hurt so I could pick you up more, like I used to."*

6. **Make sure your child knows he still has an important role in the family.** He's always been the baby in your family, and he may well feel displaced. Be specific to help your child feel

seen and valued for who he is and all the ways he contributes to the family: *"Carlos, I love the way you help me when we grocery shop . . . We're such a great team!"* or, *"Sara, I love the way we laugh together . . . it's so much fun to be with you!"*

7. **Give a context if you can't relate as usual, to reduce resentment of the baby.** Explain that it's hard for your body to carry a baby inside plus carry him outside for a long time, but that you love him and want to hug him and hold him as much as possible. Find as many opportunities to do that as you can.

8. **Be aware that your child may hear things that will worry him.** For instance, one five-year-old I know happened to see a soap opera at a neighbor's in which a pregnant woman's baby died at birth. Frightened, but scared to tell his mother about what he saw as a likely tragedy ahead, he became miserable and difficult. Luckily, instead of punishing him for his belligerence, his mother told him she thought he must be worried and upset. *"Are you worried about whether I will have enough time for you when the baby comes?"* she asked. *"No,"* he responded, *"I'm worried the baby will die!"* His mom was able to explain to him that most of the time in our country, modern medicine is able to keep babies and mothers completely safe. She pointed out all the families they knew who had babies, and how these babies had been safely born. After this conversation, the five-year-old relaxed and returned to his usual cheerful and cooperative self.

9. **Keep your relationship with your older child as smooth and affectionate as possible**, sidestepping power struggles and minimizing conflicts. She needs to be secure in your love

to handle the arrival of a sibling with equanimity. Naturally she'll be testing you to be sure you still love her.

10. **When you pack your bag for the hospital, involve your child. Prominently include a photo of her.** Also secretly pack a small present that you have bought and wrapped that will be from the new baby to each big sibling. You might want to include a card from the baby to the older sibling saying something like, *"Thank you for singing to me while I was growing. I am so excited to finally be ready to be born so I can be with you. I can't wait to learn from you and be friends with you. I feel so lucky that you are my big brother. I love how strong and gentle you are. I am tiny now but I promise to grow as fast as I can so I can play with you. I love our family."* Some parents object to this, because of course the baby had nothing to do with this card and gift. But I have never heard of an older sibling questioning it; they all love it. If your child does ask, you can simply explain that the baby can't talk yet, but if she could, this is what she would say.

Weaning Versus Tandem Nursing

Tandem breastfeeding has built the most beautiful and loving bond between my toddler and baby. They love interacting with one another and the toddler has always been very tender and sweet with the baby. Breastfeeding has been such a wonderful way to reconnect and help my toddler come to terms with the big change in his life of a new sibling.
   —Grace

When I got pregnant with my daughter, my breasts were so sensitive that nursing my son made my skin crawl with revulsion. I finally decided that it would be better for my son to wean him than to grit my teeth every time I nursed him.

—Tara

If you are still happily nursing an older child, and plan on nursing your new baby, you have a big decision to make. Should you wean your nursling, or plan to tandem-nurse?

This is a very personal decision. It depends on how old your child is, and how ready he or she is to wean. It also depends on your own reactions, which might be hard to predict right now. Some experts think that the pain or revulsion sometimes felt by pregnant women toward their nurslings is nature's way of letting them know their body can only grow one child at a time. Of course, extended nursing with a limited food supply probably also meant that in the past, menses returned more slowly after childbirth, so children were naturally spaced farther apart than in many families today.

Deciding whether to tandem-nurse is a big decision, one that it's worth doing some research on, to find out what other families have experienced. Many mothers swear by tandem nursing, saying that it fostered a close relationship between their children. Since babies receive oxytocin in breast milk and their bodies make more of it in response to nursing, it makes sense that they feel warmth toward the sibling with whom they share their nursing experience.[5] Most mothers say that the pain and revulsion vanishes once the baby is born, and having an older child helps regulate the amount of milk, so it's easier to begin breastfeeding your infant.

If you decide to tandem nurse, it often works best if your older child is night-weaned, and has set nursing times (such as bedtime and waking up) rather than nursing on demand. That way, you won't feel so overwhelmed by your child demanding to nurse while you're first starting a nursing relationship with your new baby. In the meantime, manage any negative physiological reactions by shortening nursing times during your pregnancy. Tell your child that you will sing a very short song or count to a certain number, and when you finish, he needs to be done nursing.

If you decide to wean, I assure you that your older child will adapt. The best way to support her through that process is to start now so that you can proceed gradually and have her completely weaned at least three months before your infant arrives. Weaning is beyond the scope of this book, but there's more advice on gentle weaning on AhaParenting.com.

Preparing Your Child for the Separation During the Upcoming Birth

Many women worry about leaving their older child when they go to the hospital to give birth to their baby. It doesn't help that labor is by definition unpredictable in both onset and length, making it even harder to prepare a child who is often little more than a baby himself.

It is, of course, possible for the older child to stay with the non-pregnant partner, rather than being left with a friend or relative. But we also know that labor advances faster when women have support from a loved one, so most of the time families choose for a woman's partner to stay with her during labor, while the older child is left in someone else's care. (Planning a home birth, so there's no separation? Skip ahead to the next section.)

How do we prepare our older baby, toddler, or preschooler for this separation from Mom, and maybe even from home?

1. **Strengthen your relationship with your child now.** Your little one might well have a hard time during your absence from her. But a close relationship with you will provide the buffer she needs to recover quickly.

2. **Pick the person who will take care of your little one while you are having the baby, and start working with that person to prepare your child.** Leave him with that person as often as possible, for short and then increasingly longer periods of time. Try to arrange, after months of this, for your child to nap there in order to get comfortable falling asleep. If your child does well napping, consider a sleepover—but don't push it. If your child isn't ready, it isn't worth the potential trauma. If the birth requires a sleepover, so be it because it's unavoidable, but that one night should be the only night unless your child is completely comfortable with this person.

3. **Don't try to get your child used to separation in general by leaving her with other people frequently.** That will just traumatize her. The goal is not to help her get used to separation and being with random people, because that is not how attachment works. The goal is to help her build a relationship with your designated person, whoever it will be, so that person can comfort her during your absence. The only thing that will help her cope with your absence is the presence of someone she trusts.

4. **Your goal is to help your designated person learn to calm your child.** It's okay if your little one cries. What matters is that he has someone to comfort him while he cries, who won't just leave him to cry himself to sleep. Kids can make it through anything if they have a trusted person to give them love and empathy when they're upset.

5. **Start preparing your little one by talking** about how you will go to the hospital to have the baby and she will be with (your friend? Grandma?), but you will come to retrieve her

soon. You should stress that you *always* come back to her. Make it a little mantra: *"And then Mommy will come and scoop you up because Mommy ALWAYS comes back!"*

6. **Make a transition book for him.** (Discussed later in this chapter.)

7. **Help your little one develop some feeling of being comforted by a stuffed animal or lovey or a clothing item of yours,** preferably smelling like you. No object will ever substitute for a person, but children can find comfort in a familiar object that they associate with safety and with parents. Let the person who will care for your child during your labor use this comfort object to help your child when she's upset.

8. **Stay positive and have confidence in your child.** Your little one will weather this, even if he cries himself to sleep in the arms of his caregiver. Your love and attention before and after will make all the difference in his being able to handle the challenge.

If You're Planning to Have Your Child at the Birth

For us what has worked like a charm three times was having the older child be present when the new baby is born. They have felt each child is part of the family in a way that we don't need to preach. They were there to see the new baby arrive into their lives and to this day they love each other.
—Atzimba

Many parents who had an uneventful first delivery are excited about the idea of including their older child in the magical moment of birth.

My own four-year-old son came to the birth center with us and built a new Lego while I labored. He was present for his sister's birth, up near my head, holding my hand. He loved welcoming his baby sister into the family, and even though he has certainly felt normal sibling jealousy, he has always been very protective of his little sister.

Given the unpredictability of the birth process, this is only a desirable plan if you've arranged for a relative—someone your child is close to—to be with her during labor. This person's job is to whisk your child away if the birth gets complicated, or she gets overwhelmed or simply bored. The support person has to understand that she may miss the actual birth.

If you decide to go this route, be sure you prepare your child so she knows what to expect.

1. **Read lots of birth books together.** There's a list of recommended books on AhaParenting.com.

2. **Watch birth videos** that are appropriate for children. You can find "Birth Day" on DVD on Amazon, or "Gentle Birth Choices" on YouTube, and your local library may have other videos that you can watch with your child. Her reaction can be a useful indicator as to whether she's ready to attend the actual birth.

3. **Let him help you push a large piece of furniture across the room.** Point out that "labor" means work and is even more work than pushing furniture, and that making loud noises, straining, and sweating help you work harder.

4. **Explain in detail what will happen.** It's important that your child know what to expect, including that the cord bleeds when it's cut, and that it doesn't hurt the baby.

5. **Prepare your child for the way the baby will look.** Newborns famously look red, pinched, and wizened.

6. **Tell her about her birth.** Children love to hear their own birth stories. It makes them feel special, and it prepares them to attend the birth.

Creating a Transition Book for Your Child

Stories that reflect their experience help children make sense of their world. Books explain what to expect, so kids feel less frightened and more able to cope. A book also gives your child the "happy ending" that is vitally important in how we remember and process events. That's why making a personalized book that includes a happy ending is useful whenever your child is faced with a big transition.

Since the separation from you when the baby is born can set the tone for the sibling's arrival, you might want to create a book that focuses just on the pregnancy and separation. Later, once you're sleeping through the night again, you might want to make another book about the sibling relationship (see page 187 for making a sibling book). Even if your little one doesn't have a lot of words yet, his receptive language capacity is far beyond his expressive language abilities, so he understands much more than you think. A personalized book of his own will help him understand even more.

You can find an example—*Nate Gets a Baby Brother*—at AhaParenting.com, which you can download as a Word document and personalize.

Making an Activity Box for Your Child

You'll be feeding the new baby many times each day, and you'll need something for your older child to do. I suggest that you find a plastic bin—your child's new activity box—that you can lift with one hand. Then, set up twenty-one different activities, such as sensory bags or bins, so that you can rotate them, putting three new ones a day in the activity box. By the time your child sees each one again, it will be a week later, and he'll still be fascinated by it.

Wondering what a "sensory bag" is? It's a heavy-duty zip-lock bag that you fill with clear hair gel and tiny objects like toy fish or animals. You can add food coloring and sparkles, and be sure to reinforce the seal with duct tape so when your child mashes it around to examine the contents, it won't pop open. "Sensory bins" are simply plastic containers with objects that your child can safely play with, like a funnel with some black beans. They're a wonderful way to contain a mess while you give your child an open-ended play experience. You can find hundreds of wonderful, easy sensory bin and bag ideas online for babies through preschoolers.

Round out the activity box with some bubble wrap, stickers, and a small colander with pipe cleaners to thread. And of course, when anyone asks what you need for the baby, ask for activities your older child can do alone, and add them to the activity box.

Is this overkill? I don't think so. Given how much time you'll spend feeding the baby or getting her to sleep, and how that's guaranteed to push your older child's buttons, this is a really smart way of tending to your child's needs and protecting your relationship with him. In my view, it's a lot more important than painting the baby's room (the baby doesn't care) or most of the other things we do to get ready for a new baby.

Work Through Your Own Emotions About Having a Second Child

When Asher was born, I grieved daily for the loss of my exclusive relationship with Everest. Just as becoming a mother for the first time is accompanied by a panoply of sacrifices, so there's an inevitable and essential grieving process when becoming a mother of two.

—Sheryl Paul, *Conscious Transitions*[6]

Most parents experience both excitement and trepidation as they look forward to the arrival of their second child. If you notice that you're feeling some anxiety about the changes ahead, don't ignore it. Address it. Notice if you have some particular thought that's creating these feelings. For instance: *"I still remember how upset I was when my little brother was born. I'm afraid I'm re-creating that situation, and ruining my daughter's life."*

Ask yourself if that thought is accurate. Sure, your daughter will have a big adjustment. But maybe her little brother will be a blessing to her, one of the very best things in her whole long life. Don't let your own experience shadow hers.

Once you've looked at the thoughts that are creating your feelings, notice the feelings themselves. Once we're feeling something—regardless of the thought that triggered that feeling—the only way past that emotion is through it. Sit, notice the feelings in your body, and watch them change and dissipate as you breathe through them.

Loving Each Child Best

If you have only one child and are looking forward to another, you may well wonder how you will ever love your second child as much as your first. Most parents feel some apprehension about this. And many parents say that when the second child is born, they felt fiercely protective of the new baby, but they worried because they didn't feel the same depth of love immediately. That's natural. While protectiveness of our children is instinctive, love is something that we create. Every interaction with a new baby is another brick in the foundation of our relationship with this new person and builds the connection. Over time, you will find yourself in a relationship with your second child that is equal in power to the relationship you have with your first—but different, because each child is a unique person, and also because this time around you're different, too. Each child needs different things from you, and you naturally respond to meet those needs.

What does this mean for sibling rivalry? It means that despite the fears that most parents have as they move toward welcoming a second child, you can, and will, love your second as much as your first. What's more, as Nancy Samalin says in her book *Loving Each One Best*, you can love each child *best*, which means you fully meet each child's needs so he isn't craving what someone else is getting.[7] Every child needs to feel seen and valued, but because each child is unique, children need different things from you to feel loved. Maybe your oldest feels deeply loved when you hold him on your lap to read to him, while your second child feels really loved when you take the time to sew his torn Superman costume, and your third needs you to laugh and roughhouse with her. Loving each one best means you love them in the way that makes them feel deeply loved, so they know that their needs will always be met. Their siblings will become blessings, not threats, once they understand that no matter what their sibling gets, there is more than enough for them ... And that you could never love anyone more than you love them.

10

Getting Off to a Good Start: Birth and the First Few Months

You're bringing home the new baby! Naturally, what you want is for your older child to fall in love with this new sibling, so you can all live happily ever after.

Usually, just so you know, it doesn't happen quite like that. In fact, it's completely natural for your older child to have mixed feelings when you bring home another baby. While she's certainly excited about the baby, seeing you and all those visitors cooing over him may well produce panic. She knows she shouldn't feel that way, so she may stuff those feelings, but that might well end in tantrums.

Don't worry, this phase is temporary. The more you can stay calm and reassuring, the faster your child will learn that she's still loved as much as ever. This chapter has lots of ideas to support your older child during your first months as a growing family. But please don't feel like you have to do them all. The most important thing is for your child to have parents who are enjoying him. Everything else is gravy.

Introducing Your Child to the New Baby

We let the older kids kiss, hold, touch, and smell the new baby. We never say, "Don't touch the baby, come away from the baby, leave the baby alone"... The new baby belongs to his older brother and sister too, so lots of cuddling and holding needs to take place for that bond to form.
    —Kell

1. **Think through the introduction.** If your child is not present at the birth, you will want her to visit you as quickly as possible after the baby is born, when other visitors aren't there. Emphasize your joy at seeing her, rather than your preoccupation with the new baby. For her, it's likely that the separation from you was the big deal. The baby may be almost an afterthought, and that's fine. The baby isn't going anywhere.

   When you bring your newborn into the house for the first time, let someone else carry the baby in. It's best if the mother, and if possible both parents, can enter with their arms open wide to hug their older child or children.

2. **Use pheromones.** Let your child sit and hold the baby, helping him to support her head. Dr. Lawrence Aber, a bonding expert, says that babies' heads give off pheromones, and when we inhale them, we fall in love, and begin to feel protective.[1] The more your older child snuggles his new sib, the more protective he'll feel toward her.

3. **Express goodwill with a gift exchange.** Let your older child help you choose a lovey (a special blanket or soft toy) for your

newborn before the birth. Then, once the children have met and had time to bond a bit, have a little gift exchange. Give your child a card and wrapped present addressed to him, from the baby. Tell the older sib how grateful the baby is for big brother's care and protection. Let big brother "help" the baby open the lovey he has wrapped for her, and explain to the baby how the big sib picked it out. Tell big brother how much the baby loves it, and loves him. Why, she already recognizes his voice, and soon she'll be able to watch him do so many things. This little ritual goes a long way to create a positive feeling toward the baby. And because the lovey will be important to your infant, your older child will be able to take pride in it for years. (It also greatly reduces the chance that your older child will tease your younger by playing keep-away with her lovey.)

4. **Limit visitors, even extended family.** It's usually best to keep the first day just for immediate family. Kids (and parents) get overwhelmed with the stimulation of too many visitors. Some parents assume it's best to send their older child off to the park with Grandpa. But what kids need most is the chance to bond with parents and the new sibling as a family without other people around, so be sure there's plenty of time for that.

The First Week: Settling In as a Family

It seemed to help a lot when I would "tell" our infant son out loud that I needed to do something for my older son. I think that made him feel important and like everything wasn't about the baby.
   —Annie

Most children are initially very excited about the new arrival. But as they see how the baby's needs are dominating their parents' attention, they often begin to get uncomfortable. When the baby is still there day after day, and the child is continually asked to accommodate to the baby's needs above his own, he often falls apart. This is a completely normal reaction and will subside as your child realizes that his needs are still being met, his parents still delight in him, and being a big brother can actually be a bit like being a superhero. You can hasten that realization by being aware of how your child is feeling.

1. **Enjoy your older children; don't make everything about the baby.** Remember that she wonders if she's still important to you, so all she really wants is to feel the warmth of your love.

2. **Include your child as you care for the baby.** It's always more work for you to include your older child, but he needs to know that he has an important role to play as big brother, and that he is not being left out. *"Your brother is fussing . . . I wonder what he needs? He's just been fed and burped. Do you want to help me sing to him?"* Remember, you're inviting your child to participate, not pressing him into service. Most young children love to be helpful and will take pride in being your assistant, running to get wipes or throw away diapers. If your child rebuffs your invitation, no worries. Offer again next time, and every time. When your child does participate, acknowledge with gratitude: *"Thank you for getting these wipes. This is just what I needed, and it was so helpful to me not to have to get up."* Your child will glow with pride as he learns that part of becoming a big brother means being able to contribute in new ways to the family.

3. **Talk to the baby about her big sister.** Go ahead and coo to your infant. But in your older child's hearing, many of the

words that come out of your mouth could be about the big sib. *"You are so lucky to have Brooklyn for a big sister . . . she's been reading about babies and taking care of her doll; she knows just what babies need . . . And wait until she shows you how she can turn the light on all by herself!"*

4.   **When you have to leave your child to pick up the baby,** put it in context. Naturally, your older child experiences your walking away as a mini-abandonment and begins to resent hearing the baby waking up on the monitor. Get in the habit of saying, *"There's the baby . . . He's waking up . . . He wants to play with you! Let's go get him!"* Give your child an excited hug and take him with you if he'll go. If not, say, *"I'll bring him to you!"* Help your older child to feel like she doesn't always come second by telling the baby, at times when he is actually quiet and happy, *"I am helping your sister with her shoes right now, so I can't pick you up yet. I will be with you in a little bit. Everyone has to wait a little bit sometimes."*

5.   **Let your older child be the star of the show.** Call visitors before they come to suggest that instead of a "new baby" present, they consider a "big brother or sister" present. Ask visitors to greet your older child first and make a loving connection with her for a few minutes before they even mention the baby. Tell them that big sister will be the one to take them in and introduce them to her new baby brother. If visitors do bring baby presents, let your child do the unwrapping and help present the gift to the baby.

6.   **Take a photo of your older child or children holding the baby,** and send that as your birth announcement, so the lime-

light is shared. You can even say, *"Max is proud to announce the arrival of his sister, Tess,"* so Max feels that glow of pride.

7. **Keep to your older child's regular schedule as much as possible.** Of course, things will change after a new baby joins the family. But if your child is used to snuggle time as he wakes up every morning, find a way for him to still get that time to anchor him for the day. Don't expect your child to want to hang around the house staring at the new baby. He needs a larger world, to keep the baby in perspective. Take him to the playground or park to run around. Let him go on "special" errands with one parent while the other parent stays with the baby. If he goes to school, send a snack for the class with a photo of big brother holding his new baby.

8. **Remember your older child is still very little.** Even if he's five! Seriously, your child will look so big next to your infant that it will be easy to expect him to act more mature than his age. And given the stress on him, he's likely to act *less* mature, at least right now. Expect regression. He deserves your babying, too.

9. **Let your child know her needs still matter.** Your infant's needs do come first. No, an infant won't consciously remember that you left him to cry while tending to older siblings, but his brain is taking shape daily based on your responsiveness. Your older child, hopefully, has been getting her needs met all along, and will be able to tolerate short delays. Help her wait by letting her know that you *want* to help her and will be right there "as soon as my hands are free," without placing "blame" on the baby.

10. **Be sure your child gets time with both parents.** Often, parents assume that Dad should become the primary care-taker of the older child. But your child has a separate relationship with each parent (as discussed in the previous chapter). She needs both of those relationships to be nurtured. As soon as the baby is fed, give him to Dad to coo over, and let Mom have some time with big sister.

11. **Eat, love, play.** Nothing will reassure your child that she's still loved as much as your genuine enjoyment of her. A few minutes of belly laughter will reconnect you and help your child feel less worried. You'll probably feel too tired to rough-house, so try the Earthquake game from Anthony DeBenedet, which you can play lying down: Let your child sit on you, while you roll from side to side, rumbling, until you finally throw her off. The suspense should be just as much fun as the final "earthquake."[2]

12. **Postpone anything but love.** Naturally, you're exhausted. Please don't let any of these suggestions make you feel over-whelmed. The only thing your children really need is parents who love and enjoy them, and you can't be that parent unless you give yourself support. So don't add these suggestions to your to-do list. Instead, throw out the to-do list and focus on love—for yourself and your children and partner. If the rest of life seems disorganized, that's fine—it means you're focusing on what matters most. Eat takeout, or ask visitors to bring food instead of presents, or have the freezer stocked in advance. Wear clothes straight from the dryer. Don't try to do anything but love your kids and sleep for the first week. No, make that the first month. At least.

How to Keep Your Child Occupied While You Feed the Baby

Things really went bad when I started locking myself in the baby's room to nurse her. I left my three-year-old watching TV. He hated it, but I had to do it. Otherwise, he would jump all over us. But I don't think he ever got over me doing that and he's still very cold to her, a year later.

—Melanie

My two-year-old used to get so naughty when I'd sit down to nurse his sister. There was really nothing I could do to get him to obey me. So I started trying to predict when she would need to nurse, and to give him some really focused attention before she woke up hungry. Then I would read to him while I fed her. It made a huge difference.

—Becky

Our genetics are from the Stone Age, since evolution proceeds very slowly. Your children are designed to notice when your attention is elsewhere (baby, computer, phone). They don't feel completely safe at those times. What if a tiger jumps out of the bushes while you're distracted? They feel an urgent need at those moments to get your attention. It's a matter of survival.

Given that you'll be feeding your infant many times a day, and it's bound to trigger your child's anxiety every single time—really!— it's smart to give some thought in advance to how to occupy your older child while you're feeding the baby.

1. **Before you feed the baby,** be sure you spend some time connecting with your older child. It's best if you can roughhouse with him a bit to get him laughing. This will ease his fears,

help him feel more bonded to you, and make it less likely that he'll jump all over you and the baby.

2. **Welcome your child to stay close.** Even if you love rocking chairs, it's worth figuring out a way to get comfortable with your newborn on the couch or a bed instead of in a rocking chair, so your older child can snuggle up, too.

3. **Have a simple snack and/or drink ready for your child.** This is especially reassuring for toddlers who weaned more recently, because they can't help feeling a bit envious about the baby eating.

4. **Offer to read to her.** Have a stack of ever-changing library books nearby that will hold your child's interest. If she knows that when the baby eats, she gets a story, she'll be much less jealous of those nonstop feeding times.

5. **Let her engage in a parallel caretaking activity.** If you're nursing, suggest he nurse his baby. If you're bottle-feeding, be sure he has a toy bottle.

6. **Pull out the activity box** that you made while you were pregnant (see "Making an Activity Box" on page 237).

7. **If she doesn't want to play with the activity box,** it might be that she needs more connection with you. Invite her to sing songs with you while you feed the baby.

8. **What if he still acts out while you feed the baby?** Sometimes, no matter how you prepare with other activities, your child will jump all over you while you try to feed the baby.

The solution to this is roughhousing with lots of laughter *before* the baby needs to eat, which gets your older child relaxed and ready to sit and read with you. But there will be times when the baby wakes unexpectedly and needs to eat, and your older child isn't cooperating. One handy solution at those moments is to take both kids into the bathroom. Run the bath and help your older child into the tub. Give him toys or bubbles. Sit watching him play while you feed the baby. It's not the most comfortable place for you to feed the baby, but the bath will calm your child, the baby won't get jumped on, and you won't find yourself yelling. If your older child is too little to be in the tub without you right next to him, a backup plan is to strap him into the high chair with something really good to eat or play with, while you sit next to him feeding the baby.

Helping Your Child with Her Mixed Emotions About the Baby

She often said in the beginning months that she wished she didn't have a sister. I never tried to "correct" her feelings. By about six months she began to say, "I really love our new baby!" They are great playmates now at ages five and two.

—Kari

Your child is bound to have some complicated feelings about the baby's arrival. If you can accept those feelings as normal, so will he. That gives them less power. Over time, his fear will settle down, his love will grow, and his relationship with his sibling will blossom.

By contrast, if he thinks his jealousy isn't permissible, he'll push it down, out of consciousness. But stuffing emotions causes anxiety and rigidity, because we have to work hard to keep them down.

What's more, emotions don't stay stuffed; they pop out again. And because they're not under conscious control, they often take the form of aggression, defiance, clinginess, or whining. If your child begins exhibiting behaviors you can't explain—waking up at night, peeing all over the house—it's a good bet he needs some help with his emotions.

Children adapt best to new siblings when parents make it clear that all feelings are normal and acceptable, even while not all actions are permitted.

1. **If your child expresses negativity toward the baby,** acknowledge it, accept it, and let him know such feelings are okay to share with you. *"You wonder if we can send her back? . . . I know, it's a big change for all of us and sometimes you wish things could be the way they were before . . . No, sweetie, she's part of our family now just like you and me and Mom, so she will live with us from now on . . . That's making you cry, I see . . . I know that isn't the answer you wanted, and sometimes it's hard to get used to this big change . . . But you can always tell me if you're feeling like this and I will always understand."*

2. **Don't be surprised if your child grieves.** Once you've made it clear that the baby is here to stay, many children will grieve about it. That's a good thing, because once your child allows herself to grieve, she stops fighting and starts adapting. To help her through the grieving, just acknowledge her sadness. *"You're feeling sad right now, huh? It's okay to feel sad. Why don't we get your lovey and you can snuggle up with me on the couch?"*

3. **What if your child doesn't bring up any jealousy or upset?** Give permission for him to express whatever he's feeling. *"Sometimes big brothers worry that moms and dads won't have*

time for them any more once there's a new baby. I want you to know that no matter how much love and care your sister needs and gets, there will always be more than enough for you. I could never love anyone more than you. If you ever feel mad or sad or left out, I want you to tell me. I am always here to help you feel better. Okay?" No, you're not giving him ideas. He's bound to have negative feelings as well as positive ones about this big change, and if he thinks having negative feelings is a terrible thing, he'll feel like a terrible person inside. You don't want those feelings eating away at him and causing bad behavior or resentment of his sibling.

4. **But then won't he "act jealous" just to get attention?** Are you rewarding hungry, cranky children with food? Seriously, if your child needs attention so much that he acts out to get it, then he *needs* your attention! Schedule Special Time with you that he can count on every day, and he won't need to act out to get attention.

5. **When strangers admire the baby, be sure to include your older child.** *"Yes, the baby's so lucky that he takes after his handsome big brother."*

6. **Help your child conceptualize that the baby will grow and change.** Of course you know that in a few years your children will be playing together. But your child can't imagine that this screaming baby could ever be a playmate, and he's bound to feel terribly disappointed. Talk about how when he was a baby, he was helpless, too, and everyone fussed over him, and he grew and grew and look at him now! Show him pictures of when he was born and how he grew, so that he can imagine his new sibling growing, too.

7. **Get both sides of his brain involved.** Your child might not be able to verbalize his feelings, but visuals will help him understand. You might draw a heart with all your children inside. Jane Nelsen suggests using candles to illustrate to your child that your love isn't diminished by loving her sibling. *"This is the Mommy candle. This flame represents my love. This is the Daddy candle."* (Use the flame from the Mommy candle to light the Daddy candle.) *"When I married your daddy, I gave him all my love—and I still have all my love left."* (Put the larger candles in holders and light a smaller candle from them.) *"This candle is for you. When you were born, I gave you all my love. And look, Daddy still has all my love, and I still have all my love left."* (Put the smaller candle in a holder and light a still smaller candle from the Mommy candle.) *"This is for your baby brother. When he was born I gave him all my love. And look—you still have all my love. Daddy has all my love. And I still have all my love left because you can give love to everyone you love and still have all your love. Now look at all the light we have in our family with all this love."*[3]

What About Those Overzealous Hugs?

We practice gentleness daily. I hold my son's hand and teach him how to pat lightly and give gentle high fives. Once my daughter started crawling, they started a crawling game where they chase each other. He's now four and she's sixteen months. He makes her laugh more than anyone else, and although gentleness is still a daily challenge, they're good buddies.
　—Maureen

Young children are still learning to regulate themselves, so it makes sense that they have to learn how big a hug the baby likes. But often children get rough with the baby under the guise of playfulness or affection. That's to be expected. After all, they feel two ways at once—affection and jealousy. Your child is not trying to be malicious. Just take a deep breath and say, *"That's a bit rough, see his face? He's telling you he's scared. Here, I will help you be gentle."* Intercept her hands, and show her how to be gentle. If necessary, lift the baby away and comfort him.

Aggression comes from fear, so unnecessary roughness can often be solved by giving your child a chance to work though those fears by roughhousing with you. If you can work a little preventive maintenance roughhousing into your day while the baby is asleep, you'll probably notice that your child is gentler later on.

But in those moments when she's finding it hard to be gentle, redirecting that impulse toward you will help. *"Look at your sister's face . . . She looks frightened. What do you think she's telling you? That's right; that's too wild for her. Are you feeling wild right now? Want to play bucking bronco with me?"*

If your child resists your diversion and continues to press herself on the baby, set a clear limit by stopping her physically. Say, *"You really want to connect with your sister right now, I know. That's too much force for a baby. You can be wild with me."*

Either she'll take your invitation, or she'll continue to resist. The resistance is a clear indicator that those feelings are bubbling up strongly and she's ready to show them to you. In fact, she's being provocative precisely to get you to help her with her feelings. If you can summon up all your compassion and soften yourself, your child may even burst into tears at this point. Hold her and keep your words to a minimum: *"I am right here to hold you; you're safe; everyone needs to cry sometimes."* You'll find that after she cries, she'll be much more relaxed—and gentler with the baby.

Regression: When Your Child Goes Backward

The baby's arrival was a brutal experience for my two-year-old, so much so that it was heartbreaking to see her pain. Today my littlest is five months old and they love each other so so much.

—Esther

Parents often panic when their child regresses. They know he can dress himself and hold a spoon and use the potty—he's been doing it for months. Now, suddenly, he can't, or at least he won't. Shouldn't they insist? After all, they have a new baby to tend to; the older child will just have to get used to being a bit more independent.

Don't worry; it's completely appropriate for children to regress when a baby joins the family. What's regression? It's when a child finds the challenges of her life too overwhelming, so she stops tackling new hurdles, and in fact becomes unable to sustain some of her recent accomplishments. Since handling the birth of a new sibling asks so much of young children, it's not surprising that most of them regress a bit. That means she may begin to wake up more at night, or have potty accidents, or have more meltdowns, or whine for your help constantly. You can minimize your child's regression by seeing it from her point of view. She's overwhelmed, and doing the best she can to cope, and it all seems a bit much. She's also asking if you love her as much as you used to, and as much as you love the baby. The more you communicate that the answer is a resounding Yes!, the more quickly your child will be able to act her age again.

1. **Remind yourself that regression is normal and temporary.** Yes, I know, it's inconvenient. But there's no emergency. If you get upset, it will just overwhelm your child more, and make more regression more likely.

The calmer you stay about this, the more quickly your child will get back on track.

2. **Communicate acceptance to your child.** No, she won't decide that she should give up the potty forever. Discipline or shame will just set her back. Instead, say, *"It's okay, sweetie. Everything has been different around here lately... Don't worry, soon things will feel normal again, and you'll remember to get to the potty every time."*

3. **Baby her.** While it's fine to emphasize the advantages of being older (*"You get to have cookies because you're three; your brother can't have cookies yet because he's a baby"*), be sure you also snuggle her and tell her that she'll always be your baby girl, no matter how big she gets. Some older sibs will ask to "play" baby, but even if she doesn't ask, she'll love it if you kiss her toes and play the same games she sees you play with the baby. When she climbs into the baby's stroller or crib, pretend that you're thrilled by this fabulous big baby: *"Amazing, a baby who can TALK!... What a wonderful baby!"*

4. **Help him when he asks.** Most parents worry that they shouldn't do things for their child that he can do for himself. So when he begs you to help him get dressed, it's natural to tell him that you know he can do it himself. But if he can't get you to baby him by helping him get dressed, he'll probably regress in other ways that are even harder to handle. Besides, he's showing you that he needs something from you—to know that you're still available when he needs you. Every sibling needs to know that no matter what his sibling gets, his needs will be met, too. Don't worry; he won't expect you to dress him forever.

WHEN KIDS REGRESS . . .

Instead of Expecting Independence

Try Empathy

Left: Remember that your child may look big compared to the baby, but he's still very small. If you don't respond to his need to be babied, it will come out in less pleasant ways.

Right: Once children are reassured that you're there for them if they need you, they're free to move on to age-appropriate independence.

5. **What if she asks to nurse?** Most kids won't be able to successfully latch on, even if they used to nurse, so usually they try once and wonder what all the fuss is about. If you're not willing to indulge such a request, decide that in advance and come up with a way to set the limit that takes the sting out of it. To me, this is the time for a shameless sweetener: *"Your little sister can't eat food yet like you can, so we need to save the mommy milk for her. I know, let's get you a big-girl drink in a cup. How about some chocolate milk?"*

Managing Naptime and Bedtime with More Than One Child

We have had a family bed since my first daughter was born. Now with three girls (the five-year-old is starting to move to her own bed), I think it has made a difference in their relationship, having that closeness every night. No matter what happens during the day, we all snuggle up every evening.

—Kera

What's hardest about having more than one child is those moments when they both need you at the same time. Most of the time, you can multitask well enough to muddle through. *"Come sit with me while I feed the baby and I'll read you a book"* may not fully satisfy your toddler, but unless she's upset, it usually works, as long as you're doing preventive maintenance throughout the day. But what about those times when you need more quiet to put the baby to sleep and there's no other adult to supervise your older child? This is a challenge worth thinking through in advance.

First, don't expect a toddler, or even most preschoolers, to be able to entertain himself. A child left alone while you put the baby to bed is likely to make noise, make a mess, or do something he knows is forbidden, like draw on the couch. Not surprisingly, most parents react to this as willful misbehavior deserving of harsh punishment. But from the child's perspective, it makes complete sense that when you go off with the baby and shut the door, all of her jealousy gets triggered. Look at it this way. It's like watching your romantic partner go into the bedroom with someone else, someone you suspect your partner finds more attractive than you. Wouldn't you feel like acting out?

So what do you do when it's naptime?

1. **As always before devoting your attention to the baby, find a way to give your older child some focused connection first.** Getting her laughing is the most effective preparation since it helps her work through any emotions that will otherwise drive her to act out. But even a hug and some nuzzling might be enough.

2. **Then occupy your older child with something totally engrossing,** such as an audiobook or a video. Even if you're generally opposed to TV for young children (which I am), the benefit of keeping your older child safely occupied while you get the baby to sleep might make the compromise of one video a day worth it to you. Audiobooks are even better because they're actually good for children; they stimulate a different part of the brain that's linked to the imagination. If your child will wear headphones, it shuts out distractions (including you singing to the baby) and further "anchors" the child in place so he's less likely to go exploring in dangerous places. (Of course, we're assuming your house is baby-proofed, since toddlers have a way of finding trouble.) If your child is too active to settle with an audiobook, ask him to draw the scenes he's hearing about as he listens, so he can share them with you (washable markers only, of course). Another advantage to headphones is that he can sit right in the room with you (maybe set him up with his back to you?) and usually stay quiet enough to let you get the baby to sleep. (Of course, this won't work with exuberant kids who shriek with laughter at the funny parts.)

3. **"Don't wake the baby!"** Young children often feel small and powerless. So when they suddenly start hearing "Don't wake the baby!" all day long, it's not surprising that they act like

they've discovered a special superpower. How can they resist testing it out? Especially when there's the side benefit of "getting even" with the baby, who has just monopolized you for so long while you got him to sleep, leaving big sister cooling her heels in the other room.

When your child purposely wakes the baby, it's not surprising if you want to throttle her. The worst part is that your child is working against her own self-interest, since this is the time you would have been able to spend with her. That's the problem with an immature prefrontal cortex—it's not so good at thinking through consequences. Be sure you're explicit, every single day, that you can't wait to spend time with her so you hope the baby will fall asleep quickly and stay asleep. If that doesn't work, and your child just can't resist waking the baby, it often works to give him an equally enticing power—over you! Put him in charge of keeping the house quiet during naptime: *"Do you want to be in charge of keeping the baby asleep so we can have Special Time with each other? That means it's your job to make sure we all remember to use our indoor voices. If I forget, it's your job to remind me, okay? You're in charge of keeping the house quiet."*

4. **Toddler naptime.** What about getting your toddler down for her nap when you now also have a baby to look after? My favorite answer is to lie down with both of them so they both go to sleep. You may have to nurse the baby (or give her a bottle) while you're reading to the toddler, but hopefully, your calming presence will soothe both of them into sleep—and you may get a nap, too, which you certainly need in those early months. If your toddler has a hard time settling, you may have to resort to short car trips, or putting the toddler into a stroller and going for a walk with the baby in a sling.

Baby, presumably, will also fall asleep, which moves your kids toward a similar sleep schedule, always a plus.

5. **Bedtime.** It can be hard for one parent to manage bedtime for both a baby and a toddler or preschooler. The good news about the family bed is that one parent can put both kids to bed at the same time, reading to one and feeding the other, with everyone falling asleep together. (If you're cosleeping with your older child, you'll need to give thought to how you'll keep the baby safe in your bed when there's also an older child, who might sometimes "wander" in her sleep.) But even if everyone will be sleeping in separate rooms, you can often feed an infant in the older child's room while reading the bedtime story. If the baby falls asleep and you can put him down, that's a big plus, so you can focus on your older child as you're saying goodnight.

The Early Months: The New Normal

When our new baby was born, I used "ventriloquy" to help the baby and my four-year-old bond. I would talk on her behalf with a cute voice and my son would talk back to her looking into her eyes and have a conversation with her. These early conversations really made a huge difference in their bonding and helped my son develop empathy for the baby. Eleven months on, they are the best of friends.
    —Bel Inda

In many families, Dad goes back to work after a week, and Mom is home with both the newborn and the older child. This can be a trying transition for everyone, leaving both Mom and kids in tears. But there are ways to make it easier.

1. **Prioritize family for at least a few months.**[4] Research shows that children adapt better to the arrival of a sibling if both parents are very involved. Presumably, the primary caretaker is less stressed, and there's more attention to go around. This isn't the time for either partner to be working late or traveling.

2. **The partner at home shouldn't expect to handle anything but the kids.** One partner may be back at work, but he or she can bring home dinner and do laundry. Sure, you're home during the day. But that doesn't mean you have a free moment. If you do, spend it connecting with your older child, to ease his adjustment. Both kids asleep? How lucky! Join them!

3. **Find ways to help your child feel connected to the baby.** That might be baby ventriloquy, or putting your child in charge of singing to the baby, or tandem nursing. But find ways for them to relate, even at this early stage.

4. **Think about how you phrase things.** If you're constantly giving your child directives based on the baby's needs, resentment will be the natural outcome.

   Instead of: *"When baby's finished eating . . ."*

   Try: *"I can't wait to play with you. I'll be there in five minutes . . . Tell me what we will do."*

   Instead of: *"I can't carry you right now, I'm carrying the baby."*

   Try: *"I will pick you up as soon as my hands are free . . . I can't wait . . . for now, can you snuggle up to me so we can be close close close?"*

5. **If your child has a hard time with the baby crying, empathize, then explain.** *"Yes, his crying is loud, isn't it? It can hurt your ears, I know . . . Crying is his words. That's how he talks to us and tells us he needs something. Can you help me guess what he needs?"* Putting on soothing music will probably help all of you. You can also give your child headphones to cancel out the noise, so he can play in peace.

When Your Child Has a Hard Time Adjusting

Let's look at two different scenarios of what happens to a young child when a sibling is born. The scenarios are identical: a two-year-old boy, a new little sister, a father who loves his family but works long hours, an exhausted mother. The difference? The child's relationship with his mother.

SCENARIO 1: WHEN OUR CONNECTION WITH OUR CHILD GETS FRAYED

Two-year-old Daniel doesn't understand why everyone is making such a fuss about the new baby. All she does is sleep, eat, and cry. She can't even play with him. Worse, his father is usually at work, and his mother is always sitting in the rocking chair feeding the baby. Daniel feels like every time he needs her, she says, *"You're a big boy, you can do that yourself."* Daniel responds by becoming weepy and whiny, which seems to irritate his mother even more. *"You're driving me crazy, Daniel!"*

Daniel gets frustrated more easily than usual these days. When he just feels overwhelmed by frustration or loneliness, and shouts *No!* in his mother's face, she yells and puts him in time-out. Daniel feels like he's all alone in the world, on his own to manage the big emotions that swamp him. He pushes them down, trying to be a good boy, so his mom will love him again. But because these repressed emotions are no longer under conscious control, they burst out in the form of aggression and tantrums. These feelings make him unpredictably rough with the baby, so his parents get tense when he shows interest in her, and warn him tersely about touching her. Daniel is convinced that he has to fight to get his needs met, so he sees no reason to compromise when what he wants is against the rules. He's more and more frequently belligerent, which means he gets yelled at more often and spends more time in time-out.

As the days go by, Daniel cries less and lashes out more. When his parents reach out to him, he's prickly, or finds a way to start a fight. He craves the connection, but because it makes him feel safe, it opens the floodgates to all those tears. So he pushes his parents away. He gets more rigid to keep the bad feelings down, insisting on having things his way and balking at parental attempts to guide him. Driven by primal needs for safety and connection that aren't being met because he's shutting his parents out, he develops strategies to meet them that aren't constructive, such as grabbing toys from the baby. But more of what he didn't need to begin with can't fill that deeper need for connection. Every day, his sister gets more irritating. She's showing interest in his toys now, and his parents seem totally enthralled with her. Daniel ignores her as much as possible, although sometimes his hostility bursts out and he yells at her or pushes her. He knows he "should" control himself, but he has no idea how. He concludes that he's simply a bad person, not worthy of the love he longs for.

SCENARIO 2: A BETTER CONNECTION

Two-year-old Devon doesn't understand why everyone is making such a fuss about the new baby. All she does is sleep, eat, and cry.

She can't even play with him. Worse, his father is usually at work, and his mother is always feeding the baby. At least she sits on the couch to feed the baby, and she always invites Devon to join her. She has a stack of books he loves next to the couch, and she always talks to him and encourages him to pick a book and snuggle up to her. The baby is right there in her lap, but his mother puts her arm around him and reads to him just as enthusiastically as she always has.

His mother encourages him to hold the baby, talk to her, and help her feel better when she cries. Devon feels proud when he's able to help by getting the wipes or singing to the baby. He gets frustrated more easily than usual these days, but his mother seems to understand. When Devon wants his mother's help, she says, *"Did you need a little help with that? My hands are busy, but bring it over here and let's see what we can do."* When Devon feels like crying, she says, *"Everything feels hard today, doesn't it? I feel like that, too, sometimes. Here, let's sit on the floor so I can hold both of you . . . There is always room for you in my arms."*

Sometimes he feels angry, especially when his mom is too busy to play with him. At those times, he shouts *No!* in her face and hurls himself to the floor, screaming. His mother just sits down on the floor with the baby in the sling on her body, and says, *"I'm right here . . . you're safe . . . I have a big hug when you're ready."* Devon ends up sobbing, with her arm around him. More and more, he's able to use his words when he gets upset, to say, *"I need a hug, Mommy!"* Slowly, he's coming to trust that his mother is still there for him. She puts the baby in a seat to watch, and chases him around and around the room until they both collapse laughing on the couch. Sometimes she even leaves the baby with his dad to take Devon to the park and spend time just with him, like she used to. Life is different with this baby around, but it's not all bad. The baby is even starting to smile when he makes faces at her.

Is it too late for Daniel? Many parents would throw up their hands at this point and try every punishment they could come up with, but that would only further diminish the trust level and worsen the child's behavior. The solution? This hurting child needs to feel the safety and connection with his parents that will allow him to work through all that hurt and pain and fear, which will allow him to feel more connected to his parents again. He'll gain the trust to cry instead of lashing out in rage when his feelings are hurt. With time, he'll empty that bulging emotional backpack so he has more emotional control. And that deep, sweet connection to his parents will reshape his view of himself as a good person who can choose not to act on those feelings of anger and jealousy. He'll even find room in his heart to appreciate his little sister.

Daily Practices to Stay Connected to Your Child Now That He Has to Share You

When my daughter was born, I strategically used the baby monitor to tell her how lucky she was to have her older brother and tell her lovely things about him (all true) while he "eavesdropped" on the monitor downstairs. That was eight years ago and they are best of friends.

—Rhona

You have a new baby in the family, so you're by definition tired and probably overwhelmed. It can be daunting to think that now, in addition to everything your infant needs, you have to pay special attention to what your older child needs. The good news is that a little time every day on preventive maintenance will usually keep

everyone on a more even keel, so you can avoid breakdowns and
enjoy your children more. So think of these habits as a way of life
that you can develop, so they don't take any extra energy.

1. **Connect with each child physically every morning.** If
   you've been up in the night feeding a baby, it will be hard to
   welcome your older child when he comes racing into your
   room at the crack of dawn. But spending five or ten minutes
   snuggling with him can change the whole tone of your morning. Look at it this way. He's been disconnected from you all
   night. He needs to reconnect to feel secure in the world, to
   refill his love tank. Then he'll be ready to rise to the challenges of the day.

2. **Get in the habit of reconnecting warmly with each child
   every hour.** Life with kids, especially when one is a baby, can
   feel like total chaos. If it feels that way to you, imagine how
   it feels to your child. His sense of time is different. He can
   lose himself in his toy cars for an hour while you feed and
   tend to the baby, so it's easy for him to start feeling disconnected from you. When you have a moment while your little
   one is happily staring at a sunbeam, grab it to go sit with your
   older child. Be sure that when you have to excuse yourself to
   tend to the baby, you give him a warm hug and tell him how
   much you loved being with him. (Yes, I know that means the
   dishes get left sitting in the sink. Let them go. You're working
   round the clock with the new baby and your other child(ren);
   your partner can do the dishes after work.)

3. **Sit on the floor with your baby.** If your child is usually sitting
   on the floor playing, she looks up, and there you are on the
   couch holding the baby. If, instead, you can find a way to get

comfortable on the floor next to your child while she's play-ing, you ease that separation. She feels like you're more avail-able. Often, the baby will be happy on a blanket, waving her arms and watching you interact with her big sibling. Babies love to watch big kids.

4. **Wear your baby to keep your hands free for your older child or children.** Babies need a significant amount of hold-ing. But they don't need constant eye contact and interaction—that's too much pressure—as long as they can get it when they want it. In fact, anthropology tells us that babies are "designed" to learn by observing life, including family life, from the safety of the parent's chest or back. So wearing your baby is good for the baby, and leaves your hands and attention free for your other child or children. Slings have the added benefit of keeping the baby a bit less acces-sible to the older child, so he can't "share" his toys by putting them on her head. You can even nurse in the sling, so that you can sit on the floor interacting with your older child at the same time.

5. **Connect with your child after every separation.** If your older child goes to school, remember that she's returning to you with a full emotional backpack of experiences from her day. She'll need your loving attention to refuel. If someone else is bringing her home, try to put your infant down to have both arms free to scoop up your child as she returns. It's ter-rific if you can set up your schedule so that she gets some time alone with you soon after you're reunited. At the very least, be sure she gets some snuggle time with you on the couch when she gets to tell you the best and the worst parts of her day while you feed the baby.

6. **Set aside time to be alone with each child every day for at least fifteen minutes.** For most young children with a baby sibling, the baby is always present, always distracting you. Your child needs the experience of you being *all his* for at least a short time every day. Don't use that time for a bath or stories. Instead, choose a time of day when your child can decide what to do with the fifteen minutes. Set a timer and say, "I am all *yours.*" Then pour your love into your child with 110 percent focus.

Why a timer? Because you don't want the baby waking up from his nap to end your time with big sister; that leads to resentment. So set the timer to go off twenty minutes before you expect the baby to wake up. That way, when the timer rings, you have time to help your child transition to another activity. Many kids have a meltdown when the timer goes off. No, she's not being ungrateful. She's just experiencing how good it felt to have your full attention and how sad she feels to lose that paradise, yet again. It's an opportunity for her to grieve the very real loss of no longer having you all to herself. Don't extend your playtime with her, but do give her your full attention and empathize with her sense of loss. *"It's so hard when we have to stop playing . . . You love it when you have me all to yourself . . . It's hard to share me sometimes . . . I miss our special times alone, too . . . Tomorrow we will have our Mom and Morgan time again, okay? . . . I know, that seems a like a long time to wait . . . You can cry as much as you want . . . Everybody needs to cry sometimes."*

After your child cries about losing you at the end of your time together, don't be surprised if she's more affectionate with the baby. As always, when we accept our child's emotions so that she can feel them, those emotions heal, leaving her happier and more cooperative.

7. **Trade off, so each partner gets time to connect with each child daily.** Your child has an individual relationship with each parent, and he will feel the loss of either of those relationships.

8. **Be sure there's at least ten minutes of laughter daily.** In addition to your alone time with your child, be sure to schedule in ten minutes of roughhousing with belly laughs, to get your child's anxieties and fears out and do some bonding. (See "Using Games to Help Your Child with Jealousy" on page 271 and "Games to Help Your Children Bond with the Baby" on page 305.)

9. **Cultivate empathy as your "go to" response to your child.** As we discussed in Chapter 1, feeling understood is what helps your child accept the situation when he doesn't get what he wants. And it's the foundation of his feeling connected to you. He doesn't want eggs for breakfast? Don't get defensive, but don't feel like you need to make a new breakfast either. Instead, acknowledge his disappointment. *"You were hoping for oatmeal with brown sugar again, huh? And here I made eggs. You sound so disappointed. It isn't what you wanted. I bet when you're a grown-up, you'll have oatmeal with brown sugar every single morning! We can certainly have oatmeal tomorrow. Soon you'll even be able to make oatmeal yourself. Today, though, we have eggs. I know, would you like some toast with your eggs? You can help butter it."* What if he falls apart? Then he really needed to cry, and it isn't about the oatmeal. Empathize.

10. **Connect with your child at bedtime.** Maybe Mom needs to nurse the baby to sleep, so Dad puts the older child to bed nowadays. That's fine, but be sure that you include fifteen

minutes in the bedtime routine for your child to spend with Mom. Bedtime is hard enough for young children. You don't want his last feeling as he drifts off to sleep to be an ache of longing for his mother.

11. **Use the power of ritual to stay connected.** Repeated rituals take on extra symbolic weight and are understood on a deeper level of the brain, so they ground us, connect us, and help us move emotionally from one place to another. Goodnight kisses are a perfect example of a powerful ritual that helps children feel safe as they separate from us into the world of sleep and dreams. You can create small rituals to use throughout your day to reinforce your connection with your child, especially at moments of transition or separation. For instance, a good-bye ritual as you drop your child at school might include a little rhyme that gives reassurance that you always come back: *"I love you, you love me . . . Have a wonderful day, and I'll hug you lots at three!"* Dr. Becky Bailey has a whole book of wonderful reconnecting *I Love You Rituals*, such as this one: *"What Did You Bring Home from School Today? . . . When you meet your child, you say, 'There you are. I've been waiting all day to hug you. Let me see what you brought home from school. You brought those brown eyes. You brought that cute little mole on your arm. You brought your backpack and coat. Let's go.'"* [5]

12. **Become a love multitasker with your attention.** When you're with two (or more!) children and feel like there's not enough of you to go around, hold the vision of the experienced preschool teacher. She has her arm around one child, is smiling at a second child, and might well be speaking across the room to a third child. We can all find our internal version of

this "love multitasker" to help us feel grounded while we shift our attention rapidly from child to child to stay connected with all of them.

Notice the focus on connecting in these daily practices? They weave a web of love that holds your children as they move through their day. Your child will feel that connection and you'll see the difference. When kids really feel seen and heard and connected, they don't have to compete for our love, and sibling rivalry diminishes dramatically.

Using Games to Help Your Child with Jealousy

I tried to remember he was still a baby himself, but it's hard when you're exhausted and sleep deprived and giving out so much energy and love all day long.
—Nadia

Is your child acting out, despite your best efforts to ease her adjustment? When you're overwhelmed with the baby, it's hard to be patient with your older child, even when you know intellectually that he has a right to be upset. So if you're having a hard time being understanding when he acts out, you'll be glad to know there's an easy way to help kids work through their jealousy and fear. The secret is to get them laughing. Not necessarily at the moment when they're acting out—although that can sometimes work—but throughout the day. Laughter helps humans let go of anxiety (which is mild fear) and transforms the body chemistry to reduce stress hormones and increase bonding hormones.

I know you're not feeling it. Who has the energy to get rambunctious with a child when you're sleep-deprived? But the good news is that laughter helps you feel better, too, and it only takes a few minutes. If you can get started, you'll probably find that you're enjoying yourself. It might be the best connection you've had with your child all day, and she'll be more cooperative for the rest of the day because of it.

All laughter is good for your child. But since what she's struggling with is whether she's truly loved, why not address that concern directly with play? That's how children work through emotional issues. Convince her on a deep level that you love her with one of these games.

1. **Fight over her.** One parent grabs the child and hugs her. The other whines, *"How come you always get to hug her . . . I want her, too . . . I NEEEED her . . . Let me hug, too!"* and clutches at the child from the other side.

2. **Play the fix game.** This game fixes whatever's wrong by convincing your child he's deeply loved. *"Where's my Michael? . . . You can't get away . . . I have to hug you and cover you with kisses . . . oh, no, you got away . . . I'm coming after you . . . I just have to kiss you more and hug you more . . . You're too fast for me . . . But I'll never give up . . . I love you too much . . . I got you . . . Now I'll kiss your toes . . . Oh, no, you're too strong for me, you got away . . . But I will always want more Michael hugs . . ."* As always, your goal is to get your child laughing. If he's not laughing, adapt the game until he is. For instance, if your child finds this game intrusive, try pursuing without actually catching him.

3. **We always come back to each other**. Children are often scared by their deep need for us, and this fear is worsened

when we're sometimes unavailable when they need us. This game turns the tables by letting your child feel like the one who's needed. When your child has been on your lap and goes to climb off, grab her and hold her gently while you beg her, pathetically, to stay. *"Oh, please don't go yet... I neeeeed you!... I never like to let you go... I want you in my arms all the time!"* Your child will laugh and insist on going. Say, *"Well, okay... I know you and I always come back to each other."* (Be only pathetic enough to get her laughing, not pathetic enough so she feels guilty. Ham it up so she knows it's a game.)

4. **"Mommy, I need you!"** When your child suddenly has to wait for your help and attention all the time, it's natural for him to wonder if you'll still be there for him if he really needs you. Tell him, *"If you need me, I will always come as soon as I can. So if the baby is in your way, or you need my help with something, you just say, 'Mommy, I NEED you!' and I will be there. Here, let's practice."* As soon as your child calls you, come running, grab him up, kiss him all over, and toss him around. It's a guaranteed way to get him laughing. And since he loves this, when you suggest that he yell, *"Mommy, I NEED you!"* as an alternative to grabbing his toy back from the baby, he'll be more likely to try it. That gives you a chance to get him laughing at those tense moments, after which he'll be more open to trying to work out a trade with the baby—or he'll suddenly feel more generous and just let the baby use the toy while he tries a different one.

For more games, see "Games to Help Your Children Bond with the Baby" on page 305 and "Roughhousing Games for Siblings" on page 203.

Reading Books to Your Child About Becoming a Big Sib

Sibling researcher Laurie Kramer asked parents to read books to their children about sibling relationships, assuming it would be helpful. Instead, within a few weeks she began to get complaints from the parents about the children's behavior toward their siblings.[6] It certainly makes sense. Many books about siblings begin by depicting a relationship in distress, in which brothers and sisters tease, taunt, and trick each other. Even when the story ends with the siblings learning to get along, children are seeing a lot of mean behavior in these stories that you wouldn't want in your house. Kids will usually emulate a role model.

That doesn't mean that the feelings of anger and jealousy that siblings have toward each other are "wrong" or that acknowledging them will make them worse. Acknowledging emotions always helps children deal with them more constructively.[7] It means that hostile acts aren't okay, no matter what we feel, and they aren't something we want modeled for our children.

So go ahead and read books to your child about siblings. Stories can be terrific conversation starters and open the door to healing. Just be sure to read them yourself first, to assess the level of hostile actions, as opposed to simply jealous feelings. Then, while you read, engage your child in conversation. Ask questions:

- How is the girl feeling?
- Why does she feel that way?
- Do you think her parents know how she feels?
- What could she do?
- What would happen then?

Make it clear that while all feelings are allowed, it is never okay to act those feelings out by actually hurting another person. Stress that the parent wants to hear when the big sib is upset, and can always help. And make sure that the stories you share with your child provide hope, in the form of a happy resolution to the character's unhappiness.

Nine Tips to Foster a Great Relationship Between Your Children Right from the Start

I let my five-year-old son give my two-month-old a bottle. It gives the older kids a caretaking role. Now if the baby cries, they both start offering solutions. "Maybe he needs a diaper? He's hungry Mommy. He needs a binky." Then I'll suggest the wrong thing, and they'll correct me. "No, Mommy, he doesn't want his binky. He's hungry." "Oh, I see, you're right... Thank you for letting me know!"
—Laura

1. **As you tend to the baby, invite the involvement of the older child and honor her contributions.** *"Oh no, why is your little sister crying? Let's go see what we can do to make her happy ... You were right, she was hungry, see she stopped crying! Your baby sister really appreciates how you try to help her when she needs something."*

2. **Stay calm and redirect.** Of course, sometimes the older sib's help won't be helpful. Is she singing too loudly into the infant's ear? Trying to feed the baby her carrot? Take a deep breath and redirect. Suggest she stroke the baby instead of singing, or show the baby her carrot instead of putting it in

his mouth. You can also suggest that she practice on her doll. Staying calm and redirecting takes a lot of self-control for you, but it makes a tremendous difference in helping your child find constructive ways to relate to her sibling, instead of feeling pushed aside when her attempts to connect are clumsy.

3. **Talk about how each child is feeling, in front of the other.** Research shows that when parents discuss the baby's feelings and needs, preschoolers interact more positively with their siblings, even a year later.[8] *"Look at Martina's face . . . How do you think she's feeling? What can we do to help her?"* You can further humanize your youngest by using her name, instead of calling her "the baby."

   This also works in reverse. Talk to the baby, in front of the older child, about the older sibling's needs and emotions. *"Your brother is sad right now, so he needs extra hugs . . . Your sister needs time with her mom, too."* Can the baby understand? Over time, she will. Most important, this helps your older child feel that his needs are as important to you as the baby's. Acknowledging feelings raises the EQ (emotional intelligence) of everyone in your family.

4. **Give the older sib some responsibility.** Kids love to be in charge of something. How about entertaining the baby during diaper changes, or singing a song at bedtime? He'll take the responsibility seriously if you do.

5. **Use physical bonding time to foster a close sibling relationship.** Whenever possible, snuggle up with both your infant and your older child, so those feelings of big love they feel on your lap get transferred toward each other. If you can

get them both laughing, the oxytocin they're releasing will also help them bond. And whenever you can, sit on the floor next to your older child while he plays, wearing your infant and letting her watch.

6. **Encourage your child to amuse the baby.** Babies love it when big sibs are silly with them. As your infant begins to smile and laugh in response, help your older child to notice the baby's affection. Soon they'll be nurturing their own cycle of amusement and adoration.

7. **Don't belittle the baby to build your child up.** Parents often make disparaging remarks about the baby so the older child will feel better. (*"Babies sure are smelly! I'm so glad you use the potty."*) It's fine for your child to feel angry or jealous, but it's not okay to demean others. So don't be mean about the baby, even in jest, or you're giving your child permission to be mean-spirited. Instead, resist the urge to compare. Each child is wonderful, and at their own stage, on their own time-table. Appreciate *that* child without comparison to any other child.

8. **Work to create an atmosphere of appreciation in your house.** Every night at dinner, have each person find at least one specific thing to "appreciate" about each other person: *"I appreciate that Daddy cooked such a delicious dinner . . . I appreciate that Jasmine helped me so much today at the grocery store . . . I appreciate that Baby Jack took such a long nap so Jasmine and I could play that fun game with her zoo animals."* You're helping your child develop the habit of appreciating her sibling, which melts away resentment. Before you know it, they'll be appreciating each other spontaneously.

9. **Do something for yourself.** Really. Hand the baby to someone else, if that's possible, and go soak in the tub. If you have
   two or more children needing you right this moment, sit
   down on the floor and tend to everyone's needs as best you
   can, but promise yourself that as soon as another adult is
   present, you're taking a break. Your children depend on you
   to stay emotionally regulated, and that means you need to
   keep your own cup full. Figure out what keeps you centered,
   and work it into your schedule. Fostering a healthy sibling
   relationship requires that you stay in balance yourself.

If you have a new baby and you've read this far, consider this the
sound of many hands clapping. Having a new baby is an exhausting,
overwhelming job, even when you don't have any other children.
Caring for a new baby along with another young child is simply
heroic.

Given the demands on you, the idea of tackling the suggestions
in this book may well sound somewhat daunting. Please don't think
you need to try them all. Pick an idea or two that get you excited as
you read about them. Any one of these ideas will make a positive
difference, and if you have more energy, do more. But you don't need
to do them all—that would exhaust you, and the last thing your children need is a more exhausted parent. So please don't follow these
suggestions at the expense of sleeping, or taking a shower, or having
a peaceful moment to yourself. The foundation of a positive sibling
relationship is a parent who can stay calm. Prioritize taking care of
yourself so you can be that parent, and enjoy these early months
with your growing family.

11

Building a Positive Foundation When the Baby Begins to Crawl

He wanted to know if we could sell his brother. When I hugged him tight and asked him why he wanted us to sell his brother, he said he was tired of him ruining his coloring. Two days later, he said, "I want to be dead since I can't color anyway."

—Cheryl

Often, older siblings reach an accommodation to the new baby, only to experience a fresh resurgence of jealousy as the baby begins crawling and then walking. That's not surprising, since now he can get into everything, including his older siblings' art projects. Babies also start asserting their own needs more forcibly as they reach their first birthday, so it's harder to distract them. They want what big brother has, and they'll howl to get it. You can't reason with them, and they get aggressive. They also master new milestones almost daily and become impossibly cute. How's an older sib supposed to compete with that? We can forgive the older sibling for wanting to sell his brother, especially when the baby is between eight and eighteen months.

Luckily, older siblings can adapt well and even enjoy the baby's achievements, if we give them a little support. Leaving them to manage on their own makes it more likely that they'll resort to aggression, or become hopeless and resentful. They need parental coaching to learn to articulate their needs, protect their belongings, and find constructive ways to express their feelings, including their jealousy and irritation. If the baby is allowed to ruin their coloring and knock down their towers, you can't expect a positive sibling relationship.

This chapter will show you how to support each of your children through those often tricky months once your baby starts to crawl, while she's still not really verbal yet.

Ten Tips to Maintain a Peaceful Home as Baby Moves Toward Toddlerhood

I used to insist that my six-year-old play with the one-year-old, and he yelled a lot at his little brother. Once I realized that really isn't his job, things got a lot better. Of course, the little guy still wants to get into everything his big brother is doing, so it's more work for me to distract him, but now they have a much better relationship.

—Michelle

Like other humans who live together, even the most loving siblings have bad days and conflicts. But you can prevent many sibling tensions by following a few basic strategies.

1. **Be sure your older child can protect his things from the baby.** If his towers are constantly getting knocked down, naturally he'll get frustrated. Give him a table to work on that the baby can't reach. Make sure he knows he has backup (play the "Mommy, I Need You!" game, explained on page 273), and respond quickly when he needs your help to defend himself from the baby's forays into his space.

2. **Don't require your older child to play with the little one.** He must be respectful and kind, but he's not a babysitter, and it isn't his job to always include his sibling. Making older kids always responsible for younger ones often fuels resentment.

3. **Describe with enthusiasm anything either child does that has a positive effect on the other child.** Children are like little Geiger counters for our energy. If they get stronger energy from you for shoving the baby than for stroking her gently, they're likely to go where the passion is. Instead, actively encourage positive interactions. You can always find something positive, even on a day when everything seems to go wrong:

   - *"You noticed the baby was fussy and figured out what she needed. Wow!"*

   - *"Your sister sure smiles when you sing to her."*

   - *"You're letting him see your car . . . Look, he's so happy! . . . I know that car is very special to you . . . Let me know if you need help when you want it back."*

4. **As the baby gains new skills, give your older child some of the credit.** After all, research shows that older siblings are often the most effective role models and teachers for young children, who naturally want to emulate their capable big sib.[1] *"Look, he's learning to use his spoon, from watching you."* It's hard for your older child to watch you exclaim over the baby's accomplishments, but it's easier when she sees herself as his teacher. And she's more likely to take an active interest in interacting with him, too.

5. **Rethink the whole idea of sharing.** To foster generosity, help kids learn to take self-regulated turns using the ideas on sharing in Chapter 6.

6. **Don't force togetherness.** If your child really resists bathing with his sibling, try to work out separate baths, at least most of the time. If the little one always disrupts story time, put him to bed first so the older one gets a calm story at bedtime.

7. **Notice those troublesome times of the day and structure them differently.** When your older child comes home from preschool out of sorts, put your baby in a sling and shift everyone's emotions with a short "family dance party" that gets everyone laughing and singing. At that witching hour while you're trying to get dinner on the table, let your older child help you in the kitchen while the little one plays on the floor or watches from a backpack.

8. **Monitor the signals that indicate trouble brewing.** If you notice your child getting testy, step in to help her *before* she lashes out. Sometimes kids need help navigating an immediate challenge with a sibling. Other times, they just feel ornery and are taking it out on their sib. In that case, some connection with you—particularly laughter—defuses the tension, but promise yourself to start using preventive maintenance (as described in Chapter 2) to help her with her feelings, beginning today.

9. **Don't take sides.** Scolding your child to be nicer to his little sibling doesn't work. In fact, when parents are seen as favoring the younger child, the older one actually gets more antagonistic and aggressive to the younger one.[2] So treat both

children as equally involved in creating the problem, even if one is just a baby.

Instead of: *"Stop being mean to your brother!"*

Describe what you're observing, without any blame: *"I hear loud voices... It sounds like you two are having a hard time... You both want the truck... Now David has it and Malik is crying... What can we do to solve this problem?"*

10. **Instead of punishing, help kids with emotions and empower them to repair after fights.** As parents, we're understandably desperate to stop sibling conflicts. So we fly into high gear to figure out who's at fault, quickly blaming one child as the perpetrator. Unfortunately, this reinforces the roles of both victim and aggressor. Families who punish children for fighting often incite a cycle of revenge. By contrast, in families where children aren't blamed, but are empowered to "repair" their relationships with each other after a fight, the kids end up closer.

Dividing Your Time

Your mother is always calling you by someone else's name, or saying "not now" and "in a minute" and "can't you see I'm [doing something with some child that isn't you]."... But those scarce resources, the ones that leave me feeling guilty and inadequate, mean they must learn resilience. They must find a way to share, to wait, to do without, to take their turn—and to ask for what they want and need, even when no one else notices that they have a problem.

—KJ Dell'Antonia, "Motherlode," *New York Times*

This won't be news to you, but the hardest part about having more than one child is that your baby needs you 24/7, while the children you already have still need you almost that often. How can you divide your time when more than one child needs you urgently?

1. **Don't divide your time evenly. Instead, meet their unique needs.** Naturally, your baby needs you almost constantly, while your three-year-old can manage some things himself and can even play for short periods of time without your intervention. Your five-year-old needs more of your time than your eight-year-old, who needs more of your time than your eleven-year-old. So your kids don't all need the same amount of time from you. *What they need is to know that they can count on you when they do need you.*

2. **Let your baby have some quiet time to play.** It's an important developmental task for babies to learn to play in your presence, but not with you. This is a first step toward self-initiative, mastery, and learning to entertain themselves. I'm not suggesting that you leave her to cry, but that you meet all her needs, and then try putting her down to let her explore and play. If she cries, comfort, engage a bit and then back off, but stay present. This lets you turn your attention to your other children, and it's good for the baby as well. As Magda Gerber, author of *Your Self-Confident Baby*, says, "Respect your child . . . (and make life easier) by *not* 'teaching your child to play' . . . You are simply available to your child without inflicting on her your desires in regard to what she should be doing or how she should be doing it."[3]

3. **Seize any quiet moments to connect.** Every child needs to feel seen, heard, and appreciated—not 24/7, but certainly

every single day. When one child is busy playing, even briefly, resist cleaning up the kitchen. It's a perfect time to go sit with the other child. Don't interrupt his play. Just watch, and pour your love and attention into him. If he looks up, comment (without evaluation) so he knows you're really taking him in: *"It can be hard to get the tracks to hold together,"* or *"You're doing the outside edges of the puzzle first."* You'll be amazed how he relaxes and soaks in all that love, and carries it with him in the form of agreeableness throughout the day.

4. **Build time with each child into the routine.** It's fine to share your attention among more than one child most of the day. That's what it means to live in a family. But be sure that each child can count on having you all to herself every single day for a short time. Try for Special Time (see "Preventive Maintenance" on page 36) with each child daily. If Special Time is mostly on weekends, be sure your child can count on a loving chat while you gently braid her hair every morning and a fifteen-minute snuggle and chat at bedtime.

5. **Be present.** Don't multitask when you finally get one-on-one time with your child. Five minutes of your full attention is worth an hour of your partial attention. Put your phone away. Forget the laundry for now. Get down on your child's level and make eye contact so he knows you're listening only to him. Bored? That's because you're not fully present. Try just appreciating your child. Notice the curve of his cheek and the smell of his hair. When we really let go of everything else and just notice the fullness of the present moment, we don't feel bored. In fact, once you give yourself permission to do this on a regular basis, you may find a whole new dimension to life.

6. **Don't shortchange the well-behaved child.** It's very common for a child to demand less attention than her siblings and get overlooked, until she starts to act out. All kids deserve Special Time with you, not just the one who's more challenging. During time periods when one child requires more focus than another, be sure to connect with the other child with a hug, just to check in.

7. **Rely on grandparents,** if you're lucky enough to have them. Once your child is able to sleep over happily with grandparents (or a trusted friend), use those times to have special dates with your other child.

8. **Whenever possible, use prevention.** All siblings get irritated at each other from time to time. When children are tired, hungry, or cranky, their prefrontal cortex has a hard time controlling their emotions. Luckily, we can usually see the storm brewing, and step in to prevent it, if we aren't too stressed out to notice the warning signs. Gather the cranky child (or children) onto your lap for a preemptive time-in and refill that empty cup. Time-consuming? Yes, but so much better than running interference once they start lashing out at each other.

How to Help Your Older Child Solve His Problems with the Little One

When my daughter was two, her brother was born. We talked about how she already knew how to share, and not to knock down block towers, compared to what babies like to do, such as knocking down towers or taking things without asking. After that, when her brother would do something that would frustrate her, she would look at us and say, "That's just what babies do!" She would actually chuckle at him sometimes.

—Natasha

So far in this book, we've stressed meeting your child's needs for connection and attention, so he doesn't develop a chip on his shoulder toward the baby. But with most children, that's not quite enough. You also have to help your child develop the skills to express his needs and problem-solve. Why?

Because the baby creates problems for him, from snatching his toys to shrieking loudly to pulling his hair. Your child needs to know what to do to solve the problem, or he'll do what all humans do when attacked—go into fight, flight, or freeze mode. And since your child is bigger than the baby, fight will be at the top of his list.

Here are the five basic steps of problem-solving that you'll use daily to help your child cope with the problems that arise from having a younger sibling.

1. **Calm, empathize, and give your child the words to express his needs.** When children are upset, "use your words" isn't enough—they need to know what words to say. *"It's okay, sweetie, you don't have to yell at him . . . I know he's being very loud and it hurts your ears, but yelling won't help him stop shrieking . . . You can just say, 'Please don't shriek, it hurts my ears . . . I hear you want a car!'"*

2. **Model calm problem-solving.** *"You're worried that he's touching your cars . . . don't worry, it's not an emergency . . . I will help you . . . We will work this out together."* Your backup helps him to calm down so he moves out of fight mode and can think more clearly.

3. **Help your child learn to "not take it personally" by describing the problem.** *"You're upset that he wants to play with your cars? You want them all to yourself right now, but he keeps grabbing at them?"* Notice you aren't making anyone wrong. You may think it's obvious that your child should simply share one of his fifteen cars, but they're his, and he clearly wants them all right now. Putting him on the defensive will just increase his feeling of being threatened and make it even less likely that he'll decide to share. So refrain from judgment, and simply state the disagreement as a problem to be solved.

4. **Invite him to help problem-solve.** *"Hmm ... You want to play with all the cars yourself ... And he really wants a car ... I wonder what we could do to solve this?"* You aren't making him solve it himself, but you're helping him start to take responsibility to think about solutions. Remember that if you push a certain solution (*"Just give him a car!"*), your child feels pushed around and gets resistant.

5. **Help your child come up with solutions.** As they gain experience with this process, even two- and three-year-olds come up with solutions. In the beginning, though, you may need to help. *"Let's see, do you think he'd like to play with the train engine instead? Want to offer it to him? Gently, now ..."*

What to Say When Your Child Is Jealous of the Baby

When children feel understood, their loneliness and hurt diminish and their love for their parent is deepened. A parent's sympathy serves as emotional first aid for bruised feelings. When we genuinely acknowledge a child's plight and voice her disappointment, she often gathers the strength to face reality.

—Haim Ginott, author of *Between Parent and Child*

If you work to stay connected to your child, she probably won't have too many moments where she feels unbearably jealous of her new sibling. You can be sure, though, that she'll have some. Make sure she knows that these feelings are completely normal, so that she doesn't feel like a monster. Acknowledge how hard it is for her and give her permission to grieve. See if you can offer some hope that things might feel better in the future, without discounting her distress.

"DO YOU EVEN CARE ABOUT ME ANYMORE?"

"Oh, sweetie, I love you so much . . . I could never love anyone more. You are my one and only Aliyah and there is no one like you in the whole wide world. I feel so lucky to be your mom. Are you feeling like I don't care? I guess I have been very tired, and super busy, so it has been hard to show you my love in the ways I used to. I have more than enough love for both you and your sister. I'm sorry that you have felt not cared about. Let's find a way to make things better. I think we need some Aliyah and Mommy time today while the baby naps. What would you like to do with our Special Time together today?"

"IT'S NOT FAIR; YOU NEVER HELP ME. I NEED HELP, TOO!"

"Does it seem like my hands are always too busy with the baby to help you? That must feel so unfair! It's hard to wait, I know. I know you need help, too, and I will always be here to help you when you need me. I will try to do a better job noticing when you need help. But I'm not perfect, so I won't always notice. Can you tell me when you need help, with your words?"

WHEN YOUR CHILD IS JEALOUS . . .

Instead of
Denying Her Feelings

Try Connecting

I hate the baby! You never play with me now!

Don't say mean things. And I play with you plenty!

Oh, sweetheart, that hurts to miss playing with me. You don't like it when I'm feeding the baby and can't play with you.

Left: It's natural to get defensive. Instead, take a deep breath and see it from her perspective.

Right: Empathize and describe the problem.

You wish I could come right away when you want me.

It can be hard to share your mom. Sometimes kids worry that their mom doesn't love them as much.

Left: Acknowledge longings and give her her wish in fantasy.

Right: Acknowledge her deeper feelings.

WHEN YOUR CHILD IS JEALOUS . . .

Left: Reassure her.
Right: Fill the need the child is expressing.

"I HATE HAVING A BABY!"

"It's hard sometimes, having a baby in the house. I guess it makes you very angry sometimes to have to share me, and to have to be quiet so he can sleep, and to have to wait your turn . . . It can be very hard, can't it? You can always tell me when it's hard, and I will always understand, and help you." (Think the word "hate" calls for a tougher response? See "When Your Child Says He Hates His Sibling" on page 119.)

"I MIGHT AS WELL BE DEAD!"

Don't panic. He's choosing the most powerful word he knows to show you know how miserable he is. Don't argue with him. Instead, empathize and offer comfort: *"Sometimes you feel that bad, huh? Oh, sweetheart, I am so sorry it's so hard . . . Come here and let me hold you."* Hopefully, then, he'll cry. If he resists, he's using his anger as a shield for all that pain. Prioritize preventive maintenance and rebuilding your connection with him so that he feels safe enough to show you those feelings. The more you can soften your heart, the more he'll soften his, and the faster healing can begin.

What to Do About Toy Grabbing

Most older siblings grab toys from the baby. After all, anything the baby has suddenly looks pretty enticing to an older sib. But is grabbing toys always about sibling rivalry? No. Toddlers are just developing social skills, and taking toys can be a clumsy attempt to "relate" to a sibling. Babies generally don't mind when another child takes something from them, so when the toy grabbing is sporadic, there's no need to intervene.

But there's a reason "taking candy from a baby" has come to symbolize an easy but immoral abuse of power. Parents usually feel uncomfortable when their child begins to compulsively grab from the baby because the baby is defenseless, unable to express his needs. Constant grabbing isn't good for the baby—who, after all, is exploring that toy—and it's actually not good for the other child either, because compulsive behavior of any kind is a red flag that your child needs help with the emotions driving it.

1. **If both kids are laughing, don't spoil the fun.** The baby might be more interested in the game with big sister than in hanging on to the toy. The lesson you're trying to teach will be lost, because this is a game, not toy snatching by your eldest.

2. **Describe what happened.** *"Baby was shaking his rattle so hard and laughing . . . Zack wanted to try the rattle, too . . . Now*

Zack has the rattle... Baby looks surprised... Now Zack shakes the rattle... shake shake shake... Baby laughs and laughs... Zack laughs, too... Now Baby has the giraffe... He's trying to put it in his mouth... Now Zack takes the giraffe... Baby looks surprised."

Why describe in such detail? Because your toddler isn't actually aware of what he's doing and what effect it has on his brother. He's just feeling an impulse and following it. Your words help him develop self-awareness. And while your eleven-month-old isn't quite sure yet what you're saying, he knows you're acknowledging him, which matters.

3. **Empathize, and ask questions to build empathy.** *"That rattle sounds pretty great, doesn't it? You want to shake it, too... The baby looked surprised when you took the rattle... I wonder if he was done with his turn?... What do you think he would say if we asked him?"*

4. **Teach your child to offer "trades" to the baby.** But how do you know whether the baby is done with his turn? Ask the baby, using the baby's language: action. *"You want the rattle? I wonder if the baby is done with it? Why don't you bring him a different toy, to see if he's ready to swap? That way, you'll know if he's done with his turn."* Most of the time, the baby will happily switch toys. He'll probably think it's a game. That's fine. This lays the groundwork so that when the baby starts to resist swapping, your child will be prepared to respect the baby's right to a longer turn.

5. **If your child can't respect the baby's turn and keeps grabbing,** it isn't actually about the toy. Compulsive behavior of any kind signals a deeper unmet need or feeling we can't

verbally express. In other words, if your child "always" grabs whatever the baby is holding, then he has some big feelings that are driving him to compulsively take whatever he can get from his sibling. The likeliest hypothesis is that he's feeling forced to share far too much with this baby, including his parents, and he's feeling desperately needy. The best way to help your child process those big feelings is with a scheduled meltdown (see Chapter 2).

As always, you move into a scheduled meltdown by setting a compassionate limit. When your son starts to grab from the baby, put your hand on the toy to stop him. Say, *"I see you want that . . . It's still the baby's turn . . . Your turn will be next . . . I'll help you wait."*

If he's already snatched the toy, the limit is to ask him to give it back. Get down on the floor next to your child and put your hand on the toy. *"Hey, sweetie—it looks like the baby is upset. It was still his turn and he wasn't ready to give you the toy yet. Want to try a trade? Hmm . . . it looks like he doesn't want anything else, just that toy. Time to give it back now. When he's done with his turn, he'll give it to you."* Should you snatch the toy from your child? No. But if your hand is on it, he'll either give it to you or start to cry while clinging to it. Before you know it, he's showing you all those tears and fears that are driving him to grab from the baby in the first place. (See "Scheduled Meltdowns" on page 43 and "Rethinking Sharing" on page 149.)

When Your Child Is Aggressive Toward the Baby

If your child hurts the baby, naturally you'll be furious. You'll feel an urgent need to teach him a lesson, and you'll probably want to hurt him back, even if you stop yourself from doing so. It will be hard to see his perspective. But consider how you would feel if your partner suddenly seemed smitten with someone new. You might lash out, too. Any child who hurts the baby is suffering from a broken heart. He needs your help to heal it.

Henry, age three, is playing with Sophie, eleven months, by grabbing a toy away from her. Sophie loves his attention and giggles at this interesting game, especially because he restores the toy to her every time. But Henry is getting rougher each time, and Sophie is clinging harder to the toy. He wrenches it away from her. Sophie bursts into tears. Henry, feeling guilty, says, *"You act like a baby!"* and reaches out and shoves her down, hard. Now Sophie is wailing.

If Dad had noticed the game getting rougher, he could have intervened by getting between the kids and engaging in the game: *"Hey, what about me? Take the toy from someone your own size, why don't you? Waaaaaa ... You took my toy!"* There would have been giggling all around, giving Henry the opportunity to discharge some tension around having to "share" everything in his life with his sister. But Dad, being human and a parent, was trying to do three other things and simply glad for a moment of quiet. What should he do now?

Punishment of any kind will make Henry feel worse and act worse. (See Chapter 2 and Chapter 5.) Helping him with the feelings that are driving his aggression is what will stop the hitting. But that doesn't mean we don't set a firm limit against violence.

First, Dad scoops up Sophie, who is howling. He resists the urge to yell at Henry. In fact, he resists interacting with Henry at all until he can get himself a bit calmer. So he summons up his nurturing and focuses on Sophie, which helps shift him from his murderous don't-you-mess-with-my-baby self to his nurturing-parent self.

> **Dad:** Ouch! That hurt! *(Sophie nods, crying hard.)* Getting pushed can hurt your body, and your feelings, too! . . . Tell me about it, Sophie.

Sophie cries even louder for a moment, as we all do when we're hurt and receive loving attention. Soon, though, she recovers and reaches for the toy, which is abandoned on the floor. Dad puts her down with the toy, takes a deep breath to calm himself, and turns to Henry. He knows Henry is feeling frightened, and no learning will happen in that state, so he tries to be warm and matter-of-fact, not accusatory.

> **Dad:** That hurt your sister, didn't it?
> **Henry:** I guess. She's a crybaby.

Dad doesn't take the bait. He gets down on the floor next to Henry, making eye contact. He's breathing deeply, working to stay calm and kind. Naturally, his face is serious.

> **Dad:** Well, everybody cries sometimes. Sophie certainly cries when she gets hurt, like the rest of us. What happened, Henry?
> **Henry:** She wouldn't give me my toy.

Henry looks blank. Is he remorseless? No. He feels ashamed, and afraid of what Dad is about to say. He's in "fight, flight, or freeze"—in this case, freeze. So it looks on the surface as if he doesn't feel anything.

> **Dad:** That was your toy, and you wanted it.
> *(He is empathizing.)*
> *Henry nods but doesn't say anything.*
> **Dad:** You must have been really upset to hurt her . . . I'm sorry I wasn't here to help.

Is Dad blaming himself? No. He's modeling taking responsibility. That opens the door a bit for Henry to feel less defensive. He shoots a quick look at Dad—*Is it possible that he might understand?*—and then looks away again.

> **Dad:** I hear you were frustrated with her. But hitting hurts. I won't let you hit your sister.
>
> *Henry glazes over and looks away. Dad knows Henry's trying to push away some big feelings that he needs help with. Dad moves in close, pulling Henry gently against him.*
>
> **Dad:** Sometimes you get really mad at your sister, don't you?
>
> **Henry** *(looking at him, testing)*: I *hate* her.
>
> **Dad** *(ignoring the hate bomb)*: Sometimes you get so mad it feels like you hate her. *(Trying to go under the anger to the more vulnerable feelings that drive it.)* I know you tell me it isn't fair that she always gets to sleep with us. Maybe you think she gets everything, and you get left out?
>
> **Henry** *(shouting)*: I am left out! Why did you have to get a baby anyway?! You never have time for me anymore! Why can't you send her back?! She ruins everything!
>
> **Dad:** You miss the way it used to be.

Henry bursts into tears and buries his head in Dad's shoulder. As he sobs, Dad says, *"You can cry as much as you need to. I am right here. I am ALWAYS here for you, no matter what, baby or no baby."* He isn't trying to stop Henry from crying. He's helping Henry feel safe enough to show him all that pain.

Sophie is initially distressed by Henry's crying, so Dad does the hardest part of this process—reassuring her and keeping her out of reach of Henry's flailing feet at the same time as he tends to Henry. He has one arm around each child.

Dad: It's okay, Sophie. Henry's just sad right now.

Finally, Henry is done crying, and snuggles on Dad's lap. Sophie has wandered to the train track across the room and is happily chugging the trains around, no longer listening.

Dad: You know that I couldn't love anyone more than you, right? You are the only Henry I have and you have the only Henry place in my heart. You are my Henry and I am your dad and I will always love you, no matter what.

Henry nods.

Dad: I know you worry sometimes that we love Sophie more. But that is never true. No matter how much love we give your sister, there is always more than enough for you. You can always tell me if you're feeling left out, or angry, you know that.

Henry nods again.

Dad: What about hitting?

Henry: It's bad.

Dad: Well, what happens when you hit?

Henry: I get in trouble.

Dad: What else?

Henry: Sophie cries.

Dad: Why does she cry?

Henry: Because it hurts.

Dad: And how do you feel inside?

Henry *(looking away)*: Bad.

Dad: Yes, Henry. You feel bad, because when we hit, it hurts the other person, and it also hurts our own heart. People are *not* for hitting. People are for loving. Just like your mom and I love and hug you. So what can you do instead of hitting your sister when you feel like hitting?

Henry: Get you?

Dad: Yes, use your words and tell me. If you need help with your feelings, or to protect your toys, call me and I will always help you. What else?

Henry: Give her a different toy?

Dad: Yes, what a great idea! And if you're really mad, could you turn around and hit the couch?

Henry: I guess so. But what I really want is one of those punching bags. It falls over.

Dad: You mean instead of your sister?

Both Dad and Henry start laughing.

Is this mean? I don't think so. It defuses the tension. Sophie isn't listening. And Dad quickly restates the limit.

Dad: That's a good idea. Punching bags are made for falling down. Little sisters are made to love. Let's consider a punching bag. But for now, I think you have a little repair work to do with your sister. What could you do to help her feel safe with you again?

Henry: I could hug her.

Dad: I know she would like that, if you were gentle. Would you like that?

Henry: Yeah. Sometimes she's okay. For a baby.

Is it necessary to make Henry feel bad about what he did? No. He knows it was hurtful; he just couldn't help himself in the press of all these hateful feelings. Yelling, punishing, time-outs, and giving him the cold shoulder would all make him feel worse, convincing him that his parents don't love him anymore, no matter what they say. In that case, why not just make his sister's life miserable?

Instead, what does Dad do?

WHEN CHILDREN HIT . . .

Instead of Punishing

Try Prevention

Left: Kids hit when they don't know how else to express their feelings. Punishment doesn't help kids with their upsets; it makes those hurts and fears worse.

Right: When possible, prevent hitting. Acknowledging feelings helps kids manage their emotions so they don't have to act on them.

When Prevention Fails

Prevent Future Hitting

Left: First, tend to the child who's hurt. Don't interact with the child who did the hitting until you can do so calmly.

Right: Empathize while you reinforce your limit.

WHEN CHILDREN HIT . . .

By Helping Kids with Feelings

Left: Acknowledge his point of view.

Right: Once he's calm and connected, guide him to problem-solve to prevent future hitting.

1. Gives Henry the message that while actions must be limited—hitting hurts and is not allowed—all feelings are acceptable.

2. Helps Henry "express" the emotions that have been eating at him and driving his aggressive behavior, so those feelings can begin to evaporate. This melts the armor that's been collecting around Henry's heart, so he feels less angry at his sister, and more cooperative in general.

3. Reconnects with him, so Henry knows he's valued, not displaced.

4. Reassures Henry that he can tell his parents how he feels and get help. He isn't left on his own in his struggle to control himself so he doesn't hurt his sister.

5. Helps Henry notice that hitting not only hurts his sister—but hurts his own heart, too.

6. Builds Henry's capacity for self-reflection, which will help him to manage himself in the future.

7. Builds Henry's empathy for his sister by focusing on hitting being a hurtful way to interact with another person, rather than simply labeling it as a bad act.

8. Helps Henry imagine other ways to handle his feelings in the future. Henry is open to this because he wasn't made to feel like a terrible person, which would have put him on the defensive.

9. Empowers Henry to "repair" his relationship with his sister.

10. Helps Henry laugh about the situation, which discharges fear and helps Henry understand that feelings aren't permanent—they can be expressed, and then we feel better. This jumpstarts the healing process inside Henry.

11. Helps Henry past his anger to an emotionally generous state where he can acknowledge that he has good feelings about his sister.

Maybe most important, Henry learns that he has a father who loves all of him, no matter what. That's what will gradually form the core of an unshakable internal happiness that will allow him to handle whatever life throws at him—including, eventually, being a great big brother.

For more on handling hitting, see "Should You Punish Your Child for Aggression?" on page 124.

What If the Aggressor Is Too Young to Understand?

In general, young children learn language faster if you use fairly normal language, not baby talk, with them. Remember that receptive language is always well ahead of expressive language, so babies and toddlers can understand much more than we think. But since parents often tell me they want words that a little one who isn't verbal yet can understand, here's a version of what the dialogue above might look like with a young toddler.

1. **Describe what happened.** *"You hit Amelia. Ouch! Hitting hurts. Amelia cried ... You were MAD!"*
2. **Empathize.** *"Amelia pulled your hair. Ouch! You were hurt and mad!"*
3. **Help your child come up with options for next time.** *"No hitting. Hitting hurts. Can you call me for help? Say MOMMY! Call me now ... That's right. See, I'm coming. Here I am!"* Pick your child up for a big hug and get him laughing, which creates a positive association to calling for you when he's in an altercation with the little one. (See the "Mommy, I Need You!" game in "Using Games to Help Your Child with Jealousy" on page 271.)
4. **Help your child repair the relationship.** *"We touch gently like this, gently ... See, she's smiling at you!"*

What If It's the Baby Who's Aggressive?

As babies get older, they're not exempt from sibling rivalry. Your little one may very well feel worried, at times, that his siblings might keep him from getting what he needs.

1. **Model for your little one how to offer trades to the older child.** Clue in the older sibling so she understands what's going on and will take the trade sometimes, so the younger child learns how to do it and feels empowered to initiate. Of course, there will be times when the older child has no interest in the trade, and the younger one howls. You'll need to step in and commiserate with how hard it is, but of course, respect your older child's right to say no.

2. **Empathize.** When your fifteen-month-old tries to push his older sibling out of your lap, acknowledge his feelings. *"You want to be in my lap, don't you? You don't want Justin in my lap."*

3. **Protect your older child's rights by setting a limit, while finding a way to meet the younger child's need as well.** *"Justin is reading with me . . . He's going to stay right here. You can come up on my other side and read with us."*

4. **Expect the little one to be unhappy.** Most of the time, a fifteen-month-old will howl when he doesn't get his way. But what he really wants is to be reassured of your love. So as long as you offer him that, he'll stop attacking his brother. After all, big brother is only a problem if he's in the fifteen-month-old's way. So scoop him up and snuggle him in your other arm, all the while assuring both kids that you have enough arms

for both of them. Then divert his attention to the book you're reading with your older child, so everyone settles into a cozy feeling again. *"Everyone wants Mama . . . Don't worry, Mama can hold you both. Look at this picture! The baby bear wants his Mama, too!"*

What do your children learn from this? They both matter and you'll respond to both of them. As your littlest gets older, you'll have lots of opportunity to help him with his sibling jealousy. (Also see "When Your Toddler Is the Aggressor Against Your Older Child" on page 128.)

Games to Help Your Children Bond with the Baby

Your baby isn't quite ready for roughhousing, but there are ways to support her "playing" with her big sibs. Try these ideas to get started. You'll all laugh so much, you'll be inspired to come up with more ideas of your own.

- Use your little one as a "football"—run her around the rest of the family into the end zone. Your kids will love it.

- "I play a game where I hold our baby [three months] and we chase her big sisters [three-year-old twins], until we catch them for a cuddle. The baby starts giggling in anticipation and always smiles at her sisters, which in turn gets her sisters giggling as well. The big girls know they have to be very gentle with the baby."—Jessica

- Be a baby ventriloquist. Be the voice for the baby and have him say all kinds of funny things to his siblings. Be sure that he also says tender, grateful, and admiring things.

Choose Love

I hope you've come away excited about some of the powerful tools that can transform your family. But please don't feel as if you have to put every suggestion in this book to work at once. Pick *one thing* you want to change, such as doing preventive maintenance with your children. Start there. Once that's a habit, in three months come back and pick a new challenge, such as how you intervene in fights.

And please, don't feel as if you have to be perfect. The only thing harder than raising a child is raising more than one! Your children don't need you to be perfect. In fact, if your child sees you as perfect, he'll feel worse about himself, because he knows he's not. What your child needs from you is a model of how to be a gracious human. That means admitting when you've been wrong. Being willing to grow. Giving yourself support to do better. Working hard to regulate your own emotions, no matter what your child does.

Not so easy, right? That's why loving your children unconditionally starts with loving yourself unconditionally.

Parenting is the hardest work any of us do, no matter what your day job is. Every one of us has days when we feel like throwing in the towel. But no act of kindness is ever wasted. Who's to know how your emotional generosity to your child today will help him to connect to his sibling after you're gone? Who's to know how their relationship will ripple down through the generations, changing the world, creating a better future?

So on those tough days, take a deep breath and remind yourself that throwing in the towel just creates more laundry. The answer, always, is more love. More love for your children, yes, but to start with, more love for yourself.

There is *always* more love.

ACKNOWLEDGMENTS

It gives me great pleasure to acknowledge my four brothers and two sisters: David, Steven, Nadine, Robert, Claudia, and Guy. Siblings are indeed the people we practice on, the people who teach us about fairness and cooperation and kindness and caring, quite often the hard way, as Pamela Dugdale famously observed. Thanks for being my family.

My deepest gratitude goes to all the parents who invite me into their lives and share their stories with me, some of whose stories are shared in this book. I'm honored to accompany you on your parenting journey. A warm shout-out also to the readers of my books, blog, and newsletters, for your commitment to being the best parent you can be to your child, and for the steady flow of love and appreciation that keeps me going.

To the busy parents who read the initial disorganized manuscript and offered me such helpful feedback—Stacy, Sonya, Jimena, Kevin, Leslie, Liz, Justin, Abi, Sally, Jessica, Michelle, Ruth, Kate, Carla, Courtney, Kelly, Heidi, Bill, Nora, Ashley, Kelsey, Caroline, Daisy, Tamara, Claire, Sara, Nicole, Emma, Gio, Shawntell, Monique, Iris, Jennie, Megan, Madeline, Layla, Karen, Miriam, and Daisy—thank you for your time and your thoughtfulness, which made this book so much more useful to parents. I'm especially indebted to Beth Trapani for your invaluable insights.

To Marian Lizzi and her team at Perigee, thank you for believing in my work. It's been such a pleasure to work with you at every stage. I would also like to thank the artist, Bryndon Everett, who breathed life into my ideas with his warm portrayals of parents and children.

To my agent, Rebecca Friedman, what a blessing to know that I can always pick up the phone to hear your laugh and your opinions.

To my assistant, Theresa Dietrich, special thanks for your grace under pressure and for handling all the details so I could focus on writing.

To my children, Eli and Alice, who gave me so little opportunity to learn about sibling squabbles, but have taught me so much about love. How did I get lucky enough to be your mother?

To my husband, Daniel Cantor, I am reminded of what Wilbur said about Charlotte: "It is not often that someone comes along who is a true friend and a good writer." Thank you for your encouragement, your editing, your humor, and your brilliance. I hope you know how grateful I am for every day we have together.

My deepest intellectual debt in writing this book is to Haim Ginott, and to Adele Faber and Elaine Mazlish, who have kept his message alive for parents. Thanks also to Ashley Merryman and Po Bronson, who inspired me to think in fresh ways about sibling conflict, and to countless researchers, led by Laurie Kramer, Judy Dunn, and Gene Brody, who persevere in providing essential pieces of the sibling puzzle. I continue to learn from and to be inspired by my colleagues Lawrence Cohen, Jane Nelsen, Dan Siegel, Heather Shumaker, Patty Wipfler, Becky Bailey, Alfie Kohn, Gordon Neufeld, Tina Payne Bryson, and many others. As always, my work builds on the wisdom of so many gifted thinkers in this field, past and present. Without them, my small contributions wouldn't have come to be. While I can never adequately express my gratitude, the Further Reading section on AhaParenting.com will introduce readers to their work and hopefully provide inspiration for further reading.

NOTES

Please see AhaParenting.com/PPHSEndnotes for footnote citations, as well as suggestions for further reading.

INDEX

Page numbers in **bold** indicate tables; those in *italics* indicate illustrations.

ABOUT THE AUTHOR

The author's children, ages three and seven

Dr. Laura Markham is the author of *Peaceful Parent, Happy Kids: How to Stop Yelling and Start Connecting*. She earned her PhD in clinical psychology at Columbia University and has worked as a parenting coach with countless families across the English-speaking world. A leading advocate for parents and children, she makes frequent TV and radio appearances and has been featured in hundreds of publications from *Redbook* to the *Wall Street Journal*.

Dr. Laura's free coaching e-newsletter has more than 90,000 subscribers. You can sign up at her website, AhaParenting.com, which serves up Aha! Moments for parents of babies through teens. You can also join her community on Facebook (facebook.com/AhaParenting) and follow the latest research in parenting via Twitter @DrLauraMarkham.

Dr. Laura is the mother of two children. Her goal is to change the world, one child at a time, by supporting parents.

Also by Dr. Laura Markham

Peaceful Parent,
HAPPY KIDS

How to Stop Yelling
and Start Connecting

DR. LAURA MARKHAM
CREATOR OF AhaParenting.com

Foreword by Jack Canfield,
author of Chicken Soup for the Parent's Soul